Sweet Strength

SEASIDE AWAKENINGS

LINDA McDANDEL

Palmetto Publishing Group, LLC
Charleston, SC

ISBN-13: 978-1-944313-10-4
ISBN-10: 1-944313-10-9

Dedication

———

To my loving husband, Mark (November 13, 1958–January 9, 2012). My knight in shining armor. Everyone's best friend, the wind beneath my wings. My Sweet Strength. You encouraged me to write. So I wrote. This is for you.

To my son, Robert: my joy and my hero. I love you more than you will ever know.

To my brothers, Alan Keith Chandler and Daniel Laughton Chandler. Thank you for always being there and loving me through it all. I love you. To my other brother, Mark's cousin Billy, who grew up with Mark and they were as close as brothers, thank you for helping me through the summer of 2012.

Mom and Dad, may you rest in peace, and thank you for loving me. For showing me how to be strong and for giving me life. I miss you.

To Cori, my niece. Always beautiful . . . kind . . . and I thank God that you're in my life. Your mom would be proud. To Donna, my sister-in-law, who was like a sister. Thanks for all the laughs and shared secrets. Thank you for loving me. I miss you.

To Laughton. Thank you for your love and dedication to our family heritage and for always loving me. Your mom would be so proud of you.

To Kyleigh. May you always find joy in your life.

To my friends and the rest of my family . . . so many to name. I love you. You have made an impact in my life. An impact that will forever be engraved on my heart. Thank you. I value you and your friendship.

Table of Contents

Introduction

"I am certain that I never did grow in grace one – half so much anywhere as I have upon the bed of pain." —*Charles Spurgeon*

My first book is a little different than most because it has been my journey over the last four years through grief and inspiring others through my passion and love of coaching. It is not a story to read from beginning to end. It is just some of my daily thoughts as I traveled through so many losses and changes while building my coaching business. My hope is that you become inspired and encouraged by my journey, as I walked through a lot of grief and built a new career, hoping to beneficially affect others along the way. I hope that my writings on grief will give you some comfort as you walk through losses you may have had.

I don't call myself a Christian, but a follower of Christ. He has been with me every step of the way, and he is the only person I have found who has truly loved me unconditionally. Through writing this book, I am not trying to persuade you to turn your life over to Christ. You will have to find your own way to peace. My peace is Jesus Christ. This is simply my walk.

My healing and comfort came from the beach, watching the sunrise, surfing, walking, running, and some sunsets. I wish I could have added all the sunrises I watched over the last four years, but descriptions and images of them would fill this book and so many more. My healing also came through the support and encouragement of family, friends, and, yes, coaching. This is why I believe so much in what I do and why I am so passionate about my work as a life coach. We are not alone in our journey. We are here to support and encourage one another. We all want to be listened to, loved, and valued for who we are, not who others think we should be or even who we think we should be, but simply who we are today. I have found there are no exceptions to this rule.

I have such a passion to empower others to take control of their lives from the inside out. We cannot control a lot of our circumstances, but we can control how we react to and perceive them in our lives. We can create who we want to be and how we want our lives to be lived. We have that power within us.

As Napoleon Hill states in his book *Think and Grow Rich*, "You may see at one and the same time both your best friend and your greatest enemy, by stepping in front of a mirror. There is no truer statement. You are the only one in life with whom you will compete against. It is all in your thoughts, your belief systems, and your paradigms that will reflect the one you see in the mirror. Your self-image and what you believe about the world around you and the experiences you go through, good and bad, will determine how well you live your life. Only you can give yourself happiness, health, and wealth." This is what I hope you gain after reading this book.

Thank you! I am sending blessings of peace, love, happiness, health, joy, and wealth to every hand that holds this book. That is my desire for you, and it burns within me.

Finally, I want to thank Leslie Moore for her tireless efforts helping me get all my posts in one file in preparation for this book's publication.

Mark the Shark

———◦◦◦———

Mark. If I had one word to describe my husband Mark it would be loyal. He was loyal to his walk with Christ, he was loyal to his family, his friends, and his love of surfing. I loved this about him.

There are so many things I loved about Mark. His blue eyes that held the depth of the ocean. His smile and laugh that would light up a room. The way he held me and kissed me. How he showed his love to me through his commitment and loyalty. His patience to stop and smell the roses. The way he could fully be with those who sat in front of him. His humor. The way he would say…whew doggie mama when I walked out of the room in the outfit he loved on me. The way he would go all out for anniversaries, Christmas, Valentines, and birthdays. The way he would slow me down. His love for animals, he loved our dogs and would go to lengths to keep them healthy. His love of the ocean and nature. There are so many stories and memories that we shared together and a part that could fill many pages in a book. He was one of those people that make an indelible mark on your heart, that can never be erased. Everyone loved Mark. You would be hard-pressed to find someone who didn't. In fact, I don't believe you could. As, the pastor said at the funeral, "I bet you all felt like you were Mark's best friend".

Mark was my rescuer. He was like the knight in shining armor that rode up on a white horse. Some of his friends said, I rescued him. I beg to differ. I had gone through a bad divorce. We met shortly after and we were married a year and a half later. In fact, when I was talking to my mom about this man I had met she said to me does he have blonde hair and blue eyes. I was taken back because I had not described him at all. I said, yes he does. She said, when I was leaving your house the other day I saw an image of a man with blonde hair and blue eyes and God, said to me, Linda is going to be alright. And...I was. You see this is the image that will always be in my heart. The knight in shining armor. When someone dies that you love, you never remember the bad. The good gets magnified, because you never truly know what you have until it's gone. We take so many things for granted and I took so many things for granted that I wish I could get back. You just never realize the sacredness of a marriage. When we did things together you understand that it wasn't just things or experiences it was so much more. When you lose someone you realize that the marriage you held was more than just two people saying vows together, it was a spiritual joining of two hearts joined in one God. It will drive you to your knees. The gratefulness of having experienced a marriage. Having lived a life with another life so intimately. In the good times and the bad...we are still joined by one heart and one spirit. Yes, there are so many things I took for granted.

Like any married couple we had our good times and our bad times. We had times of adjustment, but we always adjusted. We never gave up on each other. We were so different in so many ways. He was laid back and easy going and I was full of energy and movement. But, this is what made, at the end of the day, a great friendship and marriage. He would calm me down and I would, as he said, make him feel alive. I think I kept him on his toes and he kept me grounded on mine. I am so thankful for the influence Mark had on my life. The time I spent with him. I love him.

Mark had an instant family. I had one son, Robert. Robert was two and half when we met and Mark loved him as his own. Robert thought of Mark like a dad. He called him Dad. They did what most dad and son's do, but their special time was in the water surfing. That was Mark's love, surfing, and he bought Robert his first board at nine years of age. Robert fell in love with surfing and to this day he has two of Mark's boards in which he surfs on and treasures.

Mark's love of surfing started when he was young. He went on to join the NSSA National Scholastic Surfing Team and won the NSSA National Championship in 1978. He was called Mark the Shark in the water and after he died my son had a shark tattooed on his back. So when Mark died we had a paddle out in his honor, the day after we had his celebration of life at the church. Surfers around the world practice this ritual, known as a memorial paddle out, usually to honor the life of a fallen surfer. There were probably hundred surfers in the water and hundred people on the beach to honor Mark. It was beautiful and it was the glue that kept me pieced together during that day. I had everyone sign his National Championship board at the celebration of life service and the paddle out. It hangs on my wall over my bed as a comforting memoir of how special and loving my husband was. I treasure the significance and the love that is written in signatures on that board.

Mark the Shark—November 13, 1958 to January 9, 2012—the legacy between the dash—will never be forgotten.

Part One:

Bereavement

"Blessed are those who mourn for they will be comforted."
—Jesus

What Now?

———✸———

Mark, I miss you so much. I feel like my insides have been ripped out of me. Mark, my better half . . . you are gone and I can't wrap my mind around it. I can't sleep. Everyone has said such wonderful things about you . . . because, well, you are wonderful. What am I going to do now? Mark . . . I love you. You were my best friend.

Rearrange

———✸———

"Shock is a merciful condition. It allows you to get through disaster with necessary distance between you and your feelings."
—Lisa Kleypus

The Monday Mark passed away will be forever etched in my mind. It was an ordinary day, nothing spectacular. Mark had gone to a business meeting earlier and was home, getting ready to take his daily run, and I was studying and working on my business.

The previous night, we'd played ping-pong, and I noticed that Mark was sweating. It was a frigid January night, and we were outside playing. I asked him if he was all right, and he said yes. I remember we had a fun night—probably the best time we'd had in a while. That whole day prior to playing ping pong that night was a good day. It was something very special about that day. It was as if God gave us a special day. We had gone to church earlier, in separate cars. We were meeting friends for breakfast, and I got there first. He pulled up, picked up a plastic poinsettia flower that was lying on the sidewalk, and handed it to me through the window. He said, "Here are your flowers today. Picked it just for you." I smiled and laughed. Little did I know how much that flower, which could never die, would mean to me. Mark used to bring me fresh flowers a lot. He knew I loved flowers. He would surprise me with them, he knew I loved to put them in our big bay windows in the living room. This was one of those little things that God gives you to show He loves you. We had a meal with two dear friends and then went home to our beachfront condo.

Monday came around, as it comes every week: Monday, January, 9th, 2012. This wasn't just another Monday. Life brings with it unexpected experiences that forever change us, after which one could say, "That was the Monday my life was like this, and this Monday my life is something different."

I went against my intuition, my spirit, my gut. Right before my husband left for his run, he came in the office, where I was diligently studying, and said, "I'm going for my run now." My gut told me to get up and hug him goodbye. Now, I don't usually hug him when he goes for a run. Because, after all, I'd see him after his run, right? I sat there, in my chair—the distance seems so foreign now—and said, "Have a good run, baby." Oh, why didn't I get up and hug him? It has taught me a lesson to listen to my gut, to listen to that voice inside.

About forty minutes later, I heard the door open, then this loud bump and a grunt. Then a thud. I yelled out, "Mark, are you okay?" I went into the kitchen to discover Mark in convulsions, blue, fingers curled up. It's a sight anyone would love to forget. He was swelling in his face and body. . . I thought he was having a seizure of some kind. I called 911, and they asked if I knew CPR. Yes, I did, but I couldn't even think what to do. I was just in shock. My mind couldn't conceive of what was happening. My heart hurt. I put the phone down and on speaker as I tried chest compression and breathing for him, waiting for the ambulance. It seemed time stopped and the seconds were hours, but the paramedics arrived in a few minutes. I was yelling at Mark, screaming at him not to die…don't die on me. I was breathing into hollowness. I was saying breathe Mark, come on breathe. The 911 operator kept asking me to feel for a pulse. My mind would trick me. I would feel a pulse and see him breathing, but the reality was he didn't or wasn't breathing. It was a complete nightmare. I could not grasp it. I mean forty minutes ago he was standing in front of me with his navy blue jogging pants and matching jacket on talking to me. His voice. Talk to me Mark. Please, let me hear your voice. I never got to hear his voice again. Please God…don't do this. Please don't let him die. In times like this you beg…beg…plead…and hope that God will work a miracle. The ambulance got there and worked on him for what seemed like hours, but wasn't. They finally put him on a stretcher and told me to follow them to the hospital. I asked if he would be all right, and they said, "Ma'am, he's not breathing on his own, but we'll do the best we can."

So I called my oldest brother, Alan; then my best friend, Vanessa; then my other brother, Danny—in that order. Vanessa was going to drive to the house and get me, but I couldn't wait. I drove to the hospital in a daze, and they took me to that damn sitting area, where I'd been once before with a friend who had lost her mom. I knew that's where you went when there was no hope. It was the "it's over" room. No more wishing, hoping, or prayers. The your-life-will-never-be-the-same room. The dreaded change room. It was done; my fifty-three-year-young husband of close to sixteen years was gone. My mind flashed back to the man I shared vows with. Words, to death do you part, hit me like a brick wall being thrown through a window and breaking it into pieces, but the window was my heart.

Eventually I had to leave the change room. The hospital staff led me to where his body was. I was so grateful to go back and see him. I guess I was hoping to find him alive. That it had all been a horrible mistake. That he was ok. But, it wasn't a mistake. He was at peace. His body was done with this time on earth, and his spirit was just beginning. For me, he was the body that I could touch and feel and see and hear, but now he was spirit that I couldn't touch, feel, hear, or see. Not that night. He was just a shell I had to say goodbye to. His body was empty, but his spirit was full.

I had to go home. I had to call my son and tell him his step-dad was gone. Robert called Mark dad. He was like a daddy to him. He had been with Robert since he was two and a half years old. Robert was hundreds of miles away and only six months into his Navy career, and about to receive the phone call no son wants to get, especially so young. I said, "Robert, Mark is gone." He said, "Mom, are you sure? I think you need to check with the doctors. Mom, you just think that." Miles away, a cold phone call . . . a familiar voice echoing some very foreign words. His dad had died.

Thus the changes began. Just like that. Just like that. In one day. One run. One life gone. How could it be?

I wanted to stay in that cold hospital room, I wanted to stay with the empty shell, lie in those white sheets. I wanted to cuddle with him. I wanted to feel his arms around me, hear his voice, see his blue eyes. The body that once had life, laughter, smiles, tears, anger, pain, was a shell now. I wanted to stay there until the nightmare was over. Until I woke up and everything was like it was before Mark went for his run.

But I had to leave. I had to do what I heard other people did when they lost their loved ones: make arrangements. That seems funny— arrangements for whom? For what? What was to be arranged—my life? My son's life? The funeral, the paddle-out? Letting friends know they'd lost Mark? Arranging what, for God's sake? My life had just *been* arranged. . . to something I couldn't bear, life without Mark. I didn't want to arrange anymore. I wanted to rearrange everything to be the way it was before Mark's run. Couldn't we just rearrange?

Labor Pains

Photo Credit: August Perry

It's been one week since you went to your real home. Mark . . . it seems like it is still that night . . . last Monday . . . when they told me you were gone. I still can't believe you aren't here. I cannot grasp it at all. But you are at your real home. Even though I know you are ok, my world has stopped, time has stood still, and I'm not sure when it will begin again.

Paul's letters in the Bible tell us to live is Christ and to die is gain. You did just that: You lived for Him and now you have gained Him. You are with your love. I am left here to carry on for . . . some purpose.

8

Mark, it hurts so bad. It's like labor pains; they come in waves, only the pain is like waves inside my heart, breaking over and over again. The pain comes faster and faster with no relief and no epidural to ease them. No birth from these pains . . . only the thought when will it ease up. The only relief I have is knowing I will see you again and that you are so full of joy right now. It's just like the relief that comes when your child is born; the physical pain ends and the joy begins. Your birth came again...heaven...Mark . . . I love you . . . I miss you.

"Let not your hearts be troubled. Believe in God; Believe in Jesus. In my Father's house are many rooms. If it were not so, would I have told you that I go to prepare a place for you? And if I go and prepare a place for you, I will come again and will take you to myself, that where I am you may be also. And you know the way to where I am going" (John 14:1–2).

Sucked Down a Dark Hole.

———— ❧ ————

"She was overstrained with grief and loneliness; almost any shoulder would have done as well." —*F. Scott Fitzgerald*

Well, Mark, today has been two weeks. You know, honey, I've been running as fast as I can, trying to escape the reality that you're in that prepared home in heaven and I'm still here. The shock began to leave me when I hit that wall—no, when I smashed into that wall. It was as if my heart and body had been broken into several tiny pieces scattered all over the place. I mean they are everywhere. Pieces. I could never even find them much less figure out how to put them back into a whole. A whole heart or a whole body. I wonder how Jesus is going to pick them up and put them back together. I can't. I wouldn't even know where to start.

Grief is a lonely place. It's as if I've been sucked down a hole that I don't want to be in; it's dark and I don't know where the end is, so I fight it. I fight it because I don't want to be in this dark hole. But, here I am. I am here whether I fight it or now. The suction from the darkness keeps me there. There's no light and there are no people. I would rather my life be like it was, Mark, when you were here. But it's not, and it will never be again.

Mark, we have all these great friends, and your friends have been so sweet to me. You have the best friends, Mark. They loved you so much. And I have the best friends, too. We are so blessed. But, that being said, I still feel so terribly alone. Most the times they really don't know what to do or say. How can they? I don't even know what to do or say. I want to talk, but I don't. I want to hug someone, but I don't. I want a friend, but I want you. No one can enter this place with me—no one but Jesus. Everyone tells me that it will get better with each passing day, they try to say the right thing, but to be honest, Mark, I miss you more with each passing day and it seems, at least right now, that it will keep getting worse. I love you so much and need your direction in so many areas of my life, and you aren't here. Honey, I pray that through your death the Lord will be glorified and I will honor you. Peace. I need Peace.

"Trust in the Lord with all your heart, and do not lean on your own understanding. In all your ways acknowledge him, and he will make straight your paths" (Prov. 3:5–6).

The Rollercoaster

"No one ever told me that grief felt so like fear."
—*C.S. Lewis*

It has been three weeks since you went home. On one hand, it seems as if time has stood still; I cling to you, and I don't want to let you go. On the other hand, it's as if it's been eternity since I last saw your face, felt your touch, or heard your laugh. I can see there are no shortcuts around this grief. I would love for there to be one. I'm not good at this sort of thing. I don't have a lot of patience with myself. I would rather skip, jump over, go around, or ignore the journey to healing.

My emotions are on a rollercoaster ride. I wish they would take the merry-go-round . . . nothing disarming about a merry-go-round. I used to like the roller-coaster ride. I used to like the thrill of being scared on rides and feeling that fear. Remember when we did ride it in Myrtle Beach acting like kids? We did ride the merry-go-round too and so many times with Robert. Robert never liked the rollercoaster when he was little, but he loved the Merry-go-round. What has happened to the merry-go-round? I don't want to feel this fear anymore. There is no comfort from this fear or is there?

"But we do not want you to be uniformed brothers, about those who are asleep, that you may not grieve as others do who have no hope."
—*1 Thessalonians 4:13*

The Identity

—∞—

I still don't feel like doing anything. My mind has to make my feet move forward. Family and friends have been supportive. And, well, Jesus . . . life is not worth living without Him. I know that when I pray to Jesus, you are right there, Mark, looking at Jesus. Wow . . . Jesus connects me to you. I like that connection. I don't understand any of this, but I don't have to. I just have to trust Jesus. It's what gets me through.

Because . . . it would be so easy to use grief as my identity. My mind keeps telling my heart, "Don't put the grief identity on, and don't wear that label." So when I read the following from *Grieving with Hope*, it rang true:

> As you are trying to adjust to your new reality, be careful not to choose grief as your new identity. Your grief and your loss should never define you. As Paul Tripp says, "Grief is a very significant human experience. It was never meant to be an identity. When I take it on as an identity, it will hurt me."
>
> If you take on grief as your identity, you'll give yourself permission to isolate yourself, sleep away the days, let your responsibilities go, ignore your family—all the while telling yourself, 'It's okay because I'm grieving' . . .
>
> Grief is not an identity, and if I make it my identity, I'll start giving way to whatever definition of that identity I've given it. Grief is a profound experience to go through, and it rocks a person to the core. It's disruptive, dislocating, and highly emotional. But this experience doesn't define me. Christ defines me.[1]

1 Samuel J. Hodges IV and Kathy Leonard, *Grieving with Hope: Finding Comfort as You Journey Through Loss (Grand Rapids, MI: Baker Books, 2011), 53 and 54.*

The questions I'm asking myself now are: What identity am I putting on? What label am I wearing? Maybe, I want to wear my grief identity. Maybe I want to get up every day and put this label on. It is defining me and I hate it. I hate it. I can't get it off. It's sewn on.

Ticket for the Next Train . . . Please

"The darker the night, the brighter the stars,
the deeper the grief the closer God."
—*Fyodor Dostoyevsky*

Well, Mark, I'm walking into my fourth week since you went home. Four weeks. Maybe it's more like stumbling into my first month without you by my side. Strange times. I have true empathy for those who lose loved ones., and I think about those who suffer losing more than one person at a time or over a short period. I cannot imagine it. I cannot fathom their pain. I can't even fathom mine.

The grief at times is almost more than I can endure. I wanted to hop on a train the other night and go . . . somewhere other than here. Anywhere fast would be good . . . faster . . . farther. To *no*where would be good. Away from the memories of you and me. To a place I could just erase everything that was happening now. To a place that everything would be like it was. Away from this sorrow.

Part of me is gone... I can't run from that. You went your way, and now I have to go mine. I have to face it. When will I believe you are really gone? You know my mind knows you aren't coming back, but in my heart there is hope.

I took all your clothes and things out of the room. Someone said it was too soon. I said, "I can look at those things for a year and it wouldn't bring Mark back." I can smell them, wear them, or treasure them, but Mark, you aren't in the clothes or physical items. You aren't here. I look for you, but you are not here.

I can't even seem to find a picture of you that is any good. Because the picture is just a memory. I want to hear your voice, hear your laugh, see your face move . . . The photograph doesn't have your varying facial expressions or your laughter.

I am thankful for the times we did have together, Mark. I am thankful for the blessings that have come in the midst of this pain. Peace and suffering, blessings and tragedies—they can be bound together as one.

My mind cannot fathom the depth of love You have for us, Jesus, or what You suffered on that forsaken cross. You, above all, know what suffering is about—what pain, loss, and abandonment are. You and You alone can enter my pain. No one else can walk with me during this time in the potter's hand. I really wouldn't want anyone to try. Because they can't. After all, Jesus, you created me; You know what is in my heart more than I do. You died for me, for us—who else has ever died so I could live again? So that I can see Mark again. So that I can find him again.

"Then I saw 'a new heaven and a new earth,' for the first heaven and the first earth had passed away, and the sea was no more. And I saw the holy city, new Jerusalem, coming down out of heaven from God, prepared as a bride adorned for her husband. And I heard a loud voice from the throne saying, 'Behold, the dwelling place of God is with man. He will dwell with them as their God. He will wipe away every tear from their

eyes, and death shall be no more, neither shall there be mourning nor crying nor pain anymore, for the former things had passed away'"
— *Revelations 21:1–4.*

Lord, may I be a light for You today.

Valentine's Day

———— ∞∞∞ ————

In a letter to Thomas Jefferson on May 6, 1816, John Adams wrote, "Grief drives men into the habits of serious reflection, sharpens the understanding, and softens the heart."[2]

Made it through another week of this process called mourning. I have to admit; last week was one of the toughest yet. Valentine's Day was almost more than I could bear. A friend came by and brought me flowers. She meant nothing but love and care. But, for me it was a stark reminder that you, honey, were not there to give me flowers, as you always did. I told her thank you quickly and practically slammed the door in her face. I thought the nerve of her to remind me of my husband's absents on Valentine's day. That's what happens. You lose your sense of thankfulness at times. You lose who you are. You forget who friends are and enemies are. My friends are not the enemy…the enemy is fear. This Valentines it sure didn't seem like my friend was a friend. Valentines was so special to us. We had even bought these champagne flutes, from Waterford Chrystal, that had hearts on them just for Valentines. I thought Mark and I would

---

2 John Adams, *The Works of John Adams, Second President of the United States, Volume 10* *(Boston: Little, Brown and Company, 1856), 218.*

be toasting good cheer with them again this year, instead I was toasting my grief. But, I allowed Jesus in after I slid down the wall with flowers in hand and the familiar tears running down my cheeks.

Another way to express this first holiday without Mark . . . through anger and tears, but I emerged from under the weight of the crushing waves that held me under, taking my breath, making me feel as if my lungs would burst from lack of air, tossing me around as I looked for the surface . . .

Only to be stronger after Valentines was over when Jesus reached down and rescued me from drowning . . . so much so that it gave me a more intimate look at Jesus; I promise you, I could reach out and touch His face. I think of Peter wanting to walk on water, then sinking, and Jesus immediately—yes, immediately—reached out His hand and pulled him up. "'O you of little faith, why did you doubt?'" (Matt. 14:31). Why *do* we doubt? Why do we doubt that Jesus will rescue us? Why do we doubt His word?

Regret

"Grief is not as heavy as guilt, but it takes more away from you."
—*Veronica Roth*

Ever want a memory to be real? Ever want reality just to be an illusion? Ever want the dream back? It just seems like too much work to begin again. Sometimes it feels like I don't have the energy to have a new dream. The old dream was once that new dream, the new hope of a wonderful life.

This morning was one of those mornings when I wish my reality weren't . . . well . . . my reality.

I was tucking away some more pictures and admiring Mark's signed surfboard last night. Everyone had signed Mark's surfboard at the celebration of life and paddle out. Mark loved that board. He was a keeper and took great care of those things he treasured. He didn't have one mark on that board and it was thirty- four years old. I will never forget the morning I looked at it and panicked when I saw all the signatures. For one small second . . . I thought Mark is going to kill me. That second between hope and reality. So, I was just doing one step at a time to help the reality not be hope that he was still here somewhere. It was therapeutic Going through some things of his . . . sorting . . . putting away. My way.

Looking at his surfboard made me flash back to an image in my mind, a memory of a dream loss and a regret.

Regret: sorrow caused by something beyond one's power to remedy.

I generally look at past experiences as learning, growing, molding experiences. In other words, I'm one who'd say, "I have no regrets in life." Even though . . . there is plenty of my life that I'd like to have not occurred. But through the years I've learned that those choices and experiences, even the ones I had absolutely no control over or didn't like, have made me who I am—strong, a survivor, and a lover of life and of others.

However, there's one regret that keeps haunting me: that I only surfed with Mark, for three times one fall. I mean, for over seventeen years, he wanted me to surf with him. I didn't. I don't know, really, why I didn't. I enjoyed watching him and being a small part of that community (which at the time I never really understood)

It was two summers ago when Mark got me out in the water at the end of August. A good friend of Mark's let me ride his board. It was a nine-foot longboard. His buddies Herb and Garrett (he took Garrett under his wing; he just loved him and wanted to help him become a better surfer . . .which he has—Mark would be so proud). Mark was so proud of me. He said I stood on the first wave and rode the line. I didn't know what that was, but hey—Mark loved it!

In fact, while going through his messages on Facebook, after he died, I saw where he told a friend about it—about how excited he was that I went out surfing. He said he couldn't wait until the next summer when I could surf again—and said how proud he was of me.

But I didn't surf that summer, the summer of 2011. I was too busy working on my personal training and coaching studies and certifications, because I needed to start working again

Then he died that January. Wow . . . regrets.

So . . . when he died, I was trying to line up a canoe or something I could go out in for the paddle-out . . . so I could spread his ashes. Well, that morning came, and I was crouching by our favorite brown chair, in which I write now, by the sliding glass door through which I could see the ocean and the cabanas. As I kneeled there, I said to God, "I don't want to live anymore. I can't live without Mark. I don't want to live without Mark." Please take me. "Why didn't you take me instead of Mark?"

Anyway, I'd planned to get someone to canoe me out at the paddle-out, because I had only surfed once and that had been two summers previously, just three times. And that day of all days, I didn't feel like it. Then, as I was asking God to take me, telling Him I didn't want to live, I heard Him say, "Get up. GET UP. You are not dead. You are alive and well, and you have a purpose—and work to do. Look around." I looked through the sliding glass door. and all of Mark's friends were there, waving at me from the beach, getting the paddle-out ready. It was life. Everyone was living life. Celebrating Mark's life. Remembering their good times with him. I was among the living. As numb as I felt, I was still alive. I hadn't died with Mark. His purpose was done. Mine purpose wasn't and neither were those of the others who still lived.

God is good like that; you know—supplying what you need at the very moment you need it. When you are broken, He sends love, grace, goodness, friends, and family your way.

Well, it was like I had this sudden strength . . . like Jesus was compelling me—like Mark was compelling me—to paddle out on a board. So, someone called Herb and he brought the board I had used a couple of summers ago. I'm paddling out. I'm not canoeing out. . . That's not who I am. I am Sweet Strength! That's what Mark told me." I paddled out there on that board: energy high, love deep, and with a spirit driven to honor my best friend. And I wasn't even cold.

Since that day, I've felt compelled to be in the water . . . to have that oneness with God, with Mark, and with friends.

But I still have that regret that I cannot surf with the one person who loved it most and who wanted me to surf with him. He would be so proud of me and probably wouldn't believe I was out there in that cold water. I would give anything for the opportunity to surf with Mark . . . to be with him in that water. I may not be that good . . . yet . . . but I *will* get better because I am determined. I know that Mark would want me to continue to live life and not have regrets, even of not going out surfing with him . . . but I do.

I hope that he's looking over me. Somehow I know he is. Hey, I have his fins on my board—and they're more expensive than the board! Mark would like that.

I love you, Mark. I hope I make you proud in the water. I'm sure going to try.

Linda McDandel

Everywhere, but Nowhere

———∞∞———

"Without you in my arms, I feel an emptiness in my soul. I find myself searching the crowds for your face — I know, it's an impossibility, but I cannot help myself." —*Nicholas Sparks*

I can't believe that on the ninth it will have been four months since Mark went home. Time has stood still for me in the midst of the movement of the clock. I still find it hard to believe that you are not with me. I mean, Mark grew up here and knew so many people, and so many people loved him. We have so many special places we went together . . . but he simply isn't in any of those places.

In fact, I went to one of those places yesterday . . . our favorite Mexican Restaurant, Fiesta Mexicana, hoping to meet him there. I was with our friends. Surely they knew where you were. I just wanted to be around who Mark was around, who loved him, who he loved; I wanted to go to our usual spots, hoping to grab a glimpse of him. I even turned my car around the other day to go back and get a better look at a bicyclist I'd passed who looked just like you, bud. I know it seems so crazy. I see you in the lineup in the water with the surfers. I could swear I see you. The guy on the bike, had your grey hair, your smile, a surf shirt on. Mark is everywhere, but nowhere to be found. Now, I know he isn't in any of those special places, just like I knew he wasn't on that bike, but my heart just wanted him to be there so badly. So yesterday was a special day of grieving, which is good. It's okay to grieve, to cry, to miss Mark . . . in fact, it's very healing. I thought it would be easier by now, but it's not. I am beginning to wonder when it will. I know to my friends I must be hard to understand. I am not who I was. I don't even know who I am now.

20

Everything has changed. I used to love change, but this is just too much. Nothing is the same—*nothing*. Even though it hasn't changed physically—where I live, the pictures I have hanging, my furniture's positions, my friends and family, the sunrises and sunsets, my daily routine—it's all changed to me because . . . well . . . I see differently now, through a different lens, because I've changed and am still changing. Yes, change is everywhere to me.

Earlier today, as I listed all the changes in my mind, wishing there was *something* in my life that hadn't changed, I heard this strong but faint voice say to me, "Linda . . . I haven't changed. I am the same yesterday, today, and tomorrow. I will never change. I am alpha and omega, beginning and end. I will neither leave nor forsake you. When your heart and flesh fail, I will be your strength forever. What a relief that was for me—a comfort—to hear that voice and to know there is *something* I can count on that does not change: God. He is always with us . . . always pulling for us, loving us, comforting us. He is the lone rock in the midst of sinking sand. As we change and things around us change, we can count on the one who never changes. He will not let you go. There are two things you can count on in this life: Your life will change . . . but God will not.

God, I pray for all those who are dealing with change in their lives, who are thinking, *this is just too much change; it's too hard*—God, I pray that You will remind them that you are God who does not change; You will bless and keep them, and will make your face shine upon them. I pray that they will be granted the grace and love to see you clearly. I pray that they will see that You are their hope and comfort in this every-changing world in which we live.

No Dinner

—∞∞∞—

"So it's true when all is said and done, grief is the price we pay for love"
—E.A. Bucchianeri

Mark, I would love to wake up this morning and say, "Happy anniversary! I look forward to more years together . . . but I can't. You are home and I am here. No flowers, no three cards, and no dinner at our favorite restaurant today. . . not this year. I remember our fifth anniversary date. You always made anniversaries so special. We went to Greg Normans Grill in North Myrtle Beach. You pulled out this little black case. You handed it to me and said Happy Anniversary! I opened it up. It was the most beautiful diamond I had ever seen. I couldn't believe it. I said, "Mark, where did you get this?" He said, "it was in my safe deposit box. It was my great aunt's ring and she gave it to my mom." It was made in 1895. I then jokily said, "What else is in that safe deposit box." I knew at that moment Mark McDandel loved me. He treasured his family's heirlooms. I knew that if he gave me his mom's ring, he deeply loved me. Mark had lost his mom and dad. He was an only child. His dad was an only child. His mom just had one brother. I never understood that about heirlooms. How important they were when you lose someone. I was the one who always cleaned out and through away. Mark used to pick on me and tell me he was glad I wasn't the one who found the Dead Sea Scrolls, because I would have said, "Look at this old thing, let's toss it." I was never a keeper, until now. I don't want to give anything away.

I miss you so much. Part of me is gone, tossed aside, thrown away. But, I know you would want me to carry on with my life. I am trying to do just that: learn to live without you, learn a new way. Thank you for living out our marriage vows. I remember the dreams I had the week before you died. I dreamed every night you were leaving me. Leaving me for another lover. I remember picking on you when I would wake up about it. We laughed, because I never had to worry about you lying to me, running around on me, or leaving me—until now, that is. It is as if the dream was preparing me for your leaving. You did leave me for another lover. You left me for a better life . . . a better love. Your true love, Jesus, and that makes me smile. Bud, I will always love you. I am so honored to have been your wife. You are gone, but babe, you are not forgotten. It was for better or worse, richer or poorer, in health and in sickness that we made it . . . until death do us part. I honor you this day . . . in love.

The World Keeps Spinning

"No matter how bad your heart is broken;
the world doesn't stop for your grief."
— *Faraaz Kuzi*

I was reading an article on grief and in it, the author talks about losing his wife and how the world is still going on around him. Boy, do I relate to him when he says something like this, "Those people don't even know that Cindy's dead, I thought. For them it's business as usual . . . just like any other day. The world is staying right on schedule and all of life is moving on. How can it be? It doesn't seem right. I felt like crying out, 'Hey folks, don't you know my wife died?

Isn't it written all over my face? My world has crashed, and you don't even care!'"

He goes on to say God gave him a crystal clear message: "Ike, all of this life around you isn't going to stop. It's up to you to decide how much time you will take out of your life before you pick yourself up and go on. You can take a month, three months, six . . . a year. Or you can take a lifetime. What will it be?"

I like that because, it is truth. The world never stops because of our pains or trials; it keeps spinning, and people keep living and going about their lives. I could so relate. My world had stopped, but no one's else life had stopped. I wanted to scream out loud so many days and say . . . the same thing . . . just the name was Mark . . . he is dead can't you understand that? But, we do have a choice to either join life again or walk out of life. Death happens to everyone, although we are never ready for it to happen to us or those we love. One thing is for sure: We are all going to die. We live in a tough world, and we aren't promised a rose garden (just like Lynn Anderson's song, "Rose Garden," says). When these things happen to us, we can choose to linger there or search for the answers to some pivotal questions while we're there. This way we can become stronger and help others as we move forward, out of that feeling of hopelessness and helplessness, and start living again. It's just some days I want the world to stop with me. Thank you God that you are the one who keeps the world spinning even if I want it to stop.

My Home

—⊶∘∘∘⊷—

*"Deep grief sometimes is almost like a specific location, a coordinate
on a map of time. When you are standing in that forest of sorrow, you
cannot imagine that you could ever find your way to a better place. But
if someone can assure you that they themselves have stood in that same
place, and now have moved on, sometimes this will bring hope."*
— *Elizabeth Gilbert*

Wow, seven months have gone by so quickly as I sifted through the debris in my life . . . the fallout . . . the change. Debris always comes with a fallout and then sorting through it all: the treasures and the trash. The death of a loved one and all the trash and treasures that come with it. There are times when the memories seem so haunting that I want an escape, and yet there are days they can be so comforting that I want to engrave them in my mind . . . brand them there so they are seared forever, never to leave.

There are days when I feel like I'm on the non-threatening merry-go-round. Round . . . round . . . and round we go. It's the same scene . . . not going anywhere, but always moving. Then there are days when I feel I'm on a runaway horse that's weary to get back home . . . racing, fast and furious, to that old familiar place he knows as home. I try to guide him but realize I have absolutely no control. I hold on to the reins, hoping to stop him but all the while praying he'll take me home with him to somewhere familiar . . . somewhere comforting. My arms are burning from the grip and my legs are gripping so tightly that they've become numb. Part of me is fearful, but another part is excited about the freedom of not knowing where we're headed. I know he knows the way home, so all I have to do is not lose my grip. I just can't lose my grip and he will take me home. To the familiar. To safety. To security. To my home.

Pain . . . change . . . loss . . . distraction. Please distract me from this loss. Seven months closing in . . . seven months of finding my way . . . losing my way . . . wondering where home is…missing my family, my home. Missing who I was as a wife, all the while moving forward to embrace this new single way of life. Missing my only son, Robert, who is in the Navy now. Missing our family life. Embracing a new life and living it the best I can . . . because I love life. Trying to figure out who this new person is and how I got here and where the heck I'm going. Where is my horse that knows the way…that is going to take me home? It's as if I'm observing myself from another place and time. Then there's the solid rock I always try to stand on, but sometimes in the midst of shifting sand, I lose my balance and fall. Jesus is so aware of where I stand or fall. I know He is with me in my heart and in my soul . . . but honestly, there are days when I want Him here in human form . . . not just in spirit. I long for that embrace. I long for that shoulder to cry on—that human touch. Jesus I need your touch.

Why cry? There is no one here. I can almost go into that place that Pink Floyd so eloquently sings about. I have become comfortably numb. I think after you've experienced so many changes in your life, year after year—big changes and small—you begin to live differently. You realize that nothing is secure. This is not our home. We are truly strangers in this place and time. We really own nothing, and tomorrow could bring another change.

There are days when I say to my friends, "I really want some stability. I need stability." But God says, "I am stability. . . I'm all the stability you need." Can I trust that? Do I have a choice? Stability . . . what is it? Are any of us so sure we have it? When everything is so unsure, it is that faith . . . that truth . . . that love that will bring you through.

This is not our home; this is not our destination. We have a more awesome destination where we will again meet those we have lost . . . but there's healing to do, a life to live to the fullest, and love to be given to those who are still with us . . . because those who have gone before us are . . . well, they're just fine. Their horse took them home; they don't need us anymore. Faith is the confidence of things hoped for and the conviction of things not seen . . . hold on . . .

Memories Rewritten

———— ❦ ————

"When a relationship of love is disrupted, the relationship does not cease. The love continues; therefore, the relationship continues. The work of grief is to reconcile and redeem life to a different love relationship."
— *W. Scott Lineberry*

Memories etched and memories rewritten. Eight months today. I miss you, honey. Thank you for the words this morning . . .

About once a month, I like to look at cards Mark gave me, and sometimes I look at messages he sent people through Facebook. The following was written about a month before he died. What a special gift to leave me with. He was talking with a friend whom he evidently hadn't seen in a while.

"I had a heart attack in May 2007, and it is a miracle I'm here, but the Lord saved me that day. I had 100 percent blockage in the 'widow maker' artery, and 97 percent of people don't make it through that. I was under a lot of stress at the time, developing some condos. My family also has a history of heart disease. But I'm doing great now! I'm eating healthy, running, walking, bicycling, and, of course, surfing. The economy did have an effect on me financially, but everything is okay, and I'm married to a wonderful, beautiful woman who stuck with me through all of it."

Now . . . that will make a girl smile. I am no expert on relationships, but I do know that any day could be your last to spend with your partner, friend, or family member. So is it really worth arguing over who took out the trash or was supposed to drive the kids to school? Over who did what to the other?

Going back to memories . . . There are times at night when I'm lying in bed in the darkness, loneliness, and that deafening silence—I think silence is an oxymoron because it can be so loud. Maybe some of you know it . . . the silence of loneliness. The thoughts of memories reverberating with a sound that becomes etched in the recesses of your mind. You can hear the sounds of the memories. You can see the images so clearly that they become like a tattoo you got in a drunken stupor, and now you want to get rid of it. But it's there, etched on your skin, with the sounds surrounding the whole thing. A reminder . . . a reminder of a night you wish you could erase . . . Or maybe the silence is the lack of that other breath that used to be beside you in the darkness of the night. It felt safe, hearing that breath . . . If you listen closely enough, you might be able to hear it.

What a different meaning breathing and breath have to me today. There are some memories you never want to forget . . . Trying to bring the good memories to life, you squint your eyes so hard and squeeze your teeth together in hope that you can bring the memory of the one you lost to life. Like, maybe if I squeeze my eyes together hard enough and think hard enough, I can bring Mark's touch to me, hear his breath beside me, feel his eyes penetrating my very soul, his smile, his voice and his love. Then there's the horrid memory—the one you wish you could forget: the thud as his body hit the kitchen floor . . . that haunting image of his body in convulsions . . . then the stillness . . . the stillness of his body as I tried to breathe life into it . . . into hollowness, while I hoped that God would come down and breathe for him—knowing He could, if He wanted to. That is something you can never forget. In fact, it's so loud it sometimes drowns out those memories you want at the forefront of your mind. You can't just turn the noise down or off—it keeps your mind wide awake . . . and sleep doesn't come.

Well, this morning, during my run, I began to see that memory differently on this eight-month path to healing and peace. Peace does come, rewriting that memory and taking the place of that haunting night, making it beautiful in its own right. Rewriting your story, your life—kind of like if you were to laser off that old tattoo and put something new in its place. I thought to myself this morning, I am going to rewrite that memory. Yep—erase it and rewrite it into a beautiful story . . . the right story . . . the true story.

As I was trying to breathe life into Mark, Jesus was breathing a new life into Mark—a better breath, and a better life than I could ever give him. His home . . . his better home . . . his real home—*that* is the beauty in death. I got to be with Mark as he breathed his last breath with me and as Jesus gave him his first breath of his new life with Jesus, his real love. That is reality, that is truth, and that is well . . . like a breath of fresh air with a gentle wind. And, oh . . . the sound of that memory is like my favorite place . . . the ocean . . . the lullaby of the waves crashing on the shore.

So now, instead of seeing Mark's lifeless body on the floor and feeling the hollowness I felt when I breathed into empty lungs, I see nothing but a beautiful beginning of an everlasting life for Mark.

Mark, I love you, and I thank you for giving me love. And Jesus,

I thank You for allowing me to rewrite my memory so I can see it for what it really is—life, not death.

Encourage

———∞∞∞———

"Maybe everyone can live beyond what they are capable of."
— *Markus Zusak*

On this cool cloudy morning, I'm missing you, Mark. Grief is like that. It just has no rhyme or reason. It's no particular anniversary, holiday, or birthday . . . just a day like any other, and yet I'm struggling with my grief. But I just have to go with it . . .

In Loving Memory of my Husband and Best Friend, Mark "the Shark"
November 13, 1958 - January 9, 2012

In 1995, I met Mark. I had just divorced and was the mother of a two-and-a-half-year-old. Mark and I fell in love and were married in 1996. We bought our dream home in 1997 and lived our lives fully. Like most married couples, we had our ups and downs, and we both chased our own careers. Mark had a couple of different adventures, but he decided he was going to develop some condos because at that time, the real estate market was booming. Mark put his heart and soul into developing condos. And Robert, our son, was enjoying his childhood in an awesome neighborhood, doing what boys love to do best when they live at the ocean: surfing and hanging out with his friends while investigating life.

Meanwhile, my husband was wrapped up in the process of building and trying to sell condos while the market slowed. There were several challenges that arose in the process of building these condos, too, and I could see my husband's stress level rise. We put both our house and the condo's on the market and neither ended up selling. But, Mark would smile in the midst of it.

You know, Mark, I miss your smile more than anything. And on my run this morning, I was thinking how you would say, "Whoa, doggie mama," when I came out of the bedroom dressed to go out to dinner or somewhere special. You gave me that grin and that look . . . You gave me that same grin and look the night before your last run . . . the day you went home. I will never forget it . . .

Mark always encouraged me and built me up, telling me I was smart and beautiful . . . that I could do anything I wanted, and that if anything ever happened to him, I would be fine . . . and to move forward. That, my friends, enabled me to take a class for life coaching two weeks after he left me. That encouragement and strength has enabled me, even in the pain, to smile and try to encourage others. That encouragement over the years has allowed me to grow, love who I am, and love others where they are.

Mark always had that smile. He cared for others and wanted them to feel encouraged and like they were his best friend. No one but me ever knew how stressed he was . . . how he hated what he was dealing with financially . . . all the debt. Mark and I never liked self-pity. It can be fun for a time, but there are so many people worse off than you, people who have been through or are going through incredibly tough times. All you have to do is walk out your door and look around, read the paper, or just look on Facebook. Now, I'm not saying you should ignore what you're going through because there are others worse off . . . because there are also others in a better place than you.

But sometimes, by encouraging others, you're helping yourself heal. And it's okay to grieve, to feel pain, and to be in a bad place . . . You just don't have to stay there. There is always a choice, and only you can make that choice. So . . . I would rather smile and encourage than stay in grief. Mark would want that. He would smile.

In all of this, I am trying to encourage people to love, to laugh, to encourage one another in their relationships . . . to give each other strength so when something happens to one person, the other will be able to move forward and not to have regrets.

I am going to share my smile today . . . Mark would like that.

Displaced

I'm sitting here, thinking about the rolling out of the ninth month and heading to the tenth month since Mark went home. I've been pondering about what is now a recurring feeling . . . trying to identify words that could describe this feeling. Displaced, misplaced, missing

. . . I think those could sum up and describe my journey thus far. Kind of like a puzzle that hasn't been put together yet. I've been trying to figure out the theme or one word that could describe my journey, and for me it's the word "displaced"—you know, moved from a normal place or position. Change . . . disarranged . . . the dictionary describes these as the state of being displaced, of having been moved from the usual or proper place. Maybe it's similar to misplaced. Yes, that is how I feel displaced and misplaced. But, in the middle of displacement I must learn how to live life again. To use my displacement as a bridge to learning how to live in my new arranged and disarranged life. Maybe I feel displaced because part of me is missing . . . not necessarily the physical aspect of feeling like I don't have a home, but the heart of it. Yes, my heart is displaced…Maybe part of it is because I am not home yet, my real home. I mean we are all going to die.

Death happens every day, and you never know when your time is. That's why it's so important to live each day with a purpose, like Mark, to love Jesus and others. So I'll live today and love today and weep today for those I miss . . . It's okay. It isn't Mark's death; he lives on in glory and is resurrected, but to lose him feels like the death of part of me. But I know Jesus will sustain me, because that is His promise . . . and I will see you again, Mark. The displacement will be gone and I will be home. It's ok for now to feel displaced…it makes you search for life.

"Can one be fully human without experiencing tragedy? . . . The only tragedy there is in the world is not awake and unawareness. From them comes fear, and from fear comes everything else, but death is not a tragedy at all. Dying is wonderful; it's only horrible to people who have never understood life. It's only when you're afraid of life that you fear death. It's only dead people who fear death . . . The end of the world for a caterpillar is a butterfly for the master."[3]

---

3 Anthony de Mello, *Awareness: The Perils and Opportunities of Reality* (Colorado Springs: Image Books, 2003), 150.

Pushing Yourself

———— ⚉ ————

This morning I woke up really missing Mark. Grief had found me once again. It was one of those mornings when I just wept for the loss . . . the closeness . . . the love . . . the hugs, snuggles, and smiles . . . the smell of his coffee brewing . . . the sound of him breathing beside me. My heart aches. Like Bruce Springsteen sings, "Sometimes it's like someone took a knife, baby, edgy and dull, and cut a six-inch valley through the middle of my soul." That pretty much sums it up.

I guess with Mark's birthday on the horizon and the one-year anniversary of him going home just a couple of months off, it's really, really hard.

So . . . how do I even manage to get going on this cloudy, cold day? I'm not much of a cold-weather person. In fact, the thought of moving to some warm tropical island is very tempting . . . but I'm here for a while, so I might as well embrace the fact that winter is coming and enjoy it. I mean, I could complain about it and hate it, but that wouldn't make it go away, and it certainly wouldn't make me any happier . . . So I've decided to somehow embrace this.

This morning, when I pushed myself to get out there and run, it was so refreshing and exhilarating. I felt great. I am alive and still here for a purpose. Making yourself do those things you don't always feel like doing—that's how you begin to change, to grow, and to break through those invisible barriers that try to crush you and keep you down. The feeling of doing it is so much stronger than not doing it . . . not moving . . . not growing . . . not stretching. I want to live and live life to the fullest, until it's my turn to go home. Life is so short . . . Mark would want me too.

I knew I could keep crying or that I could do what has kept me going and moving forward through this grieving process—running on the beach, surfing, learning new stuff, exercising, eating healthy, keeping my mind positive, praying, building my business of helping others. *I love to help others.* All of these experiences build my strength. It's how I manage to walk through this incredible pain with some laughter, love, fun, and a positive view of life.

Runner's High

"The gift of grief is that it presents us with the opportunity to heal and grow." —*Jewish Proverb*

Ever heard of 'runner's high'? That's no myth—your body rewards exercise by releasing endorphins (the feel-good hormone). But more than just the temporary feeling of wellbeing 'runner's high' brings, exercise has proven very effective in relieving symptoms of mental health conditions like anxiety, seasonal affective disorder, and clinical depression. New research shows thirty to sixty minutes of daily exercise to be as effective as antidepressant medication in the treatment of mood disorders. If team sports are your thing, they add still another dimension to the mental wellness effects of activity—the social benefits of combining activity and teamwork are undeniable.

"Exercise reactivates your mind-body connection, putting you back in touch with your creativity and problem-solving abilities, ultimately improving mental clarity. So go ahead: Write yourself a prescription for exercise and banish your winter blues or creative blockages for good!"[4]

Yesterday, my gynecologist and I were talking about how I was handling my grief and how much exercise and healthy eating helps with depression. What an effect lack of exercise and poor nutrition have not only on our health but also on our emotions and our minds.

Depression is real. I know about depression it is something that I battled for a few years. But with prayer, exercise, healthy eating, keeping my mind and thoughts positive and true, I know that I can do anything. You are the only one holding you back. Learning to look at yourself . . . well, outside of yourself, from a non-judgmental view, is one of the best things you can do. I love you Mark, thank you for loving me. As Friedrich Nietzsche said, "One's own self is well hidden from one's own self; of all mines of treasure, one's own is the last to be dug up."

Love Bigger Than Anger

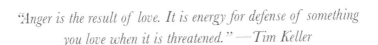

"Anger is the result of love. It is energy for defense of something you love when it is threatened." —Tim Keller

I'm optimistic, motivational, full of life. A weight was lifted off of me this morning. I didn't even know it was there until it was lifted. Wow.

Jesus is *love* . . . and He loves, even when we can't. I didn't think I would be angry during this grieving process. Because I love Jesus

---

4 Brendan Brazier, "How to Use Fitness to Create Mental and Physical Strength for Life Part 2," *Shanghai Veggie Club, December 30, 2012, http://www.shanghaivegetarians.com/vegan-fitness-with-brendan-brazier-activity-how-to-use-fitness-to-create-mental-and-physical-strength-for-life-part-2/.*

so much, I didn't think I would ever get angry at Him. My faith is strong, but this month I've been angry. Sunday night was the height of that anger, and self-pity was running a close second. I believe they go hand-in-hand: anger and self-pity or anger and pride. It's hard to be full of love and anger at the same time. It's hard to be humble and angry too.

I wonder if I'll ever be the same. Two weeks ago, I hurt my arm skiing, I was missing my family, missing Mark, and the silence was too much to bear. . . My financial state was rocky, and everything seemed to be crashing down on me. Physical pain, emotional pain—it felt good, actually, to be in physical pain . . . to feel it. I was so mad at God. I said, "Well, you took my husband; you've taken most of my material things; my son is in the Navy; now I'm in pain and can't continue to surf, workout, water ski, train my clients . . . are you happy now . . . are you happy now . . . is this where you wanted me broken?"

Then I heard the Lord say to me, "I am so much bigger than your anger. I love you, and I have plans for you. I will never leave nor forsake you. I know pain, I know loss, I know anger. It's okay to cry. It's okay to be mad. It's okay."

Two days later, the anger was gone.

Courage

———⟪∞⟫———

"Courage does not always roar. Sometimes it is the quiet voice at the end of the day saying, 'I will try again tomorrow.'"
—*Mary Anne Radmacher*

Yesterday, after being interviewed on Donna Tyson's "Rivers of Faith" program, I was feeling pretty good. Talking about my grief helped, talking about who Mark was helped. It was encouraging. Having a good day, which is always refreshing. Then I receive this phone call, and bam. . . It was one of those phone calls that throws you this curveball out of nowhere. You're whistling through your day, thinking, this is going to be a good day, and then something comes out of left field. Anyway, I said to myself, don't I have enough to deal with right now? I want a break. Then at the end of the day, I pray and give it to God, and I say to myself, maybe this or that could happen . . .. I have to remind myself: Don't react to something that may or may not happen. Today your daily bread has been given. Today, you are fine. Today is a gift. Tomorrow you will get up, put one foot in front of the other, smile, give thanksgiving for another day, point your feet in the direction of that straight path, and walk forward. Yes, it's easy to react during grief, it takes courage not too.

Sole Provider, Soul Provider

Sole provider, soul provider. Loneliness in the midst of people. . . there are nights I dread going to sleep . . . lying there with my own thoughts in the dark. The silence of loneliness—what an oxymoron. Loneliness isn't really silent. I mean, you have these thoughts that reverberate with such a loud sound that you wish they were silent. Maybe silence is the lack of another voice, to be heard in the night, when you are alone. Maybe that's what they mean by silence.

There are days and nights when I feel I don't have a friend in sight. There are days when I feel I have too many to even say hello to. My soul is always crying out. My prayer life seems rather weak right now. I had someone pray for me the other day I was so thankful. No one has prayed for me in such a long time. Is anyone listening . . . does anyone listen?

No one gets heard anymore. Everyone is so busy talking over others . . . trying to get others to hear their side and their story that really, no one is listening. Everyone wants to be right and to be heard. I think that's why there is such loneness no one seems to listen. Through all of this, I have learned that is the biggest contribution I want to give to others: listening . . . hugs too. Hugs and listening.

After time, people just go back to their lives . . . I mean, they have to. That's what our world does: It keeps on turning. It's funny . . . people expect you to do certain things or be a certain way. People have all kinds of advice for when you are hurting . . . when you are trying to figure it all out. But they don't listen.

Loneliness . . . Jesus knows loneliness. . .and he listens…

Perfect Time

"There is a time for everything and a season for every activity under the heaven: A time to be born and a time to die, a time to plant and a time to uproot." — Ecclesiastes 3:1-2

I have really been reflecting on Mark's death and the timing of it all. Some would say it was an accident and he was too young. Personally,

I believe it was God's perfect timing. I believe there are no accidents or coincidences with God. As painful as it is, I truly believe it was perfect. I never really question why God does anything He does. I don't understand everything, but I don't question it. I reflect upon it. Death and accidents bring us to a time of reflection. Reflection of our lives and those around us. Isn't that ironic? Death brings us face-to-face with life.

Life suddenly becomes more than the daily trip to Starbucks, the next meeting, the project that presses in on us to get finished, the petty disagreement with a spouse about who is right and who is wrong, or who's going to take the kids to soccer. Because time stops. It stands still. All of a sudden, the diaper that needs changing in the middle of a sleepless night becomes about a baby who depends on us for love and care. That friend who wants to chat at the post office when you're in a hurry becomes a chance to take time out of the day to laugh and listen. Oh, and the sunrise you fail to see in the morning when you're in too big of a hurry or too tired to get up—it seems to be the first thing you want to embrace. Life becomes bigger than our minds can wrap around. Time seems to . . . well . . . have a time of its own. It stops, or at least feels like it stops. We realize we can no longer control or manage time; there is someone bigger than time . . . someone outside our time.

"Your eyes saw my unformed substance; in your book were written, every one of them, the days that were formed for me, when as yet there were none of them"—Palms. 139:16

As I think about God's timing and reflect on Mark's life, death, and his continued life in his real home, I am in awe of our Lord's sovereignty and the preparation He makes in His perfect time. You see, He had been preparing Mark to see Him face-to-face, and He had been preparing me for a life without Mark. I see His hand over the last five years in this preparation for us to go our separate ways—together, but for now separate.

In May of 2007, as the market continued to dive, Mark had his first heart attack at forty-eight. We had gone to the doctor earlier because he'd been complaining of chest pain. The doctor gave him antibiotics and did X-rays, said he had pneumonia, and sent him home. Later that night, he was in more pain and wanted me to call the doctor, who recommended going to the ER. Mark did not want to go and stayed up most the night. By morning, he had agreed to go.

At the emergency room, Mark started sweating and turned ashen. They took him up immediately; he was having a heart attack and needed surgery. It all happened so fast. I immediately prayed, "Lord, I cannot lose him. Please don't take him from me." From the moment we arrived at the emergency room to surgery completion was seventy-seven minutes. The doctor told me he'd had 100 percent blockage in his main artery, called the widow maker. The doctors all said that it was a miracle he survived. I broke down. I went in to see him; he was hooked up to all these machines. He had less than 10 percent damage to his heart, and they had put in a stent. He was alive and going to be okay.

That's when reality crept in. All the work Mark and I were doing had us going in different directions. Within seventy-seven minutes his and my lives changed. We were connected again like magnets. One of the first questions he asked the doctor was, "Am I going to be able to surf again?" Mark: a child of God and always a surfer. He was on the NSSA team in the early '70s and was the NSSA National Champion in 1978. The doctor said yes, and Mark was ready to get out of that hospital and put his feet on the familiar feel of the surfboard in his favorite spot: on the wave. I cannot explain in words the relief and thankfulness I felt in my heart. He was going to be okay.

I told him the next day I would never argue with him or get mad at him again. He smiled and said, "Can I have that in writing?" We both got a big laugh out of it.

We came home and got settled in and I started cooking healthier foods, taking any junk out of the house, as his friends joked, "lentils and rice." He snuck his favorite foods, as I found out later, when he would meet the guys out. This was in 2007 and Mark was sure he'd get the condos completed and sold. Surely, God was going to relieve him of his financial struggles; after all, he'd survived this life-threatening heart attack. But the Lord had other plans, because Mark had not fully realized that all he needed was God. God was also preparing me in another way. Mark's heart attack made me think a lot about what I would do if something happened to Mark; it had almost happened. Well, we never got relived us of our financial burdens or of other trials we were to face and overcome in the few years we had left together. Instead, God used those years to strengthen me and to prepare Mark for his time on earth to end. He drew us closer together, and our relationships with Jesus grew even stronger, both together and separately.

Mark started using his testimony, his story of near death and of his financial demise, as a platform to show what Jesus can do in your life if you depend solely on him for everything. We began realizing that Jesus was working in the little things and the big things. We saw His hand on every aspect of our lives and Robert's life. Mark made a comment to me after we'd lost our home and the condos: "When we were going through all of that financial loss, you know what God was saying to me? He was saying to me, 'I am all you need, Mark.'"

I often say we really need to have a wide lens on what the Lord is doing, instead of a narrow lens that just captures one part of the landscape. It is like needlepoint; underneath the fabric are all these strings mixed and mangled, no rhyme or reason, but when you flip it over, it is this beautiful work. The Creator sees the big picture. God was giving us testimonies and stories to share, to show how much Jesus loves and cares for us. The Lord even used Mark's death to bring people to Him.

You see, we all have stories and testimonies. It's all about drawing us closer to the one who holds time in His hand. Life is all about God and His story. Jesus reveals Himself through testimony . . . through the times of happiness, joy, pain, and sorrow. It is what the Bible does, stories of everyday people who lived life through a time period that holds an eternal time for God.

Maybe time does heal, especially outside of this time, in another place where there will be no pain. I guess I am still being prepared; I have more stories to tell and more testimonies to give. May God bless us with eyes to see His love for us in the midst of our accidents . . . in the midst of our pain.

Thank You for the wonderful gift of a husband in Mark that you gave me. Thank You for giving us the unique preparation we need to part from this world. Thank You for the fact that no matter what we may be feeling, you never leave nor forsake us.

Celebrating

———⌘———

"Life is like riding a wave. To keep your balance, you must keep moving."
—*Eric Carlson*

Happy birthday, Mark! It's hard to believe, still, that you are no longer with me. I know you are having a celebration in heaven. I bet it's the best birthday you've ever had. You are with all your family now, and I bet you're catching the best waves and eating the best cake. And I know you are getting the best love you've ever had. Wow . . . I'm jealous. I know if you were here, I couldn't give you all that. I miss you. The grief has been difficult at times, but I know you are so much happier where you are, with God. That is what keeps me focused—well, somewhat focused . . . You know me: go, go, go! Especially now . . . even more so now . . . movement is what gets me through.

You would have celebrated your fifty-fourth birthday with me. I remember us talking about what we would do in our fifties. Well, we did some of it anyway. The tears fall; my heart is so sad . . . sad for me, not you, as I think about not being with you for your birthday. What a journey this has been. Mark, I just never knew it would be this hard. But that's life. I'm left here for a reason and you're home . . . it was your time. I don't understand it all, but I don't have to. I just trust and know that it will all be okay in the end. Thank you for allowing me to be a part of seventeen of your birthdays. Love, cards, dinners, intimacy, fights, makeups, laughs, and just dang fun and crazy years. Happy birthday, bud! You rocked and are rocking on, Mark the Shark.

And Mark, I'm rocking on too and soaking up the sun because of you. You have given me all I need to rock on. Thank you for showing me love so I know what love is . . . and I know what it can be. I will be able to love again. I'm going to try and surf on your birthday today. Hopefully there are waves . . . catch you in the water.

His Love of Surfing

"I could not help concluding this man had the most supreme pleasure while he was driven so fast and so smoothly by the sea."
—Captain James Cook

I just had my two-year breast cancer screening. I am still cancer-free. Thank You, Jesus. That was the longest dang few minutes, waiting for the results. Mark was with me last year. It seemed even longer waiting by myself. But, I felt your presence Mark. You know, I remember after my surgery the waves were good. Our little ocean front condo that a friend let us rent after we lost our home . . . it was our honeymoon spot. You loved checking the waves out the front door and walking across to surf. This day was no exception. I remember you looking at me and saying, "the waves are great, do you mind if I go surf, are you ok?" I looked at you and said, "well now if something happens to you how am I supposed to swim out and get you?" We both laughed. I said, go ahead, I will be sleeping anyway. Gosh, I miss you and feeling your love of the water.

Jesus

What's on my mind? Jesus Christ and going into the eleventh month of my grieving process. Comfortably numb, like Pink Floyd's song . . . that's how the days' end: comfortably numb.

Wow . . . has it really been almost eleven months? It's hard to wrap my mind around it. On my run this morning, I thought about the last eleven months and having Jesus with me during this journey. You know what I love about Jesus? He knows everything about me. I mean, there is nothing that I can hide from Him. He knows every dark place in my heart, every evil thought, every time I've denied Him, every lie I've told. . . He knows sin that I have committed or will commit in the future. He knows every fiber of my being, and He understands. And you know what the miracle is? He still loves me, just as I am . . . not as I think I should be or as someone else may think I should be. I can talk to Him. I don't have to hide things from Jesus because He knows me so well. He created me. . . He knows my next move. That is the miracle—His love . . . His love of me. I have never had that kind of love anywhere else before. I relish it. I love the freedom in that: being able to tell Him everything with no condemnation, no judgment—just love. Jesus has been my rock through this grief. Jesus always knows where I am on my journey. . . I don't have to explain it to Him.

Other people, with good intentions, always want to tell you where they think you are on your journey; they base it on their experiences in life. It's hard to separate our experiences when we see others in a similar situation. But with Jesus, there's no trying to convince, no trying to make someone understand.

My prayers through this have gone something like this: Good morning, God, thank you for this day and thank you for looking over my family and friends and me.

Dad's timing

I am a little overwhelmed today. Wishing Mark was here. My dad is dying and we have hospice in. We were going to transfer him from the hospital to a nursing home, but his kidneys starting failing. I was with Mom in the emergency room on Christmas day because of her heart. So my brother and I were going from the emergency room upstairs to be with my dad.

It's surreal . . . anyway. We got Mom out of the hospital yesterday and took her home. She is supposed to get her heart shocked for the second time on January 3. This will depend on when Dad passes. I really don't want to lose him now. I just don't want to lose another loved one this year. Mark, my sister-in-law in October, now Dad. But God has a plan . . . I just know it.

My brother Danny, who lost his wife, has the flu. My other brother, Alan, had to take his wife to get her kidney stones broken up today. The grace in all of this is that my son, Robert, is getting leave from the Navy and will be here tomorrow. So he'll get to see his Pop Pop, we hope, before he dies. That is our prayer. My mom is so sad and has that heart condition. They would have been married sixty-two years in February.

It has been quite the two weeks . . . here we go again. God's time, not ours.

Rescue

—⊶⊷—

"Grief wraps around people, takes them to place they would not go otherwise." —Patti Callahan

Well, bud, it was a year ago today that you went home. On one hand, it seems like a lifetime since I've seen you, talked to you, touched you. Sometimes it seems like another life. A year ago, something happened that changed my life. It was a nightmare, that night . . . a nightmare. But for you, it was a joyful homecoming. For me, though . . . well . . . it has been quite the year here without you. How I miss you.

Grief is a very lonely place. It's different for everyone and no one can understand but the one going through it. It's a path that you and you alone walk. But in my experience, Jesus entered this place with me . . . this journey. Because Jesus . . . well . . . He knows pain, loss, and how to heal. No family member, no friend, no one but Jesus. It is a lonely journey through the valley of the shadow of death. But it's okay, because even though you may feel alone, you're not. And it's okay because . . . well, honey, I know you are now full of love and joy. That is my saving grace through all of this: you are at peace . . . you are home. But my home isn't the same. Mark, what do I say . . . how do I say it? You rescued me, so long ago. And your friends say I rescued you. . . . Maybe we rescued each other.

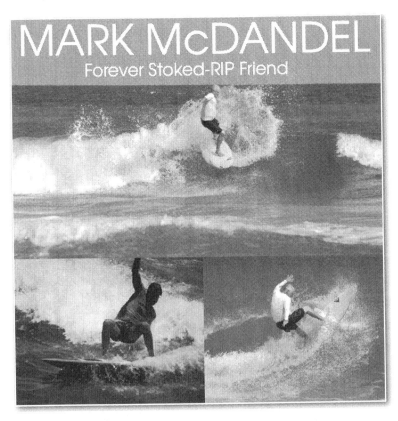

The memories of us as a family with Robert (what a great dad you were) and our times together are forever etched in my heart and mind. The good memories, the bad memories, and the tears and the laughter. I've found that time eases the pain, but it doesn't erase you from my heart. Mark—your smile, your touch, your laugh, your warm embrace, and your love. Just you. I will always have a place in my heart for you, my surfing dude, Mark the Shark.

I am just telling you, honey, it has been a pain that I hadn't known before. A pain that I find hard to articulate and express with words. A pain that made me want to curl up in a corner and cry out, "God, take me . . . please. Just take me with him. I don't want to be here anymore. I don't want to live without you, Mark." A pain that made me physically sick. There were times I thought my heart couldn't find one more heartbeat because it was literally broken . . . shattered into tiny pieces. I wondered if it would ever be put back together again. What happened to my life? My family? My home? Our friends? There is such darkness in losing a loved one. It is then and only then that I believe any of us really looks at death, at life. I think it is in the death of someone we love that we make the decision to live or die. Do we die with them, or do we live a new life without them? Do we lie down and quit, or do we get stronger and persevere? Exactly what are we to do with the life we have left? Life . . . we are all just a breath away from death and entering eternal life.

Bud, because of who you were, because of the hope I have in God, because of what I learned being married to you and what I learned by losing you, I made the decision to live without you, persevere, and become stronger and better until I come home. Mark, we went through so much together. Our faith grew together. We were challenged through sickness, the loss of financial security, the loss of those we loved, the loss of our home, people who took advantage of your trust and financial success and left you holding the debt that they owed you. And all you would say is, "Jesus may love you, but I'm having a hard time." We at times were the best of friends, and then there were times we thought we were enemies. We were challenged in our marriage, but we always worked it out. In the end, we grew closer because of the trials we faced. Dammit . . . I thought we would grow old together. I guess God had different plans.

I remember writing in my journal last New Year's Day like it was yesterday. I wrote about how we were going to have a great year. We were in this rented oceanfront condo . . . which you loved because you could give the wave report from the deck. I can still see you sitting in that chair, staring out at the ocean with your headphones on, listening to your favorite tunes, drinking your coffee . . . and finally at peace from all the struggles we encountered financially. I was journaling about how excited I was about the New Year because it was going to be like a honeymoon; it was just you and me. Since we got together, we'd had Robert because he was almost three at the time; we raised him together and were so proud that he had joined the Navy. So we were excited about our life together, just you and me in this beach bungalow. The New Year looked promising. Then, nine days later, you were gone. Life had it owns plans and we weren't consulted about it at all. Someone said to me after the death of their loved one that it felt like they had no control over anything anymore. We don't, do we? At least not over our circumstances. The only control we have is how we react to and handle those circumstances.

Mark, this year without you has been filled with so many emotions, challenges, highs, and lows. There were times when I thought I couldn't stop the flood of tears that came and times when I couldn't shed a tear. I've made some very stupid decisions and some very wise decisions. I have felt pain so deeply that I didn't want it to stop because it was better than feeling numb. I've been so lonely at night, only to wake up in the morning with a renewed spirit. I've been full of fear of the future, only to be challenged by that same fear to face it and do positive things within it. I've become so angry with God only to find that He loves me more than I ever knew. Even when I backed away, He never ever left me. He has always been by my side. He has carried me through every one of my dark, angry days. My faith has changed so much through this. It has humbled me and made me look at my walk with Jesus . . . what it was and what it is. I no longer see my walk with Him the way it was. I see people differently—I love them more. I see the world differently—I love life more. God is love. A love that I have never known.

I've seen friends who I never thought would leave me do just that, but I've seen friends stand by me when I never thought would. I have made new friends and renewed old friendships. It amazes me how easy it is to find out who your real friends are when something like this happens. And it's okay. It's good to know these things, and I still love them all.

And, Mark, you would have been so proud of your cousin who was like a brother, Billy; he has walked with me through all of this. He helped me get out and go. He made me laugh. We have talked and cried together . . . about you . . . over you. And we've gotten mad at you for leaving us here. He misses you so much.

I couldn't have gotten through this year without my friends' love and support, our river days and my surfing days, my surfing buddies Inga and Sunyata. Oh, how I looked forward to surfing with those two beautiful girls. You would be so proud of me, Mark, for surfing even in cold water. The river, skiing, the healing of the ocean, working out, running, my personal training, my family at the gym, my coaching, taking continuing education courses, boxing, moving forward, growing, learning new things, playing, working, all these are the things that have carried me through and helps me heal.

Mark, I remember us holding hands walking down the sidewalk and talking about a name for my business. I asked you to help me with a name . . . something feminine, but strong. And you said, "Name it Sweet Strength." You always believed more in me than I believed in myself . . . as I did with you, bud. I always believed more in you than you did. You always told me I was smart and beautiful and that I could do anything. You made me feel special. You were special. I miss your encouragement, but I thank you for my name, Sweet Strength. Somehow it has given me the strength to encourage others, and it has made me want to continue this journey, even without you. It has given me a purpose.

Thank you, Mark, for seventeen and half good—no—*great* years. The best years of my life. You may be gone, but you will never be forgotten. You rock, my friend, and I will see you when I come home.

The Fall

"Man maintains his balance, poise, and sense of security only as he is moving forward" —Maxwell Maltz

For some time, I felt like I walked a balance beam of faith. Like I was walking that beam, that thin line, teeter-tottering between the different sides that lay beneath. If I lost my balance and fell to one side, it would crush me; I'd become weak and helpless. I'd lose my faith, my perseverance, my life, my peace, who I was, my purpose. I would fall flat on my face, never to recover, because life was so hard and I was so very tired. Tired of life . . . tired of losing those I love, illness, of working to rebuild my life, of my work when I hadn't been in the workplace for so long because I was a mom and wife. Tired of seeing those I love in pain . . . tired of looking at hate, war, prejudice, hunger, and death.

Then there was the other side of that fall, when I'd land on my feet, ready to run, ready to face life instead of death, ready to encourage others because of what I'd seen and been through, ready to live my life with meaning and purpose, ready to have peace instead of anxiety, ready to run the race marked out for me instead of giving in, ready to succeed, ready to grow stronger and stronger, ready to heal instead of hurt, ready to become the person that God had created me to be, ready to stand tall in victory—yes, ready for everything that life would throw me, because I would know that in my inner being I have a force . . . a power that compelled me forward, making me stronger than anything that would try to conquer me, calling me to live out my purpose to love others and have hope for better days because I believe . . . I believe I was made to stand, not fall; to love, not hate; to conquer, not quit; to inspire, not tear down; to give, not receive; to make peace, not war; to live life every moment of every day; to forgive as others have forgiven me; to reach for the stars; to dream; to take care of myself so I can take care of others; to be thankful for the illusion of time between sunrise and sunset; to hope for a better day.

I have felt for some time like I don't know which side I'll fall toward, and I especially had this very vivid view yesterday of walking that beam and thinking to myself, I could go either way after this . . . I really could. After losing three family members within a year, trying to build a business, and losing everything financially . . . it has been not only a long year, but a long five years. First there was my husband. Then in October, 2012 it was my sister in law. My brother's wife of thirty-four years. My niece and nephew's mom. I tell you it was a rough day for my family on that faithful day October 12, 2012 as any death in the family is. Making arrangements for my sister in law with my family brought back that day we did that with Mark, except I wasn't as numb. It's difficult to watch your brother go through the pain of losing his wife of thirty-four years unexpectedly. It's hard, because you know the pain he will have to endure as the days turn into lonely nights and haunting memories of what was. It's hard to watch your niece and nephew lose their mom at such a young age. Donna was a wonderful woman. We had lots of fun and she would do anything for you. She loved her family so much. She had been in my life since I was sixteen. She was like a sister to me. We had so many good times together. We shared life's secrets and helped each other through the child rearing age. I miss her friendship and love. She always had the ability to make you laugh. Her and Mark were the jokesters in the family. They were so funny together. We spent a lot of time together sharing our lives, our losses, our children's experiences and so much more. I will miss her greatly. Then two months later, I watched my daddy die, lying on that bed, looking like a man I had never known, I was thinking I may teeter toward the side of despair and weakness. And then the following day watching my mom pick out his casket. Death and life, living and dying, dying to live, or living to die—or is there a line that separates the two? I mean, we must die to live. We must all face death to live, or we will surely all die. My mom was so fragile, so sad, picking out how she wanted to see her husband of almost sixty-two years put in the ground—his body, that is, not him really. But that's how we know and love our loved ones, isn't it? We interact through our bodies . . . our touch, our voices, our faces, our smiles . . . or maybe we interact through the pain we share in our bodies . . . our tears. . . Yes, God's grace is to give us a face and a body to love and hug, to argue and make up with . . . to hold. God's grace gave us this way to feel a touch, to hear a voice, and to see a smile. God's grace, it always amazes me.

As we made arrangements for my dad in the very room that we'd been in two months earlier to make arrangements for my sister-in-law, I thought to myself, I am very close to falling over and landing on my face. It was almost as if I wasn't there. . . I was watching myself closely on that balance beam . . . walking . . . trying not to fall yet . . . trying to make the decision on which way to go. I remembered Mark and making those arrangements for him. I felt sorry for myself but, all the while knowing that others have losses too, which way am I going to fall? How do I stay balanced on this beam in the midst of this crazy, surreal scene in this funeral home? The funeral home director's voice was like that of the adults in the *Peanuts* cartoons . . . blah . . . blah . . . blah . . . blah . . . I looked at Mom, wondering if she was walking that same beam. She has had such a hard life. She was so strong, but so weak. I thought how happy I was that Mark, Donna, and Dad didn't have to walk that beam anymore—the beam that leads us to Jesus—because they are with Him . . . healed, loved, and at perfect peace.

I wonder sometimes why we have to walk that beam at all and why things can't be easy . . . why we have to choose a side. But I read something today in one of my favorite books and I was reminded that it is these times that make or break us, build us up or tear us down, make us love or hate, make us bitter or better, and that is why we always have that solid beam beneath us—Jesus. Because if we keep our feet on the beam and don't let distractions and circumstances get us off balance, we won't have to worry about to which side we'll fall . . . we will simply make the choice to jump off and land on our feet, then take off running the race that's set before us.

"Contrary to what might be expected, I look back on experiences that at the time seemed especially desolating and painful with particular satisfaction. Indeed, I can say with complete truthfulness that everything I have learned in my seventy-five years in this world, everything that has truly enhanced and enlightened my existence, has been through affliction and not through happiness, whether pursued or attained. In other words, if it ever were to be possible to eliminate affliction from our earthly existence by means of some

drug or other medical mumbo jumbo . . . the result would not be to make
life delectable, but to make it too banal and trivial to be endurable.
This, of course, is what the cross signifies, and it is the cross, more
than anything else, that has called me inexorably to Christ."
—*Malcolm Muggeridge*

For today, I'm still balancing . . . because I hurt and I'm not ready yet to fall on either side . . . just simply to feel the beam beneath my feet.

The Married Life

"A great marriage is not when the "perfect couple comes together.
It is when an imperfect couple learns to enjoy their difference."
— *Dave Meurer*

I miss the married life and most of all miss the one I was married to. It's hard to adjust some days, but I am . . . and I know there is good in the midst of all of this and that one day I'll be on the other side. There is nothing on earth that can replace a great relationship full of fun, laughter, and intimacy. There is nothing that can replace learning together with the one you love. There is nothing that can replace even the times of misunderstanding and arguments…those times where you think there will be enough time in the day to make up and the gentleness and freshness of making a compromise. Sometimes we forget that there's no point in getting stuck in the little stuff . . . time is too short for arguing . . . or not playing together …or not loving one another.

Fake It Until You Make It

———— ✺ ————

"Your biggest challenge isn't someone else, or your circumstance. It's the ache in your lungs, the burning in your legs, and the voice inside you that yells, 'Can't!' But you don't listen, you push harder. You hear the voice whisper 'Can,' and you discover that the person you thought you were is no match for the one you really are." —Unknown

It has been one year and a little over two months, and it has been one of the most challenging experiences of my life, losing Mark, my partner. I've been through a lot of difficult times and have experienced a lot in life. But the death of my husband trumps it all. Two thousand twelve was quite the year of deaths for my family. First Mark, and then my brother lost his wife of thirty-four years, my sister-in-law, Donna. Both Mark and Donna were in their early fifties. Then Dad on New Year's Eve, so my mom lost her husband of sixty-one years.

I'll never forget when Donna died. I was on the river on a warm day: October 12th. My oldest brother, Alan, called me and said they couldn't find my sister-in-law. She had gone to the cabin that Danny, my brother, had built, but wasn't answering their calls. They lived by the beach, but had a cabin on the farm where my family grew up. The door was locked, but her car was there. Her husband, my brother Danny, was working and had asked my other brother, Alan, to check on her. Alan, said to me, "You may need to come home." As I headed in to get ready to help, I got the dreaded phone call. I call them the cold calls because they seem so cold . . . so distant . . . so foreign. Donna's body had been found inside of the cabin. She had died suddenly, at fifty-four years old.

They had been together for thirty-four years. Thirty-four years! I had grown up with Donna; it seemed she'd always been in my life. She and Mark had loved to cut up and joke. Now they were together.

I remember my brother Danny saying to me, "I will be fine; I'll get through this easier than you." I said, "No, you won't. No, you won't." It was the shock. He was trying to absorb the shock of someone alive and present yesterday and gone today. There's no smooth way to experience that transition. There's no easy way.

I remember being at the funeral home, thinking, here we go again, the arrangements. I felt nauseated; it was too soon to be there again . . . too soon to feel those emotions rushing through. I mean, I was just beginning to feel steady again. But life isn't steady. Life is a never-ending journey of change that wants to test our balance. It took every fiber of strength I had to try and be there for my brother and my parents.

Mom and Dad seemed to float in and out of the hospital that year. They weren't able to come to any of the funerals. Mom hated that and felt so guilty. She wanted to help me, but was doing all she could to take care of herself and Dad. She's a strong woman—a woman who knows firsthand about Sweet Strength. She grew up during the Depression, with a mom who had depression. Mom and I talked daily and encouraged each other.

Then that December, the week before Christmas, my oldest brother called me. Mom had fallen and Dad wasn't doing well—bronchitis, they thought. So the doctor was admitting both of my parents to the hospital. In her fall, Mom had hit her head. She was fine, but needed to be under observation, and she was worn out. Dad had bronchitis and COPD.

The next thing we knew, Dad's kidneys started failing. He had never had kidney issues before. On New Year's Day, our daddy—my mom's husband of sixty-one years—passed away. Another funeral, another set of arrangements to be made. Could we all do it again? What choice were we given? Death . . . death is like that; it gives us no choice.

But life gives us the choice to live or die . . . we have to decide.

I don't remember much about my dad's funeral or making the arrangements. But I did realize that I couldn't grieve for Donna or Daddy because I hadn't even finished grieving for Mark.

Death and losing loved ones happens every day, somewhere and to someone.

If I had known or someone had told me how hard it would be to continue to live each day to its fullest and not fall prey to the battle within my mind, I would have never believed them.

But, beginning the very day after Mark went home, I realized if I didn't choose to change everything about what I understood as seventeen years of my life, and make it into something completely new, I would lose the battle with life and living . . . really living . . . and I would die.

I'd been in this most familiar, yet unfamiliar on a totally different level, place before with my thoughts and my mind. The games my mind will play on me at times. The war . . . the battle . . . the confrontation between thinking positively, creatively, optimistically, hopefully, and thinking negatively, fearfully, confusedly, closed-mindedly, and narrowly. The mental challenge to overcome circumstances that seem impossible to overcome. Circumstances that only me and my spirit and soul understand. That only the faith I have in God to get me through will lend a hand to the battle for my mind. My trust and faith have come from my Jesus.

We live in such a world that the media seem to thrive on turning diversity into negativity and focuses on every evil that happens, feeding it to us on a regular basis, regurgitating the same crap over and over again, and we eagerly receive it like a mother bird's babies receiving food. As if we don't have enough on our plates with everyday living. You hardly ever hear about the good things that are going on in the world, the hope, and the miracles that occur every single day. You really have to make an effort to change your mindset and perspective to look for the good, not the bad; to hear the positive in each situation, not the negative. It takes effort, especially in the fast-paced, high-tech, stressed environment and society in which we live.

There have been many times during this period of totally new way of living that every fiber in me has told me to quit. My mind plays such games with me. Missing Mark, my family, my sense of security (which is an illusion anyway; the only security for me personally is my Jesus), my way of life. There were days when I thought, what are you going to do? How are you going to live without Mark? How are you going to earn an income? Where are you going to live? You aren't strong enough to do this; just lie down and quit. Run and don't look back. You can't do this, Linda.

My mind was tired, my heart was broken, I was confused and struggling in a different way with my faith, I felt alone (in the midst of so many people, I still felt very alone), and my body was exhausted. There were days when I didn't want to get out of bed. There were days I didn't feel like smiling, talking, or seeing anyone.

However, deep within my spirit and my soul, there is this small voice pushing me forward, enticing me to live differently; to think differently; to be stronger; to be better; to not give up; to run with the horses, not walk with the turtles. Well . . . it was better than the other option. So each day, I made a choice . . . I made an effort . . . I made myself smile, get up, be positive, share my gifts and talents with those around me, work out, eat healthy, learn something new, be with friends, go out, just *go*. In other words, I knew that I needed to fake it until I could really make it. If you can think negatively, you can think positively. If you look for the bad, you'll certainly find it . . . but if you look for the good and challenge your thoughts, you'll find the best.

Our minds are a powerful gift we were given by our Creator. Our thoughts are what make our lives. They can either propel us to create a new us, hold us back, or take us back to places we aren't supposed to be. Thoughts . . . battles in our minds . . . challenges to stay motivated, positive, hopeful. Hopeful that we have a purpose and an opportunity to share with others in this life.

There were days when I literally talked out loud, arguing with myself about my thoughts and how I could be positive just as easily as I could be negative. How only I could make my life . . . could choose how my life is going to be lived out. I argued until the right voice, the right thought was in the forefront of my thoughts: You are beautiful, you are talented, you love others, you have lots of support from family and friends, you have a lot to offer. Your body, your health, your mind are given to you for a purpose.

That's how we relate to others—though our body and our words. They both need to be at their best for us to be able to care for or love others. We really can bring sunshine to our lives and to others' lives . . . or we can bring hell to our lives and others'. And it all begins with our thoughts. Everything in our world started with a thought . . . either a great thought or a bad one.

There are four questions from Byron Katie that have helped me when my thoughts want to run on that path to disaster. They are: Is it true? Can you absolutely know that it's true? How do you react when you believe that thought? Who would you be without the thought?

Sitting With Pain

————◦⊶◦————

"I can bear any pain as long as it has meaning." —Haruki Murakami

The dictionary describes pain as suffering, distress of body or mind. I feel so much pain right now . . . not that I haven't before. Not that any of us have never felt pain. We all have carried the burden of pain in one way or another. Losing Mark has brought me much affliction, in both my body and mind. Today, I cried out and said, "Lord have mercy on me. Please . . . enter this place with me." Because I've embraced the realization that I have to learn to sit with this grief at times and let it come. That's the hard part: sitting . . . allowing Jesus to enter here with me. I really want to numb it on days like this, when it gets so bad, when I can only cry out for Jesus to have mercy on me. Those are about all the words I have today.

People want to cure my pain. People who love me want to take away my grief, and how thankful I am for the people who love me . . . who loved Mark. But only God can enter my pain, and sometimes, in a strange and foreign way, it's comforting to sit with my pain . . . not really reacting to it—just sitting with it . . . processing it. It provides great insight into who I am as a person. I know this is why God allows us to feel pain: to know Him more, to love others at greater depths, and to be able to get a glimpse into our souls. I cannot even imagine the pain Jesus felt on that cross . . . or the pain that God felt, allowing Jesus, His one and only son, to be on that cross. Who could wrap their finite mind around something so far from our comprehension? Not me. I try, but I cannot. Jesus, He sat in his pain, He cried out in his pain, and in His abundant grace He loved through the depth of his pain.

One time when Robert, my son, was little, there was this bad thunderstorm on the horizon; lightning was crackling all around and the thunder sounded like it was going to rattle every last pane of glass. Robert must have been about six or seven. I was upstairs reading a book to him, which was my favorite thing to do. He looked up at me and said, "Mom, I'm scared." Trying to be an optimistic mom, I said, "Robert, there is nothing to be scared of . . . all that lightning and thunder is how much power God has, and with that very power He watches over you. You don't have anything to be scared of. In fact, even if we were to die tonight in this storm, we would be alive with Jesus and all that power and glory." Robert looked up at me and said, "Mom, you always try to be positive . . . I just want to be scared for now; can I be scared?" Well, I just wanted to feel my anguish today, to feel the loss, and it was okay to feel pain and not try to bury it or numb it . . . just to sit with it, ponder it, get to know Jesus more intimately, get to know myself a little better. That bittersweet pain. . .

Pain can be covered up; I do it now and then, going through this grief, and have done it in unhealthy ways in the past. Anything to stop the pain, the affliction. We do that, don't we? Immerse and enmesh ourselves with friends, exercise, music, wine, drugs, pornography, shopping, overeating, under-eating, overworking—you name it, we do it . . . anything to stop the pain. And we don't even recognize that it only prolongs and increases the pain. It's an illusion that it will help. There is only one thing to do: sit with it and let God enter it with you. It will pass. All emotions do. They're like visitors coming and going . . . some stay longer than others, some are more intense than others, some are gentler, but eventually they all leave. If I sit with the sorrow, it passes quicker than when I try to dull it with other stuff.

If we didn't have pain, we wouldn't be able to even begin to understand or appreciate the sweetness of life. We wouldn't be able to empathize with others' pain, nor would we ever see ourselves in a way that stops us . . . slows us down . . . beckons us . . . calls us into transformation into the likeness of he who enters the pain with us—he who knew real pain. He is the only one I know who dared to die for our pain, for our healing, for our life: Jesus. We find out a lot more about who God is, about who we are, and about who others are by sitting in silence in the unwelcome but necessary pain.

Not Stopping

———— ✸ ————

Ever since Mark died, I have felt like stopping.

Sometimes I lie in bed at night wondering what happened to seventeen years of my life. Wondering how I got here . . . going home to an empty house night after night. Staring at the ceiling, working on avoiding the trap of fear of the future, making myself regain control of my thoughts . . . bring them to the present and what is going on right now . . . and right now, everything is good.

What a journey. I mean, it's an adjustment to go from partnership to figuring it all out on your own. Going from not having to worry about an income to learning to make one and not just that, but build a successful business. We all have a journey to live out. We have to live it out and not stop, because . . . you see, life doesn't stop for us. Life keeps on, so even if we decide to hang up the towel, to stop life . . . it's only your life that will stop. Remember it's never over . . . not until we stop.

So, stopping is not an option. We have to keep moving. Because as we continue to move; to live life no matter the circumstances; to take responsibility for our lives, even if the circumstances are beyond our control, we have to take responsibility for our lives and choices. And our choice not to quit is the most important. If we stop, then there is no option to improve. If we stop, there is no opportunity to succeed. If we stop, we will never reach our goals and our dreams will never have a chance. If we stop, we may never have an opportunity to love again. If we stop, we will never know what could have been.

We are here for a purpose: to live up to our full potential. That is what God has planned for us. He has a perfect plan for us, but we can't stop. We have to believe . . . we have to hope . . . and we have to see beyond what's in front of us.

So, really, my struggle doesn't matter. I can do this. I just have to say to myself, "Don't stop." It is always darkest before the dawn. You are always about to break a barrier when you seem at your worst. You are always on the brink of success when you feel like you've failed. We can't stop . . . because life won't stop for us.

Surfer Dude

―◦◦◦―

"Sometimes, only one person is missing,
and the whole world seems depopulated"
—Alphonse de Lamortino

It is a beautiful day in the neighborhood. That's what Mark would say. This morning, a year and half later, I'm thinking about my surfing dude. I guess the Surf rider Expo this afternoon makes me think of his love and passion for surfing, and not just surfing, but the surf community and his large array of friends. He loved people; he loved me so much.

I love this time of year. Spring and summer in the air―my favorite time. Mark and I would head to the beach; I loved watching him surf. I don't know . . . he left such an impact on my life and on his friends' lives.

I hope this day those who knew Mark will remember his smile, his laughter, his love of the ocean, his love of surfing, his love of Jesus, and his love of his friends. I hope they'll remember the way he spread love, through being a best buddy . . . the gift he had of making everyone feel special. I hope it will inspire them to do their best surfing and to be thankful that they live at the beach where they can surf (even though they may get frustrated because there may not be the waves they like). Mark always said, "If you can surf here, you can surf anywhere," and he proved it! I hope that knowing him inspires his friends to love others as they are, not as another else thinks they should be. I hope they never forget him, but remember he would want them to live their lives to the fullest, enjoying each moment, never being in a hurry, but enjoying who they're with . . . enjoying life, this ocean, this beach community, and people.

Finding The Peace

———∞∞∞———

"Peace is a journey of a thousand miles and it must be taken one step at the time." —*Lyndon B. Johnson*

This morning is cloudy . . . overcast, yet again . . . ugh . . . where is my morning sunrise, which compels me to get up and get going? Well . . . it failed this morning. It fell into a foggy, dreary day.

I typically get so excited in the morning. I love the thought of going on the beach and watching the sunrise and running. It just gives me hope that everything is going to be okay . . . that God has given me another day to spread sunshine to others. I just don't do well with the clouds and cold.

This morning, I decided I needed a bigger challenge than running my usual run on the beach. Some days I just need to push myself a little harder . . . to see if I can do it. Most days, I find the hard sand to run on, but because I was feeling a little down this morning, I knew that I needed that extra push, so I decided to do my time on the soft sand.

Halfway through my time, I said to myself (yes, I talk to myself), "I can't do this. . . well, why can't you do it? Does your body say you can't? No. Do you not want to do it? Yes, I want to do it. Do you need to do it? That could be debated. Does your mind tell you to stop? Yes—that's it. It's my mind, not my body, that wants to stop. Well, Linda," I said to myself, "you have a choice, you know. There's no one out here you're racing against but yourself. You can stop anytime . . . or you can do your time." That was what I needed to hear. "I can do this," I said. "I want to do this . . . I need to do this for myself." I run in soft sand once in a while, but this morning it seemed extremely difficult. I felt as if I were in quicksand at points. I felt as if I couldn't make my running stride . . . that I was bogged down—and I was. But I kept going until I met my time, so another challenge met . . . another struggle defeated. I had the patience, the fortitude, and the peace that came with the accomplishment.

I thought, That's how I feel about my grieving process. I don't want to do the time. I'm tired of the struggle. I don't want to continue going through this. And the grief isn't just about losing Mark, but it's also about losing who I was, and it's about all the changes that have occurred since Mark's death. I usually thrive on a good challenge—I don't like it when I think I can't do something or someone else says I can't do something. It makes me work harder to accomplish it. But I just don't have a lot of patience for this grieving process . . . so there are many times I have no peace. I believe peace and patience have to go together . . . like a pair of scissors that can't cut unless both blades are there. Now, I know where my peace lies, and to a certain extent, I have that underlying peace propelling me to live the next day out, but there are times I just can't find it. Times when I don't accept Jesus's gift of peace. I would rather struggle a little more.

Anyway, a friend who is very special to me said, "Linda, you have to find peace in the midst of this process." I think she was really saying that I needed to be patient, because if I have patience, then I will have peace. Patience with myself, with all the things I'm dealing with financially, with the decisions I have to make now that Mark usually made, with just living this single life when I'm not used to the single life . . . and I must have patience with others, because the ones you think will be there so often aren't, and the ones you didn't think would be there are.

I have to do my time in the grief process. I have to find the peace and the patience . . . because I learned that whether I have the patience for this grief or not, it has the patience for me.

"Now, may the Lord of peace himself give you peace at all times in every way. The Lord be with you all" ⸺ *2 Thessalonians. 3:16.*

Move Just Move

⸺⸺⸺⸺⸺

"It takes courage to push yourself to places that you have never been before . . . to test your limits . . . to break through barriers. And the day came when the risk it took to remain tight inside the bud was more painful than the risk it took to blossom." —Anaïs Nin

This is certainly true in my life. This is what I experience as I walk through this season of grief. This time of reflection, of life—of living, not dying. There are so many things I don't want to do right now. But I find as time goes on that I'm embracing life in a different way and that it would be so much more painful to stay here, in this place. I want to grow and learn through this time of change, this time of leaving the security of the known to move into uncertainty. I want to experience life in a new way. I want to be the woman that God created me to be . . . to risk . . . to love . . . to grow . . . to give . . . to be stretched . . . to run, not walk . . . to soar like an eagle . . . to live life to the fullest and to take care of myself so I can be of value to others.

I don't weep for Mark. Mark is good—he's better than good. He's at his best and being loved more than our humanity can even comprehend. No . . . instead, I get sad when I don't move forward, when I feel frozen. I weep for those who can't move past pain and grief and are immobilized, those who can't break through the barriers. Because I know . . . I have experienced, not only in this, but during other painful times in my life, that it is so much better to blossom through risking it all than to remain inside the bud.

We are here just for a short time; we are not promised tomorrow. It's critical to live in awareness of the life going on around us . . . in us. And to do those things we've always dreamed about doing so we can become the people God created us to be.

Run With The Horses

I have a painting of horses running hanging above my computer. I love it because it reminds me of one of my favorite verses in scripture. "If you have raced with men on foot and they have wearied you, how will you compete with the horses? And if in a safe land you fall down, how will you do in the jungle of the Jordan?" —*Jer.* 12:5

Eugene Peterson wrote a book about Jeremiah called *Run with the Horses*. In it, he talks about this verse:

> There is a memorable passage concerning Jeremiah's life when, worn down by the opposition and absorbed in self-pity, he was about to capitulate to just such a premature death. He was ready to abandon his unique calling in God and settle for being a Jerusalem statistic. At that critical moment he heard the reprimand. Biochemist Erwin Chargaff updates the questions: "What do you want to achieve? Greater riches? Cheaper chicken? A happier life, a longer life? Is it power over your neighbors that you are after? Are you only running away from your death? Or are you seeking greater wisdom, deeper piety?"
>
> Life is difficult, Jeremiah. Are you going to quit at the first wave of opposition? Are you going to retreat when you find that there is more to life than finding three meals a day and a dry place to sleep at night? . . . Are you going to live cautiously or courageously? I called you to live at your best, to pursue righteousness, to sustain a drive toward excellence. It is easier, I know, to be neurotic. It is easier to be parasitic. It is easier to relax in the embracing arms of The Average. Easier, but not better. Easier, but not more significant. Easier, but not more fulfilling. I called you to a life of purpose far beyond what you think yourself capable of living and promised adequate strength to fulfill your destiny. Now at the first sign of difficult you are ready to quit? What is it you really want, Jeremiah? Do you want to shuffle along with the crowd, or run with the horses?[5]

I want to run with the horses. Mark would want me to do that, too.

---

5 Eugene H. Peterson, *Run with the Horses (Downers Grove, IL: IVP Books, 2010).*

The Raspberry

———✺———

I love this short story that's inscribed on five of the six pillars in the Holocaust Memorial in Boston's Quincy Market. The stories speak of the cruelty and suffering that was endured in the camps. The story I love follows:

> The sixth pillar presents a tale of a different sort, about a little girl named Ilse, a childhood friend of Guerda Weissamn Kline, in Auschwitz. Guerda remembers that Ilse, who was about six years old at the time, found one morning a single raspberry somewhere in the camp. Ilse carried it all day long in a protected place in her pocket, and in the evening, her eyes shining with happiness, she presented it to her friend Guerda on a leaf. "Imagine a world," writes Guerda, "in which your entire possession is one raspberry, and you give it to your friend."

I would give my raspberry to Mark, my best friend. In fact, I would give all my possessions to have him back one more time . . . just to see him once more, to hear him, to feel him. But one day soon I will be able to give him my raspberry, as we will be together with hope and love for eternity. Can you imagine the eyes in which Ilse looked through? The soul . . . what she experienced: the pain she felt, the fear? It was real, not imagined. And yet through this pain and fear she chose to see the sweetness of one raspberry and the love that drives out all fear . . . and she extended that love, that one sweet glance of life in the middle of death. She let love rule. It was probably the only piece of food she'd had in a long time . . . probably the only piece of life she'd witnessed in a long time . . . probably the only piece of color in that godforsaken place that she'd seen . . . and she chose to give that precious gift to her friend. In the midst of suffering, of fear, of control, of death . . . she chose friendship and love. She chose to live.

I doubt anyone I know or most of us have never experienced what Guerda and Ilse did in their little six-year-old lives, but some have. Some people have experienced so much horrific pain that I wonder how they survived to tell their story. Pain, depression, suffering—it's all relative to what we know, what we have grown up with and experienced as individuals . . . as Americans . . . as free people. Pain is so different for everyone. It really doesn't matter what someone else may think pain is, or how hard it is to endure . . . we all have it, precious pain. We all cling to a certain fear. We all hide some kind of scars . . . sins . . . guilt. It all gives us a reason to give up, and we can find all kinds of excuses because of it to abandon our goals and our plans. Hell, it can cause us to abandon our lives . . . our hope . . . our reason for pressing on to love and give to others. It can cause us to give up those dreams that lie dormant at the bottom of our shattered hearts and souls. Pain can give us a reason not to change. It keeps us in invisible chains . . . but, Ilse saw life in the pain. She saw love in giving the only thing she had to offer: that raspberry. Maybe, just maybe love would be enough to free her and her friend from the dark walls that surrounded them. Maybe love would drive out their fear.

I ran into a friend of mine in the grocery store today, and she was in pain. She was depressed. She said she had been that way for two years and that she couldn't feel God. Well, I talked with her for a short while and had much empathy for her pain. She said she felt so alone. Oh, how I could relate. Yes, I think we can all relate at one time or another to loneliness. But without loneliness we wouldn't be able to understand what it is to not be alone. We wouldn't be able to understand love.

I have felt so displaced since Mark died . . . kind of lost. But if I wasn't lost, I wouldn't know what home was. Home is found in your heart . . . cliché, but so true.

You know, loneliness is designed to help you discover who you are and to help you stop looking outside yourself for your worth. I bet that on that day, Ilse knew who she was. She didn't look outside of herself. She discovered love . . . a love so sweet . . . a love of who she was . . . so she could think of nothing else but giving.

I tried to understand my friend who's been struggling with depression. I tried to have empathy for her pain and loneliness. And I could definitely relate to her not feeling God . . . but I know that as I give to others and as I try to inspire and encourage others . . . as I try to move in my pain . . . I feel God there. I feel joy, not pain. I feel hope . . . because you have to give that last possession to live, to love, and to feel. I pray that my friend will pick the raspberry, put it in her pocket, and give it to another so she will lose her chains of pain . . . of fear . . . of loneliness.

I wonder if Ilse "felt God" in that godforsaken place. I told my friend that if she waited to feel God again, it may never come . . . that you have to know He's there. Because, to be honest with you, I rarely "feel" God . . . but I know He's there because He's in my soul. He created me, and I trust He's there. I know He's there . . . otherwise, I would have never made it this far, and I sure as hell wouldn't have gotten out of bed after Mark died.

I bet Ilse knew that God was with her. How else could she give her last possession to her friend? How else could she have *joy* in the midst of darkness? How else could God have given His last possession for us to live—Jesus? God gave him to us, his friends. We didn't earn it . . . there's nothing we can do to earn it, nothing we can say to be given pure love. God didn't base it on a feeling. No . . . it was based on something bigger than a feeling. It was based on an action of love.

Love, you might be surprised to know, isn't a feeling—it's an action. It's willing good to another person. The feelings come as fruit to love. Ilse performed the action of love. I hope that we would all have the possibility in our hearts to be an Ilse.

Somehow, I know that if we could reach that state of giving our last possession for love, all our fears would be driven out.

Come Sit Down

"If you have no time for rest, it's exactly the right time."
— *Mark Twain*

As I begin my rest and respite for the week . . . a much needed break . . . I realize I haven't had a break—mentally, emotionally, or physically—since my husband died. I am tired. We all need breaks. I'm so wired, and Mark used to be the one to say, "Linda, come sit down with me. Come sit . . . and relax. Linda, let's enjoy where we are . . . not where we're going next." He was the most laid-back guy, and I was full of energy. We were different in so many ways, but it was a yin-and-yang kind of relationship. I knew how to keep the excitement, and he knew how to calm me down and ground me. One night I was painting and had been all day. Mark sat on the couch and was watching me paint. I said, "You could help." And he said, "Or you could sit down on the couch beside me and relax . . . it will be here tomorrow." He knew how to calm me.

Oh, I miss that in my life . . . that yin to my yang. I haven't had that other side of balance in my life since he died. I'm having to learn to be the yin and yang in myself . . . to be whole without Mark. That in itself is a journey . . . a learning process. He was my calmness in the midst of my overzealous passion to move and go and do . . . and my desire to empower others to live with zest, passion, health, and self-love.

I, of course, can coach others in peace, calmness, stress management . . . isn't that the way it usually works? I mean, I'm trained in it. But it's very hard for me. I've been working on it and working it out, and I'm getting there. I take time. Often it's in the activeness of my life that I find peace and renewal . . . by building my business and learning everything I need to know about business, waterskiing, boxing, weight training, surfing, and other things. Being active is somehow my peace . . . my healing. But I need complete rest now. No schedule for a week. No expectations, no agenda . . . just being. Being in the present . . . in nature . . . with those I love. No coaching, no training, no business-building business. Just being, resting, and listening to God . . . the one who calls me to rest.

Angels Come in Many Forms

"Angels appear in many different forms to hold your hand through difficult times." —Doreen Virtue

I decided to walk on the beach earlier. Sometimes I just need to slow down. I've been running as fast as a cheetah after its prey since Mark died. I still haven't caught my prey . . . still running. You see, Mark was gone a second after he died. He's still gone and he'll still be gone in ten . . . twenty years. So my belief is I have to move forward; even a second ago is the past. Besides, if I slow down, the past that is gone pounces on me and traps me. The loneliness wants to hold me hostage… but I don't dare stay there because it threatens to keep me prisoner, no hostage bargaining or release.

As I walked, my angel, hostage negotiator, showed up in a seagull. He followed me down the beach as if to talk with me. During Mark's paddle-out, there was a lone seagull that flew over us. I know it was that same seagull walking with me today, letting me share my pain so I wouldn't be captured by it, but instead released from it. That seagull followed me all the way to my path back home . . . and he flew away when the tears were gone. God sent an angel to carry the weight of the pain away.

Free Bird

If I leave here tomorrow
Would you still remember me?
For I must be traveling on now
'Cause there's too many places I've got to see.

But if I stayed here with you, girl,
Things just couldn't be the same.
'Cause I'm as free as a bird now,
And this bird you cannot change, oh, oh, oh, oh.
And this bird you cannot change.

This is for us, Mark. It's been a year and half later and we're both free . . . just on different sides of the world. I look forward to the day when all is completed with my side of the world and we're all free to be with you and God. Free to believe and accept his gracious offering of everlasting life. "Free Bird" reminds me of Mark and our journey to our separate worlds.

I often think of stories I've read of people who die and are hovering over their bodies. They are looking down at loved ones, at the nurses and doctors who are trying to save them. They are then presented with a question or a conversation allowing them to go with the light or stay with their families. They are given a glimpse of the other side, the indescribable beauty. Everlasting life, with unconditional love and shared with those who have gone before them.

Of course, you only hear the stories of those who return to life. Who decide, or for whom the light has decided, that it's not their time.

I often think of Mark doing this, watching me trying frantically to bring him back to life, and debating if he should stay or go. Well, Mark had lots of family whom he loved, who passed before him. He told me several times that he was ready to go. He had a lot of stress here on earth. I know he loved me and wanted to stay with me, but the pull of freedom and unconditional love held him that afternoon. It comforted him. It was his time . . . the decision was made. He was going home, to be totally free, once and for all.

I picture him making that hard decision, but the only one he could. We all need to be free . . . free from worry and stress, free to love, free to give, and free to accept the grace and forgiveness that Jesus has so freely offered us. Some of us learn how to be free on this side of the world. I believe when you can learn to be free with yourself, who you are and who God created you to be, you become a free bird. You begin to have a small taste of the freedom that's offered in another world, which also offers pure unconditional love and grace . . . heaven . . . our true home. All you have to do is believe.

Mark, your freedom is true freedom, but I'm thankful for the freedom I have here on earth for the time I have left. I am free to love my singleness, to love others, to love myself, and to accept and believe what's offered by our Savior. Everlasting love, unconditional love, a home with no pain and no suffering . . . until then, my love, we'll be free in different worlds.

Invisible Walls

"Limitations tend to be illusions or self-created barriers."
—— *Steven Redhead*

When I run on the beach in the mornings, there's a place I can't seem to pass. No matter what, since Mark's death I haven't been able to run past these condos that Mark built. I always turn around when I reach them. There are too many memories . . . too many reminders of prayers gone unanswered. It's funny, how we have these walls in front of us that seem so silly, but they are so real in our heads.

Mark built the condos in 2007, and they became the beginning of the end for us financially and for Mark financially, emotionally, and physically. They weren't even considered risky at the time. However, as everyone knows, the real estate market at that time . . . well, we all know that story. Six million people lost their homes and financial security.

For years, I would run to those condos and pray over them. I would pray that they would sell and Mark would keep his health. Then Mark had his heart attack, and he thought surely they would sell. Of course, they didn't. So I would run to them every day and pray over them. We even had people come and pray with us. I tried to get Mark to let them go, but he couldn't—he was just like that. He said he had to do what he could to keep going and making payments. The banks wouldn't work with him at all; he tried everything he could. Ultimately, we lost them and everything else. Our home, our financial security. We had the best home. It was built in 1935, by a New York Architect. Mark loved older homes. He researched found out who the owners and the architect was. There was not landscaping when we bought the house so we got the advantage of creating what we wanted. Mark loved this. He designed the pool and worked with the landscaper on the design of the yard and the plants and trees we wanted. I loved palm trees and we put nine around our pool. The big joke with our landscaper was "More Palm Trees Please" because I loved them so. There was this stream in the back yard and beyond the stream was this area of wild growth and bamboo. Mark loved going back there to work and cut back the overgrowth with his big machete. That's how he relieved his stress. We always knew where to find Mark if he had a stressful day... surfing or cutting down extra bamboo. He loved working in the yard and found solace there as well as his surfing. He was so proud of that house and it was so unique. We lived there over thirteen years before we lost it to foreclosure. He was devastated. Mark never got over that. He never truly healed from all the loss.

So... God never answered my prayers, at least not in the way I wanted them answered. I mean, the condos didn't sell . . . we lost our home and ultimately God didn't answer my prayers of keeping Mark healthy.

Well . . . Mark, you're free from that now. You don't owe anyone . . . not one penny. You carry no debt now. Honey, it's all okay now.

I've had this huge wall in front of me at those condos. I've tried to go around that wall (run past those condos in the mornings), and it just seems to stretch so far that I can never find the end. . . So I turn back. I've tried scaling that wall only to find myself sliding back down, landing on my back, the weight of my body making an imprint in the sand . . . only to get up, turn around, and go back. Then I was thinking maybe I could pole vault over that wall . . . but I always came up short, and the wall just seemed too high.

Well, this morning I decided I was just going to surrender to that wall . . . and that I needed to pray . . . maybe thank Him for this wall, this barrier, and give it to Him to handle. I closed my eyes, stretched out my arms, and I ran right through that wall . . . yes, right through the center of that concrete wall. I ran right past those condos. I kept running and running and crying and crying. Guess what I discovered? It didn't stop me . . . it wasn't hard at all. There was no wall—it was all an illusion. I imagined it . . . I built it there.

Freedom from barriers . . . freedom from the walls we build that stop us from praying . . . from hoping . . . from moving forward. False illusions . . . appearing real. I did it, Mark.

Traveling Abroad

As we head into fall, walking into twenty-one months later, it's bittersweet for me. One, because summer is coming to a close and it's my favorite time of the year. The hotter, the better for me . . . maybe it's because I was born in June. I mean, I am a flip-flop, bathing-suit, water-fun kind of girl. Another reason is that it means memories of loss come creeping in.

This summer has been tougher for me than last summer. July through September has been quite the battle for me, emotionally. It seems the longer my husband has been gone, the quieter it gets, and the stillness is just plain spooky at times. I'm a people person and love being in a relationship, and this experience has really given me another perspective on those who have lost loved ones, relationships, and live alone. It's given me empathy for those who feel like they're walking alone in this world, even if they're surrounded by friends. Empathy for those in a foreign land.

Those of us who feel as if we're traveling alone in a foreign land for the first time, surrounded by multitudes of people, but no one seeming to speak our language, and we feel totally displaced as we try to learn fragments of the language so we can ask for directions . . . so we can fit in . . . so we can navigate around their streets and community. No one wants to feel like they're displaced or lost.

Yes, the attack from that enemy called loneliness snuck up on me like a cat sneaks up—slowly but with perfect pouncing precision on her prey. The single little sparrow busy finding straw for her new nest doesn't even notice what lurks behind her.

What an emotional battle it has been. I'm thankful I have my protective shield around me . . . because without God, it would have been tough to get through these last months unscathed from the soreness caused by loneliness's laceration.

My battle with loss and loneliness is that: a battle. It's not the end; it's the beginning . . . the beginning of finding my adventure in a new land. It brings opportunities for new relationships, new sights, a new way of living. It's kind of like after you get rid of the anxiety and fear of being in that foreign land alone. You start to want to thrive there . . . You want to enjoy it. You begin to learn and understand the language of those around you better. You begin to learn about the area . . . you get a road map . . . you ask for directions . . . you suddenly find the streets in the community becoming more familiar. You're finding your way around. You're beginning to feel more comfortable in your own skin, even though you may feel a little different on the inside. You're starting to understand the culture. You're even starting to dress like the natives. Yes . . . the foreign land becomes another part of who you are. . .

So when you it's time to go home to what you know . . . the familiar . . . you will have gained from your experiences in that foreign land. You will have become stronger. You'll be able to understand those around you better. You'll be able to help them navigate through a foreign land because you learned how to do so. You'll look at those you love differently because you'll be empathetic, remembering that they may be in a foreign land too . . . learning their way around.

The Line Up

"Her happiness floated like waves of ocean along the coast of her life.
She found lyrics of her life in his arms but she never sung her song."
— Santosh Kalwar

Some mornings, I love to walk down to where the surfers are and watch them in the lineup. The sight is absolutely beautiful . . . serene: all of them waiting for their opportunity to do what they love best. Riding the wave as it rolls in against the beautiful vast horizon of the deep blue sea as the sun prepares for its day to rise high in the September sky. They make surfing look so easy . . . but that's the talent of any good athlete. When they're engaged in their favorite sport, they make it look as easy as walking.

I like to look for Mark in the lineup. It brings me peace, thinking I may see him . . . at least envision him out there. I keep thinking if I look hard and long enough, maybe I'll glimpse his white hair and his style of controlling his board, moving it where he wants it to go on the wave . . . carving out his own style with each drop-in . . . making his presence known without having to say, "Here I am, look at me! Look at me master this wave!" He loved surfing . . . the water . . . his friends. And he was humble. I loved that about him.

I often asked him why he didn't try to make surfing his career. He would tell me that his mom got sick and he felt he needed to help his dad with the motel and get his college degree. Just like Mark, sacrificing for others. That's who he was. But he never lost his love of surfing and the salt water, which kept drawing him back, wave after wave.

Yes, I know I won't really see him in the water when I look for him. It's just a place to connect my mind, heart, spirit, and soul . . . because sometimes your mind and heart want to tell you something different. They're not in sync with each other. So I have to learn how to get them on the same page. After all, we are all one heart, mind, body, spirit, and soul. To heal and be whole, I have to solve the mystery of keeping the inside and outside on the same wavelength.

I may never be a great surfer, but it's a place that brings me peace because I feel Mark's spirit . . . because I'm sitting in the middle of God's creation, which is so much bigger than me. It humbles me. It brings me peace because I'm surrounded by others who are there for their own reasons and their own passion for surfing. It heals me. It congeals my heart, body, soul, and spirit together in a rhythm. The ocean . . . the peace . . . the action . . . learning a new skill moves me forward. It keeps me strong and moving forward in life, which I've done since Mark died. I've moved forward, not staying in the grief . . . not staying in the sadness of it all.

I searched for the place where I could feel peace that transcends all understanding. I needed a real place to pull it all back together when it wants to come unraveled. I also understand that, for me, it was someone bigger than myself who pointed me to that place . . . who continued to give me strength. . . That person is Jesus Christ. Without Him, I wouldn't have the inner strength to enjoy this life that I don't understand. He gives me a survival instinct that just won't let me give in. He gives me hope that this is not all there is, but that this is what I have now . . . so I should live it to the fullest: laugh, give to others, and above all have fun!

A day doesn't go by that I don't think of Mark and miss him. I know he would want me to continue my life, because he would be the first to let me know that life is short.

Sweet Strength is always moving forward with a zest for life.

Familiar Brown Chair

"We are torn between nostalgia for the familiar and an urge for the foreign and strange. As often as not, we are homesick most for the places we have never known." — Carson McCullers

They come so suddenly as I slide into my favorite chair with journal and pen and a cup of hot green tea comfortably held in my hands. I was really hoping that the time had come . . . that the drops wouldn't come. I mean, it's been awhile since I sat here. I mean it's close to two years. Surely, I thought, they won't come this time.

Avoidance is so comforting when you don't want to be in a familiar place . . . a spot that takes your memories on an emotional ride to another place and time. It gets tiring sometimes, having to face reality . . . having to battle. But the battle always brings freedom with it. Reality is like an internal dialogue. It has a blatant voice that I would just as soon not hear . . . especially today . . . because this morning, I was dancing with the stranger called a new life until I melted into this chair of familiarity.

By all accounts, I'm doing great with this new change, and I love who I'm becoming . . . but today, there is no avoiding who I was. One by one . . . pain by pain . . . the moisture falls so effortlessly, containing who I was and holding the joy of who I'm becoming. They roll down my cheeks . . . falling on my freshly composed thoughts . . . smearing and staining my paper. Dammit. I hate this. I hate being weak and afraid. I don't like falling victim to my own cocooning memories of who I was . . . of my life before . . . or to the fearful thoughts that threaten to hamper the release of this new, beautiful, strong, strange woman. Weakness seems to come so easily, preying on my fears and loneliness. And this strength that I fight for . . . well, it's a fight to stay strong . . . to move . . . to be alive . . . to embrace this stranger in my life. Weakness has never been something I'm comfortable with . . . but this morning I seem to be chained in these memories and this weakness and these tears. Change and transformation . . . release the chains. . . I'm so afraid to listen to the words I'm thinking and so afraid to feel the tears that are falling.

But I will not be afraid of the memories of who I was or of this stranger and this strange life with which I've become intimate. This stranger has compelled me to leave it all behind and be bold in my newness. This stranger looks back at me in the mirror, imitating my face and body. But she has crept into my heart and mind, shaping and molding them into her new home . . . into her new rhythm of single life. Suddenly this stranger has become my best friend. She has become . . . me.

Maybe this morning I'll sit in my brown chair and feel the weakness leave with each tear, and the strength come in with each word said in prayer. Sometimes it's good to sit in our weakness . . . in our loneliness . . . so we can find strength from the one above. Sometimes we have to say goodbye to those memories that haunt us and threaten us in our change to become better. Sometimes we have to let go of what we knew or who we are so we can discover what we need to know and who we can become. When we allow the stranger of transformation, it will know how to navigate the strangeness of life . . . the changes . . .

It doesn't matter how much I may want to go back—I can't. I can't grow myself into what used to be. But I can grow myself into what is now . . . what is going on at this moment. The brokenness is healed in the butterfly, not in the chrysalis. I can't find freedom in the chrysalis . . . in the safe brown chair. I can't find freedom in wanting things to be the same. I can't find strength and hope unless I'm willing to get out of the chrysalis. I can't find strength and hope in staying the same when nothing around me is the same. I can't find strength in what ifs. I release the chains by creating new memories . . . by releasing the what ifs. I become the beautiful butterfly by embracing a new way of living life. I get my wings to soar when I realize the pain I feel today will provide me with the strength to fly tomorrow . . . to break out of the chrysalis.

We cannot stay the same and move forward in life in a healthy and productive way unless we somehow come to the understanding that we are always changing and that everything and everybody around us is changing. We can't live in the brown chair. We have to learn how to become different people with each change or we'll die where we are. We'll be thrown in the back of a truck, headed to the trash heap of other brown chairs, unless we change. Yes, change is scary . . . but regret is scarier. Change is scary . . . but not doing something about our lives when we can, can be scarier.

As my tears start to be spaced father and father apart and my tea is half gone, I think about how different I was couple of years ago, sitting in my safe brown chair. It was Mark's favorite chair too. We'd try to beat the other in gaining access to the brown comfy chair. It makes me smile, thinking of him in that chair. "My husband and I" . . . It sounds like I'm speaking a different language when I say those words. It's been difficult to let that part of who I was go . . . being married and all. A lot different, this single life . . . walking in that door alone, night after night . . . Robert gone . . . the dogs gone . . . Mark gone . . . my house gone. And here I am, learning a different road . . . a different way of life. I'm learning how to love being alone. Besides, being alone with yourself is a good thing. It's like that quote by Ellen Burstyn, "What a lovely surprise to finally discover how un-lonely being alone can be."

Another tear rolls down my cheek, this time splashing in my last sip of tea.

I don't know how to change. I'm scared.

What do you mean you don't know how to change? You already have . . . and remember, it's your reality now, being single. It's a good reality for now. It's where your growth will occur.

Really, it's so hard to look at . . . trying to remember each detail of what you had, who you were, and what you lost . . . trying hard to get those pieces back. You hope that if you can think about the way it was, then maybe—just maybe, with a miracle—you can stay there. You can sit in that brown chair and be that same person . . . But reality always knocks the door in. It doesn't matter if it was locked or if you took the trouble to put a steel door around those comforting illusions . . . trying to keep the truth out. It will bust right through and confront you face-to-face, eye-to-eye, thought-to-thought, and tear-to-tear.

There are things that will forever change who we are, and we have to embrace that change . . . learn how to become a different person . . . think differently. That's when we discover that we can choose to become the butterfly or to stay in the dark chrysalis. When a tragedy, challenge, barrier, or memories of the past threaten to make us weak and break us down, we have to change who we are and how we think.

We have to allow ourselves to do the hard stuff . . . you know . . . leave the shore . . . change the sails . . . change direction . . . swim against the current . . . take the path less traveled. Do what you don't want to do . . . but what you know will allow you to become stronger, better. Creating a new person . . . a new way of thinking . . . a new perspective . . . a new life. . . the butterfly.

Well . . . there they go, memories. Tea's all gone . . . tears are dried up. I don't think I can write another thought today. Wow, the time has passed so quickly, sitting here thinking of what my life used to be like . . . who I once was. I'm glad I made the choice to reel in those memories before they broke my line.

I think next time I want to avoid this brown chair. I think I'll let my new best friend, who looks just like me but is so much stronger, freer, and more positive, sit here. I bet the tears will be tears of joy and the memories will be of what she accomplished that day. And I bet she won't get caught up in the past . . . what she can't change. But I bet she will see this brown chair as a chance to write about how bright and different her today is and how much hope she has for the future. Yeah, next time I'll trade off with her . . . because the thought of me staying here, in the past, in who I was . . . well . . . come on now. Let's continue what we're doing and keep moving on in this new life. Thank You, God, for always making me see the butterfly.

Images of Death and Life

"The fear of death follows from the fear of life. A man who lives fully is prepared to die at any time." —*Mark Twain*

It's hard to sleep with death images in your head. Life and death. . . Each day is so fragile. We don't even realize how close we are to death . . . or life. Not much separates the two. It's almost as if they're separated by a thin glass of sorts, which can be shattered at any time by just the throw of a hard stone.

Some friends and I went to see a friend of ours who is dying of cancer. One of my friends said to me on the way home, "Dying is so ugly." I had to agree. From what I've seen of it, it's just . . . well. . . The images of those headed to another life. Images of Mark on the floor dying, the one I love leaving me, the fruitless effort of my breath exhaling into his lifeless lungs, and nothing else mattering. Images of the other people I've been in the presence of when they leave their bodies behind. And just last night, seeing our friend lying there, with absolutely no resemblance of the person we knew in the gym. Her body is struggling to take in the next breath . . . so thin, so frail, in so much pain. Thin, that is, everywhere but where that godforsaken cancer has chosen to make its home. She fought so hard through this, and some would say she lost the fight. Did she really? Or has she won?

Cancer . . . I hate it. My own journey with breast cancer brings the reality of my brush with what could have been death to my thoughts this night.

She called me back in February or March to ask me about the stomach pain she was having. She wanted to know if I'd ever experienced anything like it, since we're both such avid gym rats. We talked awhile and she asked me to pray with her, and I did. She called me a couple of weeks later. They'd found something. She wanted prayer. She was so fearful that it was cancer. I told her not to let her fears go there, that she didn't know yet. Not to assume the worst. I prayed with her. After that, I prayed for her. Her fear was so strong; she didn't want to have cancer, as none of us would. Well, her worst fear came true.

How do we face our fears? I think we have to face them head-on so they don't rob us of living.

In April, it was official: She had cancer. Eight months later, she lay dying. I didn't keep up with her like I'd intended over the months. Good intentions are nothing but that . . . intentions of doing something. But when we fail to follow through, they're no intentions at all, really.

I saw her after her surgery, spoke with her a few times on the phone, prayed with her. But my prayers seemed so empty to me. It's hard to understand sometimes, isn't it? It's hard to understand death, life, cancer, prayer.

I used to be quite the prayer warrior, or so I was told. People always wanted me to pray for them. My prayer life is different now. My prayers go something like this now: Lord, have mercy on me. Thank You, Jesus, for this day. Jesus, forgive me for those I may have hurt as I forgive those who have hurt me. Help me love like You love me. Jesus, my friend needs You and I don't know what they need, but you do . . . so please do it for them. Protect my family and friends from the evil one. Protect me. You are my Shepherd; I shall not want. Jesus, please give me strength, because I'm done. Help me encourage someone today. Help me bring light to someone and help me be light. Jesus, my mom and dad need a hand. Jesus, my son is yours; I give him to you to love and take care of. Jesus, I can't change the world; help me change myself . . . change my heart. I know you love us. I know you have won. Jesus, I just can't see today through the death, so I'm glad you can. Tell Mark hello for me. Bring peace to this world. Bring love, and may it start with me today, God.

My faith has turned into just being with Jesus . . . not a lot of doing with Jesus. All I know now is to be with Him in my day and allow Him to be with me. There is really nothing I understand anymore except that.

Sometimes there seems to be no rhyme or reason to any of it. But there is hope. You see, my friend is going home. She faced her greatest fear with courage, strength, fight, hope, love, dignity. She fought, and she lived. The cancer thinks it has won. Death thinks it has won. But guess what? She won . . . Mark won . . . she's going home . . . to her true home, where there is no more death, pain, worries, or fear.

She faced her fear with a strength that came from beyond. That body isn't who she really is. That cancer, which thought it had won in her body, will be gone . . . and she'll be alive and well. We think about the ugliness of those we care about dying, but there is really beauty. Beauty that they are taking off that body, leaving that ugliness behind, and going on to something more beautiful than we who are left behind can even comprehend.

There is beauty in death if you look for it and if you understand that death is really the beginning of life. Seeing death while we're still here makes us appreciate life and want to live, or at least it makes me feel this way. Living life to the fullest . . . give it everything you've got. Don't get worn-out and stressed-out and miss it. Don't settle. Don't quit. Don't stop the race before you reach the finish line. My friend didn't.

There is life in fear when you face it. There is still beauty in this world among all the thorns. As long as you are living, you have a choice as to how you view this world. You have a choice as to how you're going to live the life you have . . . all the way to the end. I don't know a lot about a lot of things, but I do know this. . . each minute we live our lives, we're faced with choices—all kinds of choices. Each choice we make has an impact on the kind of story we write . . . the kind of story we leave behind . . . the life we live. Each choice, every thought makes us stronger or weaker . . . healthier or sicker . . . more loving or more hateful . . . more peaceful or more stressed-out. With each choice we make, we choose to be givers or takers. Each choice we make either muddies our waters or makes them clearer. Each thought, every decision has a domino effect in our lives. We are here for a purpose, and maybe we don't understand everything. But do we really need to? Or do we need to just understand our choices, our thoughts, and our beliefs?

So this morning, when I woke up, I said, "Linda, get up. Get going. You have so much to be thankful for." I read my index cards. One says: The Lord is my Shepherd; I shall not want. Another one says: You are going to feel like quitting—don't! One says: Winners never quit and quitters never win. And then the last one says: You are here for a purpose. Now go help someone.

But it's okay. God has a plan, and it will all come together. Just keep dreaming and remember that your home is where your heart is. And this isn't your real home—just a temporary place in which you are to shine, grow, love, and share your gifts with others. Home is coming.

So out the door with a smile I went on my run, ready to conquer this year with my dreams and visions.

Sweet Strength is getting up and going no matter what.

Two Years

Well, Mark, it's been two years. Two long yet short years. Some days it feels like eternity since you've been gone, and some days it feels like you just left to go for that run and you'll be back in forty minutes, like clockwork.

I'm so happy that you made it home, bud . . . so happy. I don't know if you can see me down here. I know you're with me in some way because I've felt your presence—especially when I'm in the water. But I don't think you can see what goes on here . . . because it wouldn't be heaven if you could see all the suffering and pain on earth. Maybe you just get a glimpse of the miracles.

Bud, it has been quite the obstacle course to maneuver on this path that has been set before me. The path that led away from being with you, married, safe, secure, and protected . . . to the stark path of today's reality. Single life again and making a living for myself. Some days, I get so mad at you for leaving me. It's better now. As time goes on, I'm no longer mad at you. Who could stay mad at you anyway? I know the reality is that it was your time and God took you, just as He'll take all of us . . . in a blink of the eye. Each breath is a gift.

We're here one day and then gone the next, to another place . . . our real home. I often think about the impact you made on people's lives. You really loved those around you. Everyone misses you. You were my best friend, too. Even though we had our ups and downs, we were always there for each other. You were ALWAYS there for me . . . through it all.

I just knew we were going to spend the rest of our long lives together . . . especially since we went through so much. Like after your first heart attack at forty-seven, when you said, "I know that God is going to relieve us of these financially draining condos now, because I had this heart attack." Well . . . that didn't happen. It just got tougher after that. I am so sorry . . . so sorry that you had to go through that. But our marriage sure got stronger over those last five years, so I guess it was good to lose all of that stuff. We found out we didn't need any of it anyway. Besides, I realized how little the loss of things . . . of money . . . of homes . . . were in comparison to losing someone I love . . . someone who was by my side every day. . .

Robert misses you so much. You would be so proud of him and what he has accomplished in the Navy. He looks after me . . . always worried about me. He has had a really difficult time and even got a Mark the Shark tattoo on his back. Not sure how you would feel about the tattoo . . . but I know you would be proud of him. You so inspired him and loved him as your own. He couldn't have asked for a better dad than you . . . nor I, a husband. Today he texted me about how hard of a time he's having. He gets sick when he thinks of you . . . that familiar punch in the stomach. I know it all too well . . . the nausea feeling, knowing you aren't here. What happened to our lives?

Change . . . it comes daily, and we need to be ready to somehow embrace that change and have hope in the midst of the pain that there is a rhyme and a reason for everything . . . and a purpose for all of this. That's what I believe . . .

Another Valentine's Without You.

This is the third year without you on Valentine's. The third year of being single on Valentine's. Valentine's Day was always very special for us. I still miss you, but I am going to look at this Valentine's different.

I went for a run earlier today in the comfort of my sandy ocean asylum, taking in the blue sky and the sunshine. I was making the time for reflection and contemplation of the love that was taken from me and the hope of the best future to come.

As I reached with my mind's eye into the depths of my heart and soul, I studied with intent the place that has been bound with loneliness and a distant lover who is no more.

I thought about the past years and how my heart has been laid bare. My heart, in the best way it could survive, tried and at time was unable to distinguish between loneliness, missing my best friend, and attraction to someone new. Thinking of the times I wanted to believe the smooth talk slithering off the tongue of an unsung hero who seemed to be lonely too. Becoming wise as a serpent, but longing to be gentle as a dove. I thought about the ups and downs, the highs and lows—especially of this past year—and the lessons learned, the emotions felt during this long trudge through the deep mud of loneliness.

As the run began, I pondered and thought about this Valentine's. My heart began to beat a little faster, a smile came upon my face, and I realized the weight of dreading Valentines was gone. Some of the loneliness had gone out of my heart's door. There was a new word that became alive and in motion with each heartbeat: hope. Hope knows that the best is yet to be discovered. I became very aware of the strength that grew out of the loneliness and the lessons learned . . . the determination. My smile increased, my run became lighter, and a sense of confidence rose up in my soul. I am not really alone.

This Valentine's, I am going to enjoy being with me and who I have become: a single, strong, independent woman, soaring with the Son and enjoying every minute of where I am in life. I love every aspect of my life: my family, my friends, and my work, reminding me this Valentines, I am not really alone. It's only if I choose to be alone. Besides, I am so in love with the man who walks on water.

Rhyme or Reason

———∞∞∞———

"This moment contains all moments" —*C.S. Lewis*

You know, sometimes there's no rhyme or reason . . . seemingly to life. Or maybe it's that there's no rhyme or reason to death . . . seemingly . . . but there always is a reason and a rhyme to life, to life everlasting, and to death; for if we live, we will never die. There is a rhyme and reason because we have a purpose . . . a destiny . . . dreams to accomplish . . . passions to burn through . . . to love and embrace others . . . to walk and run the race marked out, never giving in, but forever giving out to others. Life is a mystery and a miracle . . . this life that is but a passing of time . . . and the footprints that we leave behind.

It has been over two years since Mark died . . . and Hammond, a young man and friend to the same surfing fellowship of Mark's died. Both avid surfers . . . both great husbands and dads . . . both best friends to their wives. To us, it seems they left this earth a little too soon, but there's a time for everything. God's time . . . there's no rhyme or reason to us, it seems . . . but to the one who gives and takes life, it's always the perfect time and rhyme and reason. We trust in time, which never really ends. We trust the one who gives and takes the time.

My son is home . . . whom I love deeply . . . whom Mark loved deeply as his own. We were celebrating Mark's life together tonight and wanted others to celebrate their lives. Celebrating life, which Mark loved. No anniversary, no birthday . . . just a night of remembering two men and the very special footprints they left on this earth and in people's hearts. I didn't know Hammond, but Mark the Shark did. And I knew Mark and what a footprint he left.

What footprints do you want to leave behind . . . how do you want to be remembered? If you knew it was your last night, what would you do?

Life is just a blink in the eye of our Creator, but sometimes it feels like a long journey in our eyes. Really, it's not. It's a very short one compared to everlasting life. So treasure every minute you're given to live and love others. Look around and breathe in every moment that you are graced with in this beautiful, astounding miracle of life that has been laid before you . . . and the abundant life you've been offered to embrace by choice. Choose wisely. . .

I have found such peace in who I am and who God created me to be . . . and in being single once again. Treasuring the sweet memories and treasuring who I have become through life's treasured time.

Sweet Strength is living and loving . . . and mostly, it's peace with where you are today.

The Monkey Lamp

"Neither is new wine put into old wineskins. If it is, the skins burst and the wine is spilled and the skins are destroyed. But new wine is put into fresh wineskins, and so both are preserved." —Jesus

In wellness coaching and life coaching, we're always focused on moving the client forward. We're always focused on seeing what's already working in their lives and moving forward from there. We never go back and try to fix something. Can you ever put things back to their original form? Can you ever make things the way they were? When something is broken, we can never really fix it. I mean, we can try to put the pieces back together, but they never really fit.

I remember one time when Mark was out of town, after we had just gotten married and moved in together, and I decided to paint the whole house a different color. I would have never been brave enough to do this while he was home. Mark wasn't a man who liked change, but I loved change. We would go back and forth. I would move a piece of furniture around and when I got home it would be back in its favorite place. We eventually learned to compromise.

Anyway, he had this favorite monkey lamp. It was very sentimental to him. It was beautiful. I loved it too; in fact, we went through this monkey fetish, when we would purchase just about anything with monkeys on it. Well, I thought the monkey lamp would give great lighting to my painting strokes in a room that was not well lit.

I was painting away, engrossed in the thought of how surprised and proud of me he'd be when he walked in the door. His favorite lamp was resting on a small table with the cord stretched to the socket. Suddenly, our beloved miniature schnauzer decided to challenge the height of that cord . . . and excitedly jumped over it to avoid walking through the maze of furniture so he could get to his favorite bed.

It was like a movie showing a scene in slow-motion. He tripped . . . the lamp slowly falling . . . falling . . . falling a whole two feet, which seemed like it took an hour in my dumbfounded haze. I reacted too slowly to swoop it up before it hit the hard tile floor . . . where it shattered into pieces of sentiment and beauty . . . of monkey limbs and faces . . . all over the floor. I stood stunned. My dog ran down the hallway, not looking back, in fear of the noise he'd unknowingly caused.

I could hardly believe my eyes. Newly married . . . wanting to please and surprise my husband with my hard work in our home . . . Now, the surprise wasn't the newly painted home; it was lying in pieces across the floor. My heart sunk. My thoughts went straight to the familiar sounds after a mess up: How can I fix this? How can I make this better? What am I going to do? How do I tell him?

I decided I'd call my friend . . . she'd surely have the answer to this. Well, she did. Okay . . . so now I have my partner in crime on my side. She suggested gluing it back together and hanging a tassel around the top of the lamp. She was in interior design. . . She said, "It'll work."

I got glue and starting gluing . . . piece by piece, putting it back together. Patience was my friend for the day. Once done, I put the lamp back in its familiar place on the nightstand by the bed and waited . . . waited for—I don't know—Mark not to notice . . . for the pieces to not look glued . . . for my conscience to feel better. I waited and tried hard to not see the broken pieces.

Well, that was the first dang thing he noticed when he got into bed: the "fixed lamp." We survived the fixed lamp, but we had to replace it with a new one and throw the old one out because it just never looked the same . . . because it wasn't the same. It couldn't be fixed . . . but it could be replaced.

Now . . . we aren't replaceable because we are human and the lamp isn't . . . but we can move from the broken to a new creation. We can't fix what's been broken. We can't go back and make anything what it was before. We can't go backward, we can go forward by creating a new us . . . a new way of thinking . . . a new way of believing . . . part of being broken is being able to sit with that, acknowledge that, and realize that maybe it's not about fixing it but is instead about replacing it. It is about becoming something new.

Jesus talked a lot about new creation. He never said to go back and fix something. He said He was making all things new. All things new . . . that's something to think about. If we focus on the broken . . . if we focus on continually trying to fix something that's broken . . . how can we see the new that is before us? The broken gives us a new starting point . . . a new way of looking at things . . . a new way to see that isn't how we want to do it again. The broken isn't about fixing but about starting again. . .

You Can't Do This

———— ❧ ————

"Don't ask yourself what the world needs; ask yourself what makes you come alive. And then go and do that, because what the world needs is people who are alive." ——*Howard Thurman*
"Every morning is a new beginning, a new chance for you to rewrite the story of your life." ——*Tina Su*

I love my runs on the beach, and this morning's was no exception. There's nothing like the feeling I get from being on that beach and having that time to renew and refresh my thoughts. I love the fact that it's just me . . . well . . . against me. I mean, I love that no one makes me get out and run. There's no one there to make me run farther, faster, or slower. It's just me and my mind, my thoughts, my body, and my choice to continue or stop. I always feel empowered when I run that extra time or I stop and do some pushups when I really don't feel like it. Maybe I switch to the soft sand for the last few minutes, just because I want to challenge myself. When I go that extra distance, in whatever form, I feel empowered to take the next step—and I know I can. It's always a battle in your mind, your thought process. It's just you and your thoughts. You can win battle.

I love to encourage people, believe in people, and empower people to make the changes they want to make in their lives. Our thought process and what we believe about ourselves is so powerful that it can enable us to become the people we never knew we could become, and live out the dreams we thought were impossible, or it can literally make us unable to move, unable to make a change or decision.

"People don't resist change. They resist being changed." —*Peter Senge*

Sometimes we just need someone to believe in us and encourage us, someone to be accountable to, someone to empower us and give us the confidence to make our own decisions.

There have been so many times during this journey I'm on that I've wanted to quit, when the pain from losing Mark was so deep that I felt like I couldn't move. The thoughts that can invade my space, they whisper to me, "You can't do this by yourself. Who do you think you are? You can't live without Mark." But I don't quit. I move. I go forward into life . . . you know . . . live. I change the thought process to: You can do this, you are doing this, and you will do this. Each time I choose to move forward in life, it gets easier to do the next time. It gets easier to believe that I can. I've become empowered because I made the decision—no one else made it for me.

Change comes with each day. You have the power in each second to change. With each choice comes change, whether that choice is as simple as replacing soda with water, replacing a sugary dessert with a piece of fruit. Maybe it's deciding to get up and walk for ten minutes instead of watching TV. Maybe it's deciding to get out of the bed. To put down that extra drink. To do that extra pushup. And each time you make that decision to push yourself, you empower yourself to do it the next time and the time after that, until you've won the battle. No one can do it for you, but do you really want them to?

Don't You Know?

The day before my husband's funeral, a friend took me to get flowers to place in the vase that was going to be by my husband's ashes. As we were in the store, I passed people and people passed me. I, of course, was in a haze . . . a daze . . . whatever you want to call it. Anyway, thoughts echoed in my head. I wanted to scream, "Do you people realize I just lost my husband? Do you people realize the pain I'm in? Can you hear the screaming in my heart? Can you see the shattered pieces dangling here on my sleeve? Can you see . . . can you hear?" No . . . they couldn't. Everyone was just going about their business. Buying groceries for their loved ones . . . probably going to cook dinner for their husbands. I wanted to scream, "I hate you! I hate the fact you still have your husband here . . . your wife."

You just never know what someone may be going through. That person who seems angry behind the cash register may have lost her husband, his wife, his child, her finances. The person who doesn't speak to you when you speak to them may be in a mental fog because of something horrific going on in their lives. Look beyond the emotions to the person's needs. Think about all the widows, orphans, those without shelter, those who have no one . . . no friends. Be a friend. Love others. Heck, go as far as to love your enemy. Pray for them pray for those who are hurting.

The past can really hold us back if we let it. It seems the past can become our future if we don't make it just that—the past. Even what you did a second ago is past. You can't get it back and you can't change it, but you can change what you do with it, how you think or don't think about it. People get stuck in the past; some just can't get past the anger, guilt, failure or mistakes. This will kill any hope of changing your life and making your future great. Every time you think of something unfavorable from the past, you bring with it all the associated feelings, and you can't move forward. It will make you relive it again and again.

Don't let the past become your future. Even if it was a good past, it's still the past. You can't recreate it, and the future holds more than you can even imagine . . . if you will only press forward.

Can You Feel The Rain

"Some people feel the rain. Others just get wet." —*Bob Marley*

Last Friday, I was out in the water, attempting to surf, and it was pouring rain. The waves were like rolling hills that had a beauty unbounded except by the limits of the shore. The waves had the appearance of gentleness, but they were strong enough to achieve the surfer's desire to ride them . . .

I have begun in a very limited way to understand the connection of a surfer's soul to the music of the wave, the communication with nature, the bond with others in the water. I'm not what I would call a true surfer yet; I'm more of a beginner, trying to figure it all out. But what I have figured out is it helps me to feel the rain. It's a place I can find healing. It's a place I can find joy. It's a place that makes me listen . . . not to other voices . . . and it silences my voice. It silences the world. It silences everything . . . but the wind blowing . . . the waves rolling in . . . nature . . . the rain . . . the connection to the water . . . the peace . . . the connection to God . . . to nature . . . connecting to my thoughts . . .

It was a piece of paradise in the water. A place of healing . . . of loving and feeling every pelting drop of rain in that downpour from heaven. At one point, I paddled out beyond everyone, laid on my board, stretched out, and relaxed. A surrender. I surrendered to the busyness of life, the pressures of the journey, the precious pain of living and let the rain wash over me and cleanse me. The depths of all the ocean and what it holds was beneath me. I cried. I wept for the place offered to heal . . . to be with my thoughts . . . to be intimate with Jesus and His creation. I felt the rain . . . I wasn't just wet.

The Grief Encounter

"Grief is like the ocean; it comes in waves ebbing and flowing sometimes the water is calm, and sometimes it's overwhelming. All we can do is learn how to swim." —*Vicki Harrison*

I just got back from a run. I needed it to release another unexpected grief encounter. Sometimes I feel like I could run and never stop . . . run until my heart bursts and my legs collapse beneath me. Some days are just like that. No matter how strong your faith or how many friends surround you, you're on a journey to healing. There will be good days and not-so-good days . . . but somehow the release that comes from physically stretching your body to its limits . . . heals pain. Healing is such a juxtaposition of physical strength and emotional fragility, a desire to be strong and a shattered and crushed heart. There is something about pain that helps us heal.

The good news is, tomorrow's a brand-new day with new hope, new strength, a new sunrise. I'm so thankful for pain that heals. I just heard Jesus whisper in my ear . . . He knows pain.

Home is Where the Heart Is

"Simplicity is making the journey of life with just baggage enough."
—*Charles Dudley Warner*

This weekend, I went to my new home so I could measure the small humble abode (the model like mine) in which I'll plant my new life and so I could once again contemplate what I need to purge from my material possessions.

This will be my third move in the last three and a half years. When Mark and I lost our 3,400-square-foot home and downsized to a 1,300-square-foot condo, we purged . . . sold and gave away many material possessions. It was actually freeing after it was done.

Then after Mark died . . . the owner sold the condo we were renting and I moved to a nine-hundred-square-foot space and purged once again. Now I'm moving to 670 square feet of pure paradise. I love the location of my studio, and it will be brand new. It will be finished September 16 for my move date on September 27. It's just like my new beginning . . . brand new.

I'm looking forward to purging again . . . getting rid of material possessions. I have found that less is more. And after losing three family members in one year . . . well, it changed my thought process.

Not a single one of my family members took any possessions with them. Naked they came into this world, and naked they left it.

I am becoming keenly aware of the power of loving someone over loving a material possession.

We spend our lives collecting things only to realize that it's our hearts, our messages to others, our love for others, our interactions with others that are the real possessions we need to embrace. Because our loved ones are forever in our hearts; they leave memories that cannot be erased, stolen, rusted, or sold.

Does anyone really remember all those material things they have in possession? Could anyone recall everything they own or have owned? Every piece of furniture, every dish, every piece of jewelry . . . I don't think anyone could unless they had pictures of the items or a list to refer to. But I bet everyone can recall the people in their lives . . . the ones they love . . . the memories these loved ones leave with them . . . the impact these people have or have had in their lives . . . because they're real. Relationships are real. Loved ones go on forever. The heart goes on forever. Material possessions have an ending . . . their story dies.

It's difficult to decide what to take and what to give away because Mark and I shared most of what I have. But Mark is not in those things. He's in my heart.

Yep, for me, less is more. For me, following my heart is greater. For me, living this life to the fullest and giving my heart to others is sweeter than any possession I may have to purge.

No matter how little we feel we may be doing without, here in America, there are those who have so much less . . . and there are always people who have more . . . so be thankful for what you have, great or small, and find peace in it and with it.

You have nothing to lose in possessions, but your heart has everything to gain . . . so grow in heart and soul and follow your dreams.

Please Sit With Me

"Pain Hurts, sometimes important things come from sitting with your own pain." —Lynne Naraka

I can remember the initial pain, shock, and disbelief after Mark died. It wasn't what people said that eased that pain. It was the friends that just sat with me, cried with me, let me cry on their shoulders, hugged me, smiled at me, and laughed with me . . . their presence. Because there was nothing anyone could say that would take away the pain. Nothing. They would try to say things, but it all seemed so useless. Some words seem to make it worse. There are several experiences people go through during which they really don't need a message full of words—they need a presence. Sometimes you just need to sit with people in their pain and love them, not try to fix them. Love them just where they are with a hug, a smile, a laugh . . . or maybe you need to cry with them.

My Mom

My mom, I have only made a couple of entries about my mom. My womb is still pretty fresh. It's hard for me to even grieve right now. I have felt the waves some...small...but, I am still really healing from my husband. I am really not even sure if I have grieved fully for my dad and my sister-in-law. It all happened too close together. I know that we expect our parents to go before us…I just wasn't ready…but, are we ever ready? My mom was one of the strongest woman I have ever had the honor of meeting. She loved me and believed in me . . . I could fill a book on everything the two of us have been through. There is nothing like a mother and daughter connection. I wish I could have talked to her…I never saw her conscious after her heart attack…I sang to her, read scripture to her while she lay unconscious…I believe with all my heart she heard me…God just works like that. So that be said, I know that the grief will come and time will release it as it needs to be released. I will be ready to embrace the waves when they come and let the tears flow as needed. However, I have learned staying there is not where I want to live nor would those who loved us and went before us would want us to live either. Life is for the living. As, I have said, so many times before . . . if we have a heart beat we have a purpose…let's live it out. (I wrote this in January 2016)

Mom Waiting To Go Home.

———〜〜〜———

"My mother taught me about the power of inspiration and courage, and she did it with a strength and passion I wish could be bottled."
—Carly Fiorina

Sitting in the sensory garden at Hospice Hospital. Taking a break and contemplating life and death. What a beautiful garden.

Mom is still waiting to go home. To be at complete peace.

There are so many things in this life that are out of our control. So many things we try to control. We're always trying to get on the path that makes it happen . . . whatever that path is for us. We want it our way. We want to make our own path, avoiding the path we are on. Avoiding the pain . . . the lessons . . . the failures . . . the guilt . . . the loss . . . but if we would only stay on the path that was laid out for us, we would find that at the end of that path is our peace, our destiny, and our wholeness.

May we journey on the path laid out before us. The sensory path of grace, faith, hope, and peace.

God I Miss Her.

———⦵⦵⦵———

Well now . . . it's a different morning, but a new day. One of reflection, of another change, of another challenge to move forward in strength and love despite loss. The prayers, texts, and calls I received—they made a difference in my journey with Mom. Sweet Strength is what I received from them.

On May 13, 2015, my mom died at eighty-three. My oldest brother had taken Mom to the hospital early in the morning. She was having chest pain. They admitted her, ran some tests, didn't see immediate concern in the first test, and then looked at the second test's results, which indicated she was having a heart attack. They ran to her room only to find her unconscious. They shocked her heart and got her breathing, but it was too late; she had brain damage. She'd been put in a room with no heart monitor—an eighty-three-year-old woman with a pacemaker complaining of chest pain.

She was transferred to another hospital better equipped to handle heart conditions. By the time I got there, it was early morning. My brother had called me at around two in the morning, telling me to meet him at the new hospital. I drove the two-hour route and made it. There she was, hooked up to a respirator. She wasn't breathing on her own, even though her heart was still strong. It was so sad. I knew that wasn't what she'd have wanted; she had made that clear.

The doctors wanted to try a procedure that could possibly reverse the brain damage. They would take her body back down to freezing and warm her up; the whole process took twenty-four hours. There were risks, of course, but at that point, it was worth taking those risks. I remember laying on her saying, please don't go yet, don't die. Then feeling guilty for those words. I knew that was unfair. Unfair to ask her to stay beyond what she could. She needed to hear the word it was ok. It was ok to let go. In my selfishness I was putting a barrier on her release to be with dad. The procedure didn't work, and on Mother's Day, we removed her from the respirator; she had no hope of recovery. It was a difficult decision and one no one would want to make on Mother's Day, or any other day. We later found out the heart attack would not have killed her; the culprit would have been the lack of oxygen going to her brain. But, the reality is it was her time, she was preparing to go home. God in his mercy was getting her ready for paradise.

We called in hospice, and I stayed with Mom until her death a week and a half later. She never regained consciousness. I sang to her, read scripture to her—I think I only left her side for one night.

I was a little more prepared for the funeral home this time, because I had been there so many times…I guess prepared was the word I substituted familiar with. Three years has passed now, allowing me to adjust to loss. Somehow, I felt like I could actually help with my mother's arrangements. The unfamiliar was becoming familiar. The arrangements, the changes—well, they were becoming a new normal.

It was a beautiful celebration of life for my mom yesterday. I was both honored and privileged to be a pallbearer alongside my two brothers, son, and two cousins. We carried her body to its final resting place. She and Dad are together again, along with my husband, my sister-in-law, and all the other family and friends who have gone to paradise, a place full of unconditional love, amazing grace, and incredible, indescribable joy and beauty.

You know, there is just this connection between a mother and her daughter that is like no other. I can't bear the thought of being without my mom during the next half of my journey. But it was her time. She was reunited with Dad.

My mom was so strong and very smart. I miss her so much. We had some great times together. We talked pretty much every day. She was my best friend growing up. We did so many things together. We used to even exchange clothes. She was a very snappy dresser. She and I wore the same size. She was always smiling. I really want to write a story about her life one day. The good times. I am happy she's whole and has been healed with pure love, joy, and eternal life.

My son was such a great help to me during this time. He was there for me and let me break down on several occasions while he held and comforted me. He was once the boy I held in my arms, and now he was holding me in his.

One-day last week, when I was at my lowest point, I was talking to a friend. He said that the one who created us breathes life into us . . . delivers us from evil . . . loves us unconditionally . . . gives us gifts and purpose and meaning by His grace. And then, through his mercy, He carries us home to be with those we love, forever and ever.

How could that not give me peace? I will miss my mom so much . . . but that pain needs to be recycled into something positive and good because she's home now and happier than she has ever been.

Death . . . separation . . . are only for a short time. And our family reunion at the banquet feast of pure love—well, that's eternal.

I will see you—Mama, Daddy, Mark, Donna—when I get home. I love and miss you. R.I.P.

Jeep

I've needed extra beach therapy this month. Squeezed it in. Meeting God there is just so healing.

I'm so sad. My 1999 Jeep Cherokee is headed to the junkyard. I was so attached to that Jeep. Well, I know better than to get attached to material things. After all, it's just that—a material thing. It's an illusion that we own them. They can be taken away at any time. We can't take any of it with us when we depart from this world. But there's a story behind my Jeep, and that story is enmeshed in my heart and memories. My husband and I bought it when we sold our previous car, before it got repossessed when we were losing everything. We didn't have enough cash to buy the Jeep—a 1999 Cherokee—we were short $1,500.00 so the previous owner took the amount needed, $1,500, from an emerald ring my husband had bought for me. So that Jeep was that emerald ring...that Mark had bought for me in St. Thomas. He had surprised me with it on our vacation there. It was a birthday gift!

It's my fault. I wrecked it Memorial Day weekend. Just found out today that it will cost too much to fix it. I tried everything to keep it, but the insurance company declared it as being totaled. I was told this in unemotional language. People that are detached from it and know its material value . . . not its heart value. The good news is that no one was hurt, thank goodness. Now I have to find another vehicle. It's not the best time to get another car, but God's always on time. So I have to trust. I have no idea what to get, because I loved that Jeep. But I really do need a new car, and this will be a great new beginning. I always look for those beginnings, because that's what life is really about—beginnings.

So I'm giving up my Jeep. Time for another journey. Off for my next adventure. I'm thankful that I've been given precious memories that hold my hand and heart during beach therapy. Hard times are just a test. And I like passing the test.

This, too, shall pass, and life continues. You just have to learn how to continue with more strength, more thankfulness, and a greater love of life.

Chock full o' Nuts

"He who has a why to live for can bear almost any how."
—*Friedrich Nietzsche*

It's the little things that make you smile. Those who have lost loved ones can relate to this.

Robert is still sleeping; he's on night shift. I haven't drank coffee in over four years. Well, I decided this morning I would just sit—since I have no beach to walk on—read, and have a cup of coffee. I opened the cabinet and bam! There it is: Mark's coffee . . . which he drank every morning.

Robert is drinking the same thing. Made me smile, and made a tear fall. I would try to get Mark to try other types, but he loved his Chock full o'Nuts. How about that tag line? "The heavenly original coffee."

I wonder if Mark is having his coffee, which he loved to drink in the mornings before going to check the surf. He wasn't ever in a hurry . . . something we could all learn from.

I can just picture him sitting at that big, long banquet table with his mom and dad, my mom and dad, his aunt and uncle, Donna, some of our friends, our dogs (Sugar Ray, Becker, and Evander, looking for treats that fall from the table), Andy Irons, and other surfers . . . and Jesus telling stories. And they're all laughing and so full of love . . . waiting to greet all of us when we get home . . . cheering us on. And Mark asking Jesus to come surf with him. Can you picture it? The crystal-clear colors, smells, sounds. The indescribable unconditional love that we strive for here . . . it's there in perfection. They've reached it. We think we loved them here . . . can you imagine the peace they feel with the laughter and smiles radiating in each healed soul? The peace that transcends all understanding . . . they have it. Every single heart's desire is there, in the stories . . . in the laughter at the banquet table of the unique spirits and souls. All together as one.

They're cheering us on. They're pulling for us . . . whispering to us, "You got this! Your journey is short . . . enjoy it." They want us to love and be loved here. They want us to experience joy and laughter and purpose . . . to live here, now.

Beauty . . . love . . . laughter . . . no more pain or suffering . . . no more tears where they live forever in paradise.

We don't need to wait until heaven to experience love, peace, and paradise. We can create it here by changing one person: ourselves . . . and by taking time to sit, read, and be thankful for a cup of Chock full o'Nuts.

Flowers That Live Forever

———— ⦿⦾ ————

"Here was a flower strangely like itself and yet utterly unlike itself too.
Such a paradox has often been the basis for the most impassioned love."
—*Thomas M. Disch*

I have to be vulnerable and admit that the holidays are just not my favorite. This is my third year without my husband . . . and it really isn't the same. That doesn't mean I sit around and feel sorry for myself— far from it. I stay very engaged with life. Besides, if you look around, there are many people in far more difficult circumstances.

Some flowers of the heart live on and bloom year after year— artificial flowers, unaffected by time, planted in the soil of memories and harvested when needed to feed the hunger of missed love.

One Sunday, my husband picked a bouquet of flowers out of a parking lot, off of the sidewalk, and handed them to me through my car window. He said, "I picked these just for you. I love you." We had a chuckle together. I said, "Oh . . . I just love them." He died of a heart attack the next day. I brought the flowers out for the holidays, as a reminder of the grace and love of both God and Mark. You see, God knew Mark would be gone from me the next day. He knew I loved it when Mark brought me flowers, and he knew that these last flowers I'd receive would never die . . . just like Mark—away from me but very much alive.

Now that is good. God is good all the time, and all the time He is good.

Sweet Strength. Make it sweet and keep it strong.

"Like a stone, time rolls on."
(Eric Church)

I wrote these words on Facebook on December 31, 2011. (As Mark stood behind me, waiting on me for once, instead of me waiting on him and he said, "Linda you need to write a book." I said, Mark, what would I write about? He said to me, "Linda you have a lot to write about, I am telling you need to write a book." (And honey, I did what you said, I have written a book, for you)

Here is what I wrote that night . . .

"Headed out to dinner with my favorite surfer guy! I am so blessed! I hope your New Year Challenges you to look beyond your mud puddles . . . into a vast and wide open sea of beauty and change."

Wow, words are powerful. How poignant. Little did I know that in nine days Mark would be dead, alive in spirit, dead in flesh. Total perfection after running the race of life, or surfing the waves of life. I would be living the very words I wrote, trying to look beyond my mud puddles that lie ahead over the next years.

Time is a phenomenon that escapes every grasp at trying to contain it, stop it, forget, move it, rush it, slow it down, speed it up . . . time like a stone . . . time rolls on.

Mark was never on time. When he died he had 5 watches on his nightstand. They certainly didn't give him an edge on being on time when his friends called him to surf or being on time when we went places, no for Mark they were a style. A style that only Mark had. The only time Mark showed up on the very second he was to be somewhere was when God called him home. He was not late. It was his time. He went from the clock time here. The twenty-four hours…. tick tock. To eternal time……where he is always on time now.

Mark was loved. In fact, Mark made everyone feel like they were his best friends. I have to tell you something. I miss Marks friendship more than anything. I miss his encouragement, his belief in me when I didn't believe in myself. We were far from perfect in our marriage and just like any couple or any relationship we had our challenges. It doesn't matter how in love you are; marriage takes work from both partners. But, one thing Mark and I did together we never ever gave up on each other. We were best friends. He was such an incredible friend. He loved slowing down and talking to people. If he saw you, he would talk to you as if you were his best friend. You were his focus. That's a gift. Everyone loved Mark. I miss him so much.

He loved going down to the beach, the surfing spot at 64th and 65th avenues and just hang out with his surfing buddies. Nothing gave him more joy. He used to tell this story about when he was in high school, he was dating this girl and she wanted him to go to her house and watch T.V. with him. Well he said that on that particular day the waves were pumping. So, Mark told her he was going surfing instead. She said, "It's me or surfing." He said, he drove her home. He then got out the car, went around to her side opened her door and said, "Goodbye." LOL. I can relate to her. I was told goodbye many days to surf. LOL.

We always think we have all this time with our loved ones. We always think they will be there the next day and next day and next day. Time . . . is like a stone . . . it rolls on . . . and if you aren't careful that stone will pull you under.

Mark and his love for the water and the others in the water with him. His community of surfers. He loved helping the gromes, as they call them. The younger surfers. They loved him. Mark the Shark. The only time Mark was fast was on the wave in the water. I am going out, as I do every Jan. 9th and paddle out in memory of the man who showed me what it was to be a best friend. I know he is watching me and he would love me getting out there and surfing for him. Waves or not.

I often wonder what Mark would say about everything today. Little did he know when he named my business Sweet Strength, little did he know I would need that sweet strength the next four years to live my life with . . . I wonder if he would even know me, recognize me. I have changed so much. I am not that woman I was four years ago. I became a new person on that day time threw me into another time. . . I have learned more about myself these last four years than I ever did in the fifty before. Mark taught me so much while he was alive. I had no clue how much I learned from him, until he was no longer here to share. He wouldn't know that. . . he wouldn't think that he had that impact. I didn't either. . . until, I had to live without him. Mark McDandel, the imprints you left on not only me, but Robert, my family, and your community of friends will never be forgotten. Your legacy of integrity, character, honesty, loyalty, strength, kindness, lives on in the hearts of those who were honored enough to know you.

Four years is much too long to see that smile and hear that laugh . . . but we will all see you when we get home. Surf on . . . and I hope that I have made you smile over the last four years . . . and I hope you are watching me today on the water today!!!! Sweet Strength. Make It Sweet and Keep It Strong. Carry On.

Whole Again

———⸿⸙⸿———

"Pay mind to your own life, your own health, and wholeness. A bleeding heart is not help to anyone if it bleeds to death." —*Frederick Buechner*

I went to Myrtle Beach last night, because sometimes I just need to see Billy Perry. You see he is Marks only living blood relative. The only one. When I see Billy it feels as if I have visited Mark in some way. They grew up together. I am so grateful for Billy's stories and his closeness to Mark. You know, it's been over four years, since Mark my husband died. But you see . . . love for someone never dies. You have a longing to see them again and maybe catch a glimpse of them in the story of another about them. Billy, I love you. Thank you for always being there. Sometimes the stories help to piece together what seems to be missing . . . somehow . . . sometimes it makes you feel whole again.

You do . . .you really do become whole again . . . in different way. Because, you will never look at life or your life or others' lives in the same way. And, you are always hopeful it's a positive light that comes out of the grief. Because, I couldn't get my sweet strength any other way . . . except to find the hope and good in a tragedy.

I think it gives you a higher respect of life, of hope, of love, of peace. You are just changed. For me it's been a new awaking into what's important. I have found that love is literally the most important thing. The love of another, empowering one another to live our dreams and to give to others.

Mark's love for me has helped me so much. I can love again. It will be a different kind of love and it's ok. My next relationship will look and will be different and that is ok. We are all going to be seated soon enough at the banquet table anyway.

Hearts enmeshed in amazing grace, undeserved mercy, unconditional love based on well no conditions. Perfect peace. And, when I am called home then I will be grounded. Home is where the heart is . . .

You can't go back . . . no . . . you can never go back . . . but you can take all the love, memories, pain, heartache, and make it blossom into a beautiful new spring.

May you find solitude, peace, love in the ever changing journey you are on even in the loss and pain.

A New Normal

I know this transformation is painful, but you're not falling apart; you're just falling into something different, with a new capacity to be beautiful.
——William Hannan

You can decide to live in your loss or move into your new beginning, a new normal. It's a choice we all have. We can decide to recycle our pain. That is what I've chosen to do with the book I'm writing and life coaching: use my pain to empower others to achieve their dreams. I am determined to continue this journey, living out my dreams and helping others live theirs.

I have continued to move forward in the midst of grief. At fifty, I started over in every way. If I can do it, anyone can. I started my business Sweet Strength. I learned to surf, moved to a new location to get a new start, joined toastmasters (speaking club), trademarked

Sweet Strength, completed a website, went out of the country twice by myself, wrote my first book. I've participated in four NPC Masters Figure Contests and placed in every one. It's been with the help of coaches, friends, and family, who have inspired me to continue the journey that's before me. Without God, friends, and family, I could not have found the Sweet Strength that lies inside and helps me continue to press forward.

You always have more Sweet Strength in you than you know . . . you just have to be willing to find it. It's not who you think you are that holds you back; it's who you think you aren't. Our words and thoughts create our reality, and the good news is that just with a thought, we can recreate our reality. Be aware of what you're thinking about, and use that white towel not to surrender but to wipe the sweat off so you can go the extra round. Be better than you were yesterday, day by day.

I often tell people you won't be able to love others until you learn to love yourself. You can't take care of others until you take care of yourself. And you will never live out your dreams—who you want to be and what you want to do—until you learn to smile and take responsibility for your actions. Become the victor, not the victim.

Life is truly what you make it. Those who have gone before us would be the first to say: live it to the fullest and make each day count.

Part Two:

Move, Just Move

These are some of my inspirational blogs, my thought process, during my time of grief, loss, change, and pain.

We all have to move forward or we are going backwards. There is no other way. We are here for a purpose and that purpose is to move forward inspiring and helping others on the way. Throughout my losses, grief, and change, moving, keeping my body health, and my love and passion of coaching others is what got me through. If I can inspire one person to move in difficult circumstances to understand that we have everything we need to create our new beginnings inside of us . . . I have lived my purpose. This is what will help you get on your way helping others . . . and . . . movement . . .

Amazing Grace

How do you speak the truth in a world that only wants to hear lies?

How do you take off the mask in a world that offers you a door prize for the best mask at the masquerade?

How do you begin to capture time when time is as elusive as ice melting in the summer sun?

How do you live passionately when passion is within you and not another?

How do you find peace in a world that constantly embraces war?

How do you listen when you can't even be heard?

How do you mourn a loss when losses come so readily and quickly?

How do you embrace life when you know it will end?

How do you understand pain and suffering when joy and happiness is what you seek?

How do you see beyond circumstances when you're the one sinking in quicksand?

How do you gain strength when you're weak?

How do you view the uniqueness of the world when the world rejects your uniqueness?

How do you stay whole in body, mind, and soul when this world throws you temptations that divide, part, and detach your whole?

How can we escape pain in a world that thrives, flourishes, and progresses on it?

I don't know how. I only know that the answer seems to lie dormant in my heart, waiting to be awakened by the truth, the way, the life in the one whose mastery is like the maestro conducting the answer through one passionate song. "Amazing Grace." Silencing the background noise of the question "how?" so when the heart decides to be awakened, it won't ask that question. The heart will begin to beat in rhythm to the words that make up the song. . . "Amazing grace, how sweet the sound. . ." And the grace that's accepted will now reside deep within the soul, in tune with the one who provides the eternal and everlasting answer to the question of "how?"

Sweet Strength is learning to awaken to the beat of the song of amazing grace that is so graciously offered.

The Struggle

Who do you look for to save you, to rescue you, to help you?

I don't know, but all I know is I received an honest answer to that question, when a lie would have done.

I had a dream one night, not too long ago. I was struggling that week with some goals, some challenges that I faced. I dreamed I was surfing and fell off my surfboard and it was a rough day in the ocean. When I fell, the tumbling beneath the waves was intense and strange. I couldn't get above the next set of waves that kept rolling in.

In fact, I dreamed that my leash was wrapped like a coiled boa constrictor around my arms. My arms were tied tight. I was thinking, if I could just get one arm free, one hand up, someone would save me. If only I could free myself, I wouldn't drown. Someone would see my hand above the water and save me. I was thinking under the water that I was going to die, drown, and I wasn't ready. I didn't really want to, I wanted to live.

I remember that there was this moment though, that seemed a release to me . . . the release of giving up the struggle. I remember thinking I could just quit the struggle and give up. It would be easier than fighting. You know the feeling...comfort, security, less effort. Fighting takes effort and makes you get out of your comfort zone and you have to think how to do something differently. I mean . . . after all there is the illusion of peace and no struggle there if you don't fight . . . it is less effort to give up . . . right? I thought about it, for a second, then the fight began. I said no, no, I will not give in. I have much to live for, much to change. I just need to get one hand free. So, there I was in my dream, my subconscious, fighting this challenge, these goals for my life, my mind ordering my life.

Then, through the struggle, the fight, the strength, the hand became free, it rose above the waves. Someone saw me . . . they pulled me to the top . . .they pulled me on their board.

You know who it was? It was God. It wasn't the church, it wasn't the Bible, it wasn't my friends, family, it wasn't my job, it wasn't even my prayers, it was the man, it was God, it was my creator, my savior. Wow, I woke up, only to realize that Jesus has been the one. He has been there through it all, but what I also realized through this dream is that I had to make the effort to reach out. I had to act. He didn't just pull me up, he let me reach to him.

I don't know what you are struggling with. I don't' know who your savior is, but I do know that we have to put into action what we believe, what we want. I know that we have to walk and move and act to be able to begin again. We have to be strong, we have to have hope, we have to have purpose, we have to want to change, we have to want to live, we have to want to share what we have been given, we have to want to reach for that dream, for life.

No one is going to hand it to us. No one is going to give us what we need; no one is going to be able to do it for you. You have to do it yourself, you have to be strong to get beyond your problems and your challenges, you have to believe that if you step out in faith, your savior will step out with you and not only save you, but propel you into a life that is not just fulfilled, but overflowing. Until we begin to move, to change, to realize it is our choice where we are and where we are going we will stay where we are.

You know life is so rich, so full, and you have been given a special measure of grace . . . all you have to do is reach your hand up and grab the truth. "Sweet Strength" empowering you to make the choice to live . . . not just survive.

When The Waters Are Troubled

—ꙮ—

"Your success depends mainly upon what you think of yourself and whether you believe in yourself. You can succeed if nobody else believes it, but you will never succeed if you don't believe in yourself."
—William J.H. Boetcker

What will you do when your waters get troubled? Because they will . . . will you stand with, or will you fall? When the pain is so severe that you feel as if you're going to die . . . you're not. When you feel like your heart will never mend . . . it will. When you're in the dark and silent night and it feels like you're all alone . . . you're not. When you feel like you're drowning . . . you won't. When you feel like no one understands what you're going through . . . God does. When it feels as if nothing is the same . . . it's not, but that's the time for change. To embrace it, to stand, to walk, and then to run the race marked out for you.

One of the questions I ask my clients is: do you believe you can do it? I believe in each of my clients when they come to me. I really do believe that people have what it takes to change their lives. If I didn't, I wouldn't even attempt to coach or do personal training. But, I believe in my clients with all my heart. Each client holds the key to his or her dreams, and I believe that all things are possible with and through God. I love to encourage my clients in their goal settings, challenge them in their thinking, and cheer them on during the rough spots. I give them tools and act as a great resource. I love them where they are and for who they are. I can be a listening ear, a cheerleader, their biggest fan . . . but until they believe they can change . . . it doesn't matter how much encouragement they're given, how many tools they have, how many goals they've set. Until they believe in their ability to make the changes they need to live the life they dream of, it will stay just that: a dream.

Being in the Moment

"Nothing is but what is now." —*Ron Rash*

I just got off the beach. Looking out over that vast beauty, I realized, once again, how much I love this beach . . . how much I love the beauty, the peace it gives my heart and soul. That water . . . the sand . . . the sounds . . . the feel. . . As I sat there, just *being* in the moment of that beauty, I wanted to share it with someone so desperately. I wanted someone by my side to see, to feel, to love it too. I can't describe the beauty of that blue, far-reaching water that seems to go on forever. I can't describe the indescribable: the way the clouds and colors of those clouds looked like a watercolor that was painted with love, stroke by stoke, on a canvas that stretched beyond the periphery view of my eyes, by the master artist. I want to describe the way the wind felt as it lightly touched my skin and blew across my body, but it was . . . well, the wind was illusive. It left me, going where it wanted. It was as if the wind was there to bring all my senses alive. I want to capture that wind. I want to capture the sounds of children laughing . . . of the waves as they embraced their boundary on the shore—those waves that really wanted to run wild, beyond where they're told they can go. I want to describe it and bring it to others, but it hit me—the reality that I can't. I can't capture the moment. I can't take a picture that would capture it. After all, it's just a picture.

A picture doesn't involve all senses. I know that because when I look at pictures, I don't feel the person . . . I can't touch the person . . . I can't touch his skin . . . I don't smell him . . . I can't hear his voice . . . I can't see his face make expressions. So a picture can sometimes contain more pain than beauty . . . because you can't capture that person. In the beginning, especially, a picture can be more painful than healing.

I have to just be with nature, with those I love, instead of trying aimlessly to capture them or to capture a moment in nature.

I get it. Slow down and enjoy the present . . . because you can't really capture it. You can't really capture love . . . the grace of nature . . . where you are . . . but you can enjoy it. You can enjoy the person you are within that moment. You can appreciate nature and the one you're with. You can love where you are and who you are with right now. You can't capture it, but you can enjoy the moment by just *being*. Sweet Strength is being in the moment.

The Beauty of the Presence.

⸺⊶⊷⊷⊶⸺

"Mindfulness is not chasing the moment, but beautifying the moment."
—*Amit Ray*

Well now, what a difference a day makes. Cloudy, cool, and windy on the beach this morning. But, what a beautiful morning.

There is so much beauty in the quietness of the morning light. We just have to live in the moment to experience it . . . to be able to interrupt the reflecting thoughts of yesterday and the thoughts of aspirations for tomorrow and allow the moment that we are existing in to complete us.

The moments of rest through our eyes of clarity when we discover the reflection of the one who gives us glimpses into our unique and extraordinary world. His world of purpose and design. His creation seen and His creation seeing. Peace and change always come to us in the present moments of clarity through the lens of the soul.

But, I have found that the only way to truly see . . . to believe in where your path is guiding you. . . .is in the spotlight of the moment where you know there is nowhere for you to strive to get to . . . because you're just here.

What are you striving to get to, are you already there?

One Way Conversation

*"If I speak in the tongues of men and of angels, but have not love,
I am a noisy gong or a clanging cymbal"* —1 Cor. 13:1

Is anyone listening? Can anyone hear me over the noise of their own voice? Do I protest so loudly that they can't hear what I say? By the grace of God goes I.

"Words are, of course, the most powerful drug used by mankind."
—Rudyard Kipling

What thoughts run through the mind during a conversation? What thoughts are there when I want someone to hear my side? What thoughts play like a merry-go-round, round and round in my mind when I think I know best for a friend or family member? Those thoughts that have become the forefront of my daily inner rumblings suddenly explode into a noisy gong as the person to whom I'm talking, whose mind I want to change, pushes my button one more time. Or how about in a debate, one in which I am right and you are wrong. The debates where my position is the only position. It's like you're already thinking of what point you can make next—so much so that you haven't even heard their point of view. Then, after you can deliver this earth-shattering statement, you just know that they'll stop what they're doing and change. Like the alcoholic is going to suddenly, after hearing you night after night plead for him or her to stop, come in the door and say, "You're right . . . I'm quitting."

No. Change happens from within. Change happens when you

allow someone the grace to change . . . the pain to change . . . the love to change . . . the respect to change.

It is because we care that we yell so loudly that people can't hear over the clanging cymbal. We are so right in that law, and grace is just too hard to live under or give out . . . I fear that they'll think I agree with what they're doing if I give them grace.

The wife (I use wife because I am a women and can relate better to this) wants her husband to change so badly—of course for his good—because it would transform everything if he would just change. It's never us that need to change, it's always them. As she advises him in all these modifications he needs to make, it's hard for her to see she is actually losing respect for him and he is losing love for her. Because all he heard was, "You can't live up to my expectations and I will only love you if you do these things for me." You know, the resounding gong. What happened to the grace? What happens to our unconditional love? What happens when all we can hear is our own voice? What happens when we know what another needs . . . what is best for them . . . because we know we're right and they're wrong. If only you would change . . . then I wouldn't have to look at my own stuff. I wouldn't need to have responsibility in my own choices. It's just easier not to listen. Does anyone listen anymore? Does anyone care?

What happens in Washington when everyone is right and no one wants to listen to the other or ask questions? Everyone is so busy trying to change everyone else's agenda and view that there's no room to listen. I'm right and you're wrong, and we're going to battle it out until you change. Everyone talks over everyone; there is no respect for another's view. It's an oxymoron that they all have something different to say, but they all sound like the same noisy gong. I wonder what would happen if the men and women on Capitol Hill listened instead of talking over one another? The resounding gong. . . I wonder what they hear in Washington.

I wonder if anyone thinks they need to change themselves before trying to change another. You know, to see from a different perspective and look at the landscape differently. To put all the ideas on the table and brainstorm about what would be best for everyone. To put someone else's shoes on and walk a mile in them. To go to the other side of the mountain to get a different view, for a moment. I mean, you don't have to stay there. You can still have your beliefs and values. Just because you hear another's belief doesn't mean you'll lose yourself. It just means you're willing to drop your agenda for a time. It means you're able to follow the way of grace instead of pride . . . besides it could possibly be for something bigger than yourself . . . something that could benefit a lot of people. You may even learn in the process.

I don't know . . . I don't know a lot about a lot of things in life. But I have learned that I would rather live under grace than law. I know I want to be able to give grace to others . . . because I sure love it when I receive grace. I know I want to be able to love others, listen to others' points of view, be open to hearing them . . . because I love it when others listen to me and love me. I know I want to work on taking responsibility for all my actions instead of blaming others . . . because I love it when others take responsibility for their actions and don't blame me. I do not want to be that resounding gong.

I used to be so dogmatic about everything. I used to think I knew a lot and that I could tell you a lot about what you needed to do. It sure takes a lot of energy to be a resounding gong. But as life continues, experiences explode upon my heart, the chip on my shoulder continues to get pounded out by life's hammer, and the grace of God raptures me day after day . . . I just pray that not only can I receive the grace that Jesus has given me, but that somehow I can learn to give it to others. That I can think about how I can change myself instead of others, learn that I am responsible for every choice I make, learn that I am responsible for my actions and for everything that happens to me. I might not be able to control some circumstances in my life, but I can control how I react and handle those circumstances.

Thank You, God, for not trying to change us. . . for instead loving us and giving us the grace so we can change and so we may give that to others today, so we could live without being the resounding gong.

Peace

Another beautiful morning on my beach run. I caught the sun peeking through the clouds for a few minutes. The ocean was calm, with a few small sets of quiet waves rolling in. The shells were in abundance this morning, and those beautiful creatures, dolphins, were playing and swimming near the shore. . . What a sight. It's hard to take the beauty in, but what a peace of mind it brings. I strive every day to enter that peace because without it, I can't function the way I like to, need to, or want to.

In fact, last night I went to dinner with a friend, and we were talking about success in life and success in business. He is a very successful businessman. He asked me what success would be for me. I said, "Peace of mind." As long as I enjoy what I'm doing, I have peace of mind . . . and as long as I am helping others, then I am successful. I don't worry about the money. I do what I love and experience peace doing it; the money will follow. He agreed and said, "If you have peace of mind, you have happiness." I replied, "More than happiness—you have joy. You can have the most successful business, a lot of money, a great family, a great relationship; you can be in great shape; you can travel . . . but if you don't have peace of mind, you can't enjoy any of it . . . You can't enjoy life."

I am finally getting back to having peace of mind, and it has been a turning point for me in my journey. I am at peace with my circumstances . . . all of them, good and bad. Stress will kill you . . . worry will age you . . . anxiousness will stop you from being able to think clearly. I know because stress was a huge factor in my husband's death. I have watched so many people get sick because of stress. I have seen so many people so worried and anxious. I don't know . . . I'm no expert on the matter. But I do know that stress has devastating effects on your body, mind, spirit, and soul.

In coaching, we talk about stress and how to manage it. I know where my personal peace of mind comes from: God is the peace that transcends all understanding for me. I also know that He gives me the choice to enter that peace. He won't force it on me. Reading about it doesn't do it either; you have to make a choice to enter it. You have to make the choice on a deep level from inside of yourself so that you will be able to see things differently, to react differently, and to change the things you can and release the things you can't.

Sweet Strength is peace of mind.

Unconditional Love

"Unconditional love is an illogical notion, but such a great and powerful one." —A.J. Jacobs

As I wander down this yellow brick road of life . . . as I meet people God put on the same yellow brick road . . . I feel a special honor to be with, walk beside, and journey with those that God created . . . God's special creations. I realize that we have more in common than we have differences. I mean, it's there . . . always there . . . this one reoccurring theme. This story.

I could write about how we're broken, fallen, and sinful, and the next moment I could talk about how we're all unique, that each one of us has a different gift and we're all created for a greater purpose. Yes, I know that's all truth. . . But the one thing I find so fascinating, so captivating, and so undeniable in every person, every relationship, and even every path I cross in every environment, whether in the grocery store or ball game, is that we are all searching, missing, and wanting desperately to find that one piece of the puzzle that we can't seem to find no matter how hard we look . . . the one piece that will complete the beautiful puzzle. Maybe it wasn't in the box, maybe we dropped it on the floor, maybe the dog ran off with it or someone stole it, but it's not there: that unconditional love that allows us to be who we are in all our mess, all our pain, all our struggles, and yes, in all our successes—or what we think is success. Where is that unconditional love? What is it and why do I long for it so desperately? I fantasize about it. I have desired it so much that it has infected many of my relationships.

Truth be known, as many years as I have worked and tried to inspire, help, and empower others, whether through ministry in the church, volunteer in nonprofits, founding my own nonprofit, or my wellness/life coaching and personal training . . . unconditional love is the running theme from which every obstacle, challenge, hurt, forgiveness, and barrier stems. It just sits there in the silence, actions, feelings, emotions, mistakes, failures . . . in everything. It sits there, waiting to be heard . . . waiting to have a voice in the silenced recesses of the heart and soul.

It is the unspoken desire and longing of our hearts: unconditional love . . . non-judgment. Paul, who lived in Jesus's time, talks about it: "Love is patient and kind, love does not envy or boast, it is not arrogant or rude. It does not insist on its own way, it is not irritable or resentful, it does not rejoice at wrongdoing, but rejoices with truth. Love bears all things, believes all things, hopes all things, endures all things. Love never ends" (1 Cor. 13:4–8). I think Paul knew personally about unconditional love; how else could he write about it like this? Songs are written about this kind of love . . . poems and prose . . . vows in marriage are taken hoping it will outlast the lust and the newness of one another. . .

We are so desperate for unconditional love that we guard ourselves. We guard ourselves from being open and daring to leave that intimate thought with that person, or that thought on paper. We long for someone to listen . . . really listen . . . hear our hearts, our souls, our spirits . . . to hear about our sins and our mistakes . . . to say, "It's okay . . . I love you as you are, not as you think you should be." So we hide . . . we hide behind our pride, our anger, our right to be right, our judgment, our prejudice. We hide behind others. We want so badly to be accepted that we'll do almost anything—trade our lives, our souls, our bodies, our hearts. We think that surely if we give it all away, that person will give us what we're looking for: that unconditional love. We hide behind our thoughts, which tell us that if that person knew us— really knew us—he or she wouldn't love us. We hide behind our dress, our music, our tattoos, our identities. We block the unconditional love because we don't believe it really exists.

I wonder why we can't accept it when it comes our way? I think it's so difficult for us to believe that we have God who can give us what we desperately long for and need . . . and when we accept and believe that God loves us unconditionally then we are able to love ourselves unconditionally and then and only then are we able to love others as God loves them.

He loves us . . . no strings and no conditions. He loves us where we are, broken and battered and torn. I don't understand it at all. I don't understand about God being the only way to unconditional love . . . but I don't have to understand it. I just have to believe and trust it.

Maybe I'm a dreamer, but I feel like this world would be a better place if we could love one another unconditionally, like our Creator does.

God, thank You for giving what seems to be the impossible: unconditional love.

Scars

"Those scars you have accumulated are the markings of a warrior."
—*Darla Evan*

Scars, physical or emotional. I have plenty of them, both of them. What do we do with our scars? Do we let them define us? Do we allow them to embarrass or shame us? Do we let others to use them to belittle us? Or do we let them empower us, making us stronger, better, and able to love others more deeply?

Scars, of the past, don't have to define who we are today. In fact, without them, we wouldn't become stronger . . . better . . . and we wouldn't understand life very well. We wouldn't understand that scars can be powerful tools used by God to make us unique. Our scars are just that: scars . . . reminders of the strength we had to get through . . . to make it. We are still here, alive, because of those scars. Every scar is a stepping stone to strength, change, and victory.

Good Morning!

———⊛⊛⊛———

When I run on the beach in the mornings, I love to pass people and say, "Good morning—have a great day!" Nine out of ten people will smile back. I like that . . . because it proves that one person has the ability to encourage others to smile. Maybe it is just a smile, but maybe they have so much going on in their lives that they'd appreciate a smile from someone—you know, have someone to notice them. How many people do you pass and not even notice? We are so busy and concerned about our lives—maybe we're worried about getting to work or to ministry to "save" someone—that we don't even notice the person in front of us. He or she becomes just another face in the crowd. It's like being in a restaurant, on an elevator, sitting beside someone in a doctor's office waiting room and not saying a word. Sometimes I wonder, how can we help others when we can't even say hello to the person in front of us in line, or behind us, or beside us?

Vison

———⊛⊛⊛———

I love helping people come up with vision for their health and wellness. Part of my job as a wellness coach is to help people see beyond their circumstances. Helping them paint the picture of who they want to be, how they want to feel and think and act with regards to wellness. And we talk about it in present tense so they're already there . . . because really, you are. You are just now ready to start tweaking the vision. When you see it, you can walk into it. Until then, the door will be closed. Vision, imagination, belief—all open the door to a whole new perspective. Without vision, there's no hope. Without imagining better days, you lose belief, and can even lose the motivation to try.

Think about the world without vision and imagination. . . There would be no bridges to cross, no cars, no furniture, no electricity—you get the idea. It all starts with a vision . . . then tweaking it until it becomes a reality. Then the vision, hope, and imagining slowly become the belief that you can—the belief that you will—and before you know it, you're there. Because you believed, you hoped, and someone else believed in you.

I believe anyone can have vision. Anyone can rise above their circumstances to see things from another perspective. I know . . . I've watched it happen in a lot of amazing people.

External or Internal

———⊶∞⊷———

Clients come to me thinking they'll finally love themselves when they lose the weight, start exercising, get a new job, are loved by a spouse or significant other, etc. I always ask, "What difference will that make in your life? How will that change your view of yourself and others?"

They tend to focus on the external, not the internal. They don't focus on the essence of who they are now, where they are now . . . it's always about the future or the past, or their external circumstances—never about the present moment . . . which is really all we have. Do we need vision? Sure, we do. Do we need hope? Sure, we do. But the vision and the hope are in the now. You start with where you are today. You can learn to love who, where, what, and how you are right now, whatever circumstances surround you and then you will be able to walk into who you want to be. You will be amazed at what follows. Don't let your thought process, your perception, or your assumptions stop you from loving yourself today, loving others today, and loving where you are today. This is where the new vision of the new you will begin, in the present.

How Much Is Enough?

———✁———

"Give me neither poverty nor riches: feed me with the food that is needful for me, lest I be full and deny you and say: 'Who is the Lord? Or lest I be poor and steal and profane the name of my God'" —Prov. 30:8b–9

"Each day, upon awakening, are we asked to paint the sky blue?
Need we coax the sun to rise or flowers to bloom?
Need we teach birds to sing, or children to laugh, or lovers to kiss?
No, though we think the world is imperfect, it surrounds us each
day with its perfections. We are asked only to appreciate them and
to show appreciation by living in peaceful harmony amidst them.
The Creator does not ask that we create a perfect world;
He asks that we celebrate it." —Robert Brault

"How many things are there which I do not want." —Socrates

> *"The greatest step towards a life of simplicity
> is to learn to let go."* —Steve Maraboli

Simplicity . . . it's different for everyone, isn't it? I long to live a simple life. But the meaning of simple is in the eyes of the one living that "simple" life. What is simple to you may not be simple to me. I see a lot of people stressed-out . . . burned-out . . . not at peace and striving for more. More what? How much is enough?

I was out to dinner last night with a friend, and we were talking about simplicity and peace. I told him I'd decided not to move to again right now. I know now why you wait a year to make any major decisions after the death of a loved one. I'd been thinking moving would be good for me. Where I planned on going was busy and new, and I thought it would be a great place to grow my business. And a friend told me I wouldn't be lonely, because all I'd have to do is go out my door and there'd be people. I could go to the movies, out to dinner, shopping anytime. But the more I visited the area, the less I liked it. You know, the gut thing. Then I realized I'd be paying more, and I can't really afford that right now. It would be stretching. So I started praying about it and thinking about it during my runs, and I decided I needed to listen to my gut. And besides, what the heck was I thinking? I love the beach. I love being on the ocean. I love my rented condo. I love waking up to the ocean. I've always wanted to live at the beach. I'm so glad I listened to my gut. The water, the ocean, the waves . . . they all bring me peace through the simplicity of them . . . the greatness of them . . .

When I was a nine-year-old girl in Williamsburg County, South Carolina, I would drive the tractor with the red umbrella, pulling the tobacco harvest going all of six miles of hour in the 120-degree summer heat—or so it seemed. These were the summers growing up on the farm. There wasn't a whole lot to do while driving that tractor at the speed of a turtle, so I spent a lot of time daydreaming—daydreaming about what it would be like to live on the beach and to move to my love, Myrtle Beach, South Carolina: the big city by the sea. I would say to myself, I *am* going to live at the beach one day.

I loved our one-week vacations in Garden City. We'd stay in the ocean all day on canvas rafts that took us over the waves like a roller-coaster ride on the water. We would laugh and giggle—my brothers, their friends, and mine—as we were tossed and turned and bounced and dropped in the ocean blue. The sun beat down on us, turning our already dark skin from farm life into a reddish-brown. We didn't care; we just wanted to be at the beach—sand, sun, heat, water and all—ignoring our parents' pleas to come in for lunch. But we'd finally have to succumb as the day turned into dinnertime and seafood. We'd be wrinkled, waterlogged, and sunburned . . . but happy. That was it: I was going to live at the beach one day. And so I did.

I love being on the beach, and I love surfing. I'm so glad I started. Whether I get any better at it or not, I just love being out there trying to get better. Somehow, I think I will. To me, being on that surfboard . . . paddling in and against the waves . . . being with nature . . . being one with the water . . . being with friends . . . simplicity. I would love to have a hut on the beach somewhere and surf all day with friends and family.

Anyway . . . back to simplicity. My friend and I were talking over dinner about what simplicity was, and I said, "To me, it's less." I also said how I like to get rid of the things I become too attached to—just to make sure I can let things go. Because we can take nothing with us, and anything we hold on to can be gone at any time. And usually others don't treasure your stuff like you do . . . so leaving it behind after you pass for someone else isn't always best.

Simplicity. I love life coaching and wellness coaching. I have a passion to help people become healthier . . . enjoy life more . . . live a less stressful life . . . love themselves. I love my runs on the beach, my time with friends and family, going to dinner, enjoying a good glass of wine. I think at times we need to refocus on our lives and how we can make them less stressful so we can love others and love ourselves. Life is very short. Nothing lasts forever. I want to be satisfied and at peace with what I have and where I am right now in life.

I think if I move anywhere, it will be to an island with surf and, oh, a hut . . . a little hut right there on the beach. . .

Finish Line

"Being the first to cross the finish line makes you a winner in only one phase of life. It's what you do after you cross the line that really counts."
—*Ralph Boston*

On my short run this morning I was thinking about the finish line. I always have a finish line in mind when I do anything in life.

I guess my training in wellness coaching and life coaching has transformed my thinking about goals and writing them down. Only three percent of people write down their visions, missions, and goals, and those three percent are the most successful. And I will be and am today successful, so I try to learn what brings about success. I watch other successful people, I read their books, and I write down my goals. Something special happens when you put things on paper, with the process of the hand holding the pen to create writing, and with the thought process that goes with it. And, of course, it's always great to keep learning in the field you're in so you can grow both personally and for your clients.

You also have a special edge on others if you love what you do. Most successful people love what they do; they're passionate about it. I love my business, Sweet Strength. Not only do I get to continue reading, learning, and taking classes about what I love, but I get to help others become stronger, better, and healthier by helping them see their vision, write down their goals, and meet those goals.

Anyway, back to the thought about the finish line. I always go a little bit farther than where my finish line is when I run. I don't stop there. I mean, participants of any race have to go past the finish line to win . . . don't they? Past the finish line are rest, new visions, new goals, and new adventures. It's also the time to think about what could have been done better, where there may have been mistakes or something that if tweaked would make you even greater at the race. You can always go a little farther than you think. It's only you, your mindset, that stops you from crossing the finish line.

Here is a simple example: when I box with my trainer, he's always a little ahead of me. He's faster doing burpees, pushups, etc. So in my mind, I challenge myself. I say, Today I will try to be fourteen burpees behind him instead of fifteen. I cross my finish line and do just a little more. This prepares me for the next time I want to do something better and become excellent at it. Because if I can do just one more than I think I can, then I have broken that old mindset of "I can't" or "let me stop at the finish line, because I made it and I'm satisfied there." No, we need to go on and cross over that line to win the race.

I am a believer that when we take full responsibility of where we are in life, of our choices, of everything we do, and of everything we want to be or do, then we are free to do anything. The circumstances, good or bad, don't matter, because we're going to have good and bad things happen to us. If we would just stop blaming everybody else or our circumstances and realize we have a choice of how to live our lives, we could accomplish so much more.

God created each of us with unique gifts and talents. With all that He has given us, we are to multiply it, to grow in it, to share it with others. God knows that we are capable of so much more than we think we are. He really gives us the world at our feet. He looks for people who want to cross over the finish line, rest, and then set new goals—not just stop because they made it to their perceived finish line.

I love the quote from Henry Ford: "If you think you can or you think you can't, you are probably right." It would be a shame to look back in five or ten years and have regret when it's as simple as changing your mindset and your choices. I don't want to live with regret.

Sweet Strength . . . it is sweet to cross that finish line and win.

Is It Worth It?

If it were easy, everyone would be doing it! Living life . . . digging deep, from within. . . But life isn't easy . . . or shall I say, living life isn't easy. Digging deeper with introspection isn't easy.

Winter threatens to break through the fall leaves. Clouds loom . . . it's still dark outside. Seems like it has been dark for days, because my favorite friend that brings warmth, daylight, and a smile to my face turned off the light and went to bed early yesterday . . . too early. My heart already longs for summer days. So I said, "Linda, let's put that smile and your running shoes on, and let's go find that friend. You're going to need it today. Get up . . . you can do this once again."

Ah, there you are, and at high tide. The waves were rocking and rolling this morning. Good, I thought, this will be a great jog. I need to work hard this morning, sweat, get some feel-good juices going.

I like running in the soft sand. It makes me dig a little deeper. Sometimes you have to dig a little deeper; sometimes you have to face life with an extra push; sometimes you have to let your heart beat a little harder, your body sweat, your legs burn from the extra work of digging deep. Sometimes my runs through soft sand are hard. That's why at high tide some people choose the sidewalk. It's just easier. I mean, we all like easy.

But if being successful were easy . . . if you didn't have to soul search, contemplate so much about how to get there, and conquer the fear of failing . . . then everybody would be successful. If it were easy to lose weight, exercise, and be good to your body . . . then we would all be healthy and the healthcare system might be in better shape. If it were easy, we'd all be Olympians. But it's not easy. So then the decision becomes: what do I really want to do in life? How badly do I want to run in the soft sand? Is it worth it? Is losing the weight worth it? Is being in good shape physically worth it? Is becoming successful worth it? Is facing my worst fears and understanding how they stop me from living life . . . is it worth it? Is it worth the work . . . or do I prefer easy?

Easy doesn't produce winners or satisfaction. Struggling with some soft sand that threatens my easy run makes the run a little harder. It makes my heart beat a little faster. I have to dig a little deeper and watch where my feet land so I don't trip and fall. It makes me sweat a little more. It makes me thankful that I can run. And I know when I conquer this soft sand and get to end of the run, it will have been worth it . . . and I'll be ready for the next run. Easy doesn't produce peace and freedom . . . but the struggle and the fight do.

Sweet Strength is digging deeper. I don't want easy. I want satisfaction.

Mindset

⸻ ∞ ⸻

*"Summing it all up, friends, I'd say you'll do best by filling your minds
and meditating on things true, noble, reputable, authentic, compelling,
gracious—the best, not the worst; the beautiful, not the ugly; things to
praise, not things to curse" —Philippians. 4:8*

I talk about mindset a lot because it is everything. What and how you
think about your life and the circumstances in which you find yourself
in this complicated and amazing world all come from your thinking
patterns. It's important that we understand how important it is to keep
our bodies moving on the stage in this one play . . . in this one role
called life . . . a life in which we are the main characters. And we, as
those characters, all have our entrances onto and exits off of the stage
of life. How do we want our exits to look?

I understand the importance of mind and body and keeping them
healthy. Someone once asked me if I'd always eaten healthy. . . *no.*
Have I always been optimistic? *Absolutely not.* Have I always worked
out? Off and on. Have I always been this wired? Had this much energy?
Umm . . . well . . . *yes!*

Now that we have the ability to reconnect with long lost people
from our pasts, there are certainly people on my Facebook page that
would agree to the above. Some of my friends on social media have
known me since I was a teenager. They have undoubtedly seen a
change in me and would all agree that I'm different now. I like being
different. I like changing with each day. I like who I am, and I love
my role on life's stage, playing the specific and unique part I've been
given.

I've been given the blessing of many diverse testimonies that have strengthened me, have made me a survivor and lover of life, and, most importantly, have allowed me to come along and encourage others who may be struggling with adversity. Some of my testimonies come from poor choices on my part, and some come from circumstances that were beyond my control. If you live long enough, you'll have lots of testimonies to be thankful for. You know, that's the complexity about the puzzle of pain, frustration, and suffering . . . it always makes the most beautiful masterpiece when all the impassioned pieces are connected as one. Our testimonies aren't all about us, even though we're the ones walking through them. Our testimonies are always for the glory of God and for empowering others. We need to understand as our struggles unfold that we are never separate beings . . . we are all connected. This will help us see the purpose and design of the puzzle. You see, testimonies, too, are growth for the mindset . . . if you allow them to act as such.

You and only you can change your life. Only you can change the way you view your world. If you aren't happy with something, you can change it. You really can.

Staying positive, eating healthy, and exercising aren't about trying to live forever. Because we're all going to leave this earth. No . . . not one of us is getting out alive. I believe that the only way to live life to the fullest is to stare death in the face. You have to face the fact that you won't live forever . . . at least, not on earth or in the body you have. But I believe that the time we've been given is like gold . . . very valuable. And as the saying goes, wealth is health . . . because without health, we can't enjoy the gold, can we? We can't enjoy our time here or our purpose of helping others if we aren't healthy in mind and body. But it's always up to you. You absolutely don't have to do anything if you don't want to.

You become and do what you think about most the time. How many could-have, if-only, should-have, I-wish-I-were, I-can't, I-won't, there's-no-way, I'm-so-stupid statements do you make in a day? How many assumptions? How many speculations? How many fears of the future? What are you telling yourself? And what would happen if you told yourself the opposite? What would your life look like if you focused on what you *could* do instead of what you can't? What if you focused on possibilities instead of problems? On what you can eat that's healthy instead of what you don't need that's unhealthy? On how good you'll feel after working out instead of on how hard it is to begin? What would your life look like if you changed your thoughts? What if every time you worried, you just said, "The Lord is my Shepherd, I shall not want; God will supply all my needs"?

This is how I try to change my thought patterns. I was getting back into my running one day after a foot injury. As I was running, my left foot was still bothering me some. I knew it was okay to run, but there was still that little ache, that little annoyance. Well . . . I decided I'd focus on my right foot because it felt great. So I started thinking about how good my right foot felt, and before I knew it, my left foot wasn't bothering me. Our minds are powerful. Our thoughts make our lives heaven or hell.

It's kind of like the business I've started. I just believe that everyone has this secret agenda . . . this conspiracy to help make me successful. Okay, maybe they don't, but it's amazing how thinking this funny but positive thought has brought the right people to me at the right time with just the experiences I needed to move my business to a higher level.

Your mindset is the beginning of a new life. How you view your world . . . how you see yourself and others . . . it all begins in your thoughts. Once I was able to understand that I had a choice regarding what I thought about, my world began to change. I understood that I could be my best friend or my worst enemy. No one around me can help me or change my world. Yes, they can come along and try to encourage and empower me. Yes, there are those who can help us when we become ill, get in an accident, or lose our jobs, but they can't help me handle my reaction to it or how I view it. Even the closest people in my life can't change what has happened to me or what will happen to me. Only I can change the way I handle and look at my life. I realize that I can make myself miserable or I can make myself happy. No one else can make me happy or miserable. No one else can hurt me emotionally unless I allow them to. No one else can make me angry unless I give them permission to.

Once I realized it was my choice to make myself physically and mentally stronger, *I did* . . . and I still work on every single day. It's not easy to change thought patterns, and sometimes we don't want the responsibility of our choices. We like to blame. But it's worth it . . . because that's where growth, strength, and peace come from—making the decision in my mind that I can do it. I can live the life I want to, because I have a choice. That doesn't mean we won't feel pain—we will—but we can choose to stay in the pain or move forward and find the gift in the midst of it.

I am Fabulous

"I am fabulous." Just saying.

You know, I used to not feel this way . . . that I was fabulous . . . that I was worth anything. And it took a lot of soul searching, a lot of hard experiences, a lot of heartache, a lot of life, and a lot of pain for me to love me as I am . . . and not as I thought I should be or as I thought others wanted me to be.

We are so caught up in what others think about us. Look at all the plastic surgeries. Look at all the tearing down and judgment of others. The gossip. The pressures to look and act a certain way. Man, it gets tiring to try to be someone you're not. It gets tiring trying to measure up. "You aren't young enough . . . you aren't rich enough . . . you aren't' smart enough. . . You aren't skinny enough. . . you don't wear the right clothes . . . you don't go to the right clubs . . . You don't live in the right neighborhood . . . you don't belong to the right club." FABULOUS. You are fabulous just as you are.

We live in a world that tries to make us uncomfortable in our own skin and that tries to get us to be someone we weren't created to be. It's as if they want everyone to be the same . . . look the same . . . act the same. But we weren't meant to be the same, look the same, and act the same. This world doesn't want us to be comfortable in our skin. The world tries to lure us into plastic so it can mold us according to its perception of beauty, success, freedom . . . the world wants us to wear a mask. The world wants us to step into *The Stepford Wives* . . . you know, a robotic kind of life. The world wants us to strive for perfection, which we'll never reach. The only perfect person I know walked on water.

I am fabulous just because I am. Not that I'm above anyone else or better than anyone else. I'm fabulous because God made me fabulous. I'm fabulous because at my age and with what I've experienced in life . . . well, dammit . . . I'm just proud to have made it this far, and I'm thankful for every wrinkle I've acquired. Because you know what my wrinkles scream? They scream, "Linda McDandel, you have lived life. You have not held back. You have felt deeply, loved passionately, and felt pain in your inner soul. And you are FABULOUS."

Your Creator made you to be a unique piece of the music that could not be heard without the song you sing . . . without the instrument He gave you to play so beautifully, making the music come together in perfect harmony. Yeah, I do a lot of stupid things. Yeah, I give my heart too easily. Yeah, I love too passionately. Yeah, I'm impulsive. . . Because I feel so intensely. Yeah, I fail . . . I fall down . . . I flounder . . . I get hurt . . . I hurt others. Yeah, I probably say too much. And I'm getting older . . . wrinkles and all, but I am fabulous and I believe it! I will continue to fight the battle of age. I'll fight it through fiercely working out . . . eating healthy . . . giving it my all . . . never stopping . . . being wired . . . driving everyone crazy. Yeah, my passionate heart will get hurt . . . and people will misunderstand me. But I know that through it all, I am FABULOUS and for once in my life, I'm comfortable in my own skin.

Sweet Strength is . . . well . . . it's just *fabulous*.

Perspective

"Perspective is the most important thing to have in life."
—*Lauren Graham*

I posted some thoughts on Facebook about what holds people back from their goals, and this friend of mine who is serving in the military commented, "War, stress, people shooting at us, exhaustion, DFAC food . . . those have been my roadblocks lately. Hopefully soon to come to an end."

That certainly puts things in perspective, doesn't it? Those are some real roadblocks, serious challenges. It's so easy to take things for granted, to complain, to have excuses. Earlier, I was going to post on Facebook about how I hate this weather, I don't like winter, and I want to move somewhere warm and sunny . . . but I thought about my first cousin Barbara; her husband, Ricky; and their family and what they're going through. She has a brain tumor. The cancer is very aggressive. When I think about her, I think Strength. I know she will fight with all she has. Her husband had just gotten home from the hospital from a heart attack and stroke.

Puts things in perspective. There are people all over the world facing real roadblocks and challenges in their lives. There are people who are simply thankful they have another day on earth, so they really don't care what the weather is like or if it's summer, spring, fall, or winter—they just want to be here for all the seasons. There are starving people who would love the freedom and the choice to be able to eat a healthy meal, to be able to drink clean water, to be able to work and make a living. There are people all over the world who would be thankful for a cloudy day instead of a day without food, or without love, or without cancer. There are people with knee injuries who would love to be able to run. The list goes on, doesn't it?

It makes me think about how much I complain . . . when I literally don't have anything to complain about. It makes me wonder how many excuses I make that cause me not to reach my goals. Excuses that aren't even valid.

It makes me wonder what I'm doing with the abilities I've been given. And if we have the ability and the choice to eat healthy today, why wouldn't we? If we have the ability to work out today . . . even if it's walking . . . why wouldn't we? If we have the choice to think positively and challenge our excuses and limits, why wouldn't we? If we have the choice to love someone, why wouldn't we? If we have the choice to be thankful for what we've been given, why wouldn't we?

So . . . I wonder how many of my challenges, roadblocks, limits, and barriers are *real*? Yes, there are real ones, and then there are the excuses. I wonder if I can challenge myself to discover which ones are real and which ones are excuses and complaints?

How could we see things from another perspective so we can reach our goals, dreams, and visions? So we can live out our purposes in life?

Perspective changes things. Thankfulness changes things. Not taking health for granted changes things. Walking a mile in someone else shoes changes things.

Sweet Strength is all about perspective.

Strong Soldiers

"Keep your head up, God gives his battles to the strongest soldiers."
—*Linda McDandel*

You're a strong soldier. Think about what you've been through . . . what you're going through. You were selected by the one who knows you better than you know yourself. You were selected by your Creator. Why? Because you are a strong warrior. If you weren't, you wouldn't have been chosen for such an important battle: life. We are in a battle . . . a battle for our mindsets . . . a battle for our health and wellness . . . a battle for love and peace and God, who created the universe . . . knit you together in the womb. God Himself, the King of Kings, picked you . . . His strongest, most determined, most qualified soldier . . . to fight the battle you're in. You're thinking, I didn't ask for this battle. But . . . wow . . . what an honor. What a privilege to know that while you may not have asked for it, you were qualified and specially picked—handpicked, in fact—because God knew that you wouldn't give up and He knew you could change the way the evil battle was going. He knew you could fight the battle because you had what it took in your heart and soul. You had passion . . . because you believed there was a purpose and plan to this battle, this war. And He knew you had this battle in the palm of your hand because He has you engraved in the palm of His hand. You have already won . . . and the best reward to winning the battle lies within your spirit, which lives on and loves on. You are brave warrior and a strong soldier. Go for it and receive the reward that's waiting for you at the victory celebration . . . at your real home.

Afraid of Success?

A friend asked me at lunch the other day if I was afraid of success. That stuck. Me, afraid of success? I had to think about that for a while. Was I afraid of succeeding? It's a question I've asked others before. Sometimes it is scary to think about real success with regards to the dreams we have—the big dreams. I mean, can it really happen? Do I believe in myself enough? What will my life look like if I reach my dreams? That's what I'm working toward, right? I am strong, I am tough, and I want to succeed, don't I?

Christian was taking his time to mentor me in some business ideas, dreams I have. He had been listening closely enough to pinpoint my weakness. I am my worst enemy. I have to defeat my worst enemy. I have to bring her down. I help others with becoming their own best friends. Am I listening to my own advice?

Each day, I write it down; I set goals, and I know I will meet them. I've accomplished a lot since I started my business two years ago. I have some big dreams. There's a lot I want to make happen. But I've let my weaknesses, my fears, and my old behaviors creep into the unopened dream that lies before me. My old self, she is so reliable—like clockwork. I know her so well. I've battled her before. She has defeated me many times. But not this time.

There's a lot to building a business from the ground up . . . especially when you've had to deal with the loss of loved ones in the process. It's easy to allow that to become a weakness. It's easy to become your worst enemy. We like to blame it on circumstances or on others; we want to make excuses, and we tend to find solace in our weaknesses. After all, we know our weaknesses so well. We tend to rehearse our weaknesses over and over in our minds. It's more difficult to feel familiar with our strengths, which tend to show up like a mirage, like a temporary mask we put on until we can run back home to our weaknesses. Our weaknesses laugh and taunt our strengths, like bullies in a playground taunting the children who don't fit the mold.

It's just easier to compete against one another than to compete against ourselves. If another person wins, we can claim they were smarter, had more advantage, were stronger, had more money, had more time, were lucky, were blessed. But if we win and succeed against ourselves, then we become this whole new person. We have to learn to live differently. We have to learn a new way of thinking. We have to learn to become our own best friend. It's so foreign. We have to learn to embrace our strengths instead of lean on our weakness.

I am sure it will be like the caterpillar inside the chrysalis that becomes the beautiful butterfly. It would be easier to stay inside the chrysalis; it's safe there, it's familiar, and nothing has to change. But when that chrysalis, which the caterpillar is wrapped so warmly in, is defeated and taken off . . . when that chrysalis is broken out of . . . then, and only then, does that caterpillar transform into the beautiful butterfly that can fly with its wings spread out. And only then does it realize that it no longer needed the old caterpillar and its weakness. No . . . that caterpillar inside that chrysalis began to understand the power of putting on a new skin—in fact, a whole new shape and form. It doesn't resemble its old self. It's a totally new way of life. Instead of comfort, security, and weakness in the safety of the chrysalis, there's now excitement in the adventure of new territory. Territory that's spread out as far as its eyes could see . . . as far as it could fly. There was a new life. There were colors and shapes and smells that it had never experienced before. There were sounds it had never heard. There was this incredible flow of wind beneath its wings. The awareness of wind and flying, which it had never been aware of before. Ah, the joy, peace, and satisfaction of what it felt like to leave the weakness and fly into the strength. The satisfaction in the work it took to be free to fly and free to feel . . . and the freedom of success of a caterpillar turned into a butterfly . . .

You see, Christian, my friend had listened to me and had heard me say a couple of defeating statements. And he nailed me, just like I've done to others in the past. Are we afraid of succeeding? Can we beat our old familiar calls to comfort? What are we afraid of? What do we need to do to become successful and enjoy it instead of sabotaging it? What do we need to be the person God created us to be? I went home and thought about this. I thought about how much I believe in my clients and how I love seeing them succeed. I thought about how I empower them to see themselves as successful. I thought about the satisfaction they have when they beat a weakness. I thought about how badly I want to attain certain goals and what it will take to reach them. I am ready. I'm ready to defeat her. After all, she's the only one who needs to be defeated, and that's the truth. No circumstance needs to be defeated, no other person needs to be defeated. Not only do all the weaknesses in me need to be defeated—she needs to go down, too. Any trace of the old self needs to be gone so I can embrace success.

I am ready to be successful. Are you? Because if we are afraid of success, how will we ever reach the dreams and visions that God has placed on our heart? God planted that desire for us to be successful inside of us. God gave me the tools to defeat my old self. He gave me the strength and the belief that it can be done. He believes in us. He loves us. He created us for this time and this season, and He put us in this place to live out His plan . . . and His plan is not weakness. His plan is total transformation. The butterfly. So are we going to listen? Are we going to be transformed into the beautiful butterfly?

Sweet Strength is winning the battle once and for all.

One Lone Surfer

Surf's up—at least today it was for one little ten-year-old girl who has cystic fibrosis.

When I'm on the beach, I always make it a point to walk or run in the direction of one of my favorite spots. Today was no exception. It is the surfer's domain, the small area of water where surfers are allowed to surf during tourist season. Because I love to surf, or shall I say, I love being in the water on my surfboard, still learning to surf. I also love watching others surf.

I enjoy the sight of the surfers in the lineup, anticipating the next wave to carve, to ride, and hope to control. It is, to me, both an inspiring and peaceful sight to behold. The surfers seem to be one with their boards, one with the ocean, and one with their fellow surfers, who understand and share their love of surfing . . . the feeling. Surfers just seem to have that special connection with nature and their souls.

Well, as I looked across the surfers' turf this afternoon, there was but one. One lone surfer, dressed in her warm wetsuit, booties, and gloves to keep the cold water off . . . in the middle of winter, riding her favorite lifeline to joy—her board . . . paddling out, through the cold water . . . waiting for the wave that will ignite the passion buried in her heart and soul. The passion she feels each time she catches a wave that carries her body-driven surfboard down the line. I stopped and watched. I knew this little girl had a drive about her, a determination. You could just tell it by watching her in the water.

I introduced myself to her mom, Lynn, who was recording the girl on video. She told me her daughter had cystic fibrosis and that exercise was great for the disease. Her exercise was in the form of surfing. She told me her daughter was ten years old and dreams of becoming a professional surfer. Lynn proudly said, "She entered some contest last year. She loves surfing so much, she goes year-round." It touched my heart and soul. I thought to myself, now that is indeed Sweet Strength. She said, "You'll see us out here this summer."

I can hardly wait to meet Lynn's daughter and let her know how much she inspires me. I can hardly wait to tell her how beautiful she is. I can hardly wait to meet this brave little girl who doesn't stop believing in her dream because of a horrific disease that has made its home in her body. No . . . she knows what she wants. She understands that to truly live, she needs to ignite the passion in her heart. Her dream drives her to beat the odds. She has a goal, and she isn't stopping or giving in or making excuses until she reaches it. Yes, I can hardly wait to surf with this little girl, who has big dreams and the courage to go after them in the midst of physical limitations. She's not stopping, and I somehow believe this little surfer girl will meet her dream of becoming a pro. Why? Because she believes. She believes in her own beauty.

Yes, what a beautiful image to behold: a little lone surfer girl with that huge vast body of water as her backdrop for the day. Her battle for the day won once again as she rides the wave with her heart lying comfortably on her treasured board . . . seeking and finding her place, her appointment with healing and strength for her body, her mind, and her soul. No, nothing is stopping her.

There *is* a journey through loneliness to the other side. But you have to be willing to not settle for good because you're lonely. You are where you are for a reason, so embrace where God has you, because the best is yet to come.

Spring

Where are you, spring?
This cold weather joke . . . well, it's just mean.
Flip-flops, sandals, and running around on bare feet.
Dang, I can't wait for some summer heat.
My surfboard is dry,
Me oh me.
The days on the river seem a distance past.
Lord, please don't let this cold weather last.
Cabin fever is taking its toll.
Damn that groundhog coming out of his hole.
He lied to us all
When he made that spring call.
So when summer finally gets here,
From this face there will be no tear!
Surfing, waterskiing, running in the heat—
Now that's a summer that can't be beat.

Uncomfortable Change

———⁂———

I don't like to be uncomfortable. It's safe, being comfortable. We don't have to test ourselves . . . our beliefs . . . our limits . . . who we are as a person. It's safer not to challenge ourselves to change. But we want to change . . . we really do. We want to lose the weight, run the marathon, open ourselves to love, build our business . . . but we can't do those things without changing who we are, how we think, what we do. We can't reach our goals, our dreams, our visions for our lives . . . by doing the same thing we're doing now.

Sweet Strength is being uncomfortable.

Outwit Our Bodies

———⁂———

"Health is not valued until sickness comes." —*Thomas Fuller*

We keep trying to outwit our bodies' desires for good, healthy, clean foods by fad diets and weight loss schemes that make millions of dollars off of us. Do we just need to learn to clean our palates and retrain them for healthy, clean, nutritious foods that lead to a lifestyle change so we'll never have to diet again?

Our bodies tell us what they need and desire, if only we'd listen. Our bodies don't want to be tricked, deceived, overfed, underfed, starved of a balance of nutrients and fuel. If we eat poorly, consume chemically designed foods, or overeat, our bodies will react by storing fat cells and we'll begin to gain weight while being starved for nutrients. We'll become sluggish and moody. We'll become more susceptible to heart disease, diabetes, high cholesterol, cancer, and many inflammatory diseases.

We cannot hide what we put in our bodies. We're only given one body. It's your best friend. Treat it as that, and your body will reward you by being your best friend . . . not your worst enemy.

We All Need a Coach

"A friend is what the heart needs all the time." —*Henry Van Dyke*

I am strong and I am a fighter. I love life and the challenges it brings. I don't ever want to quit. I want to and will persevere. I have a will to survive—and not just survive, but thrive. I want to be the best I can be in every endeavor I attempt. Even though I'm all these things, if it weren't for my friends—who came along beside me, believed in me, and wouldn't let me quit—I'm not sure I could have made it through this life . . . especially through the last year.

You know, I'm very good at motivating myself. I mean, I'm a coach—I coach myself in my mind all the time. But sometimes I need to be coached by someone else. Sometimes I need a cheerleader, someone who really knows me, who has seen me in action or non-action.

Like yesterday. I went to my boxing training with Brian Barnes and I was so tired. I didn't feel good. I sure didn't *feel* like being there. But

I knew I needed it to ground me . . . to get me back in the game of life. Eating healthy and exercising are my ways of releasing stress. It's part of my quiet time inside while my physical self is being challenged. It's part of what keeps me strong and able to handle life and what it throws at me.

There are times I have to have discipline instead of doing what I may *feel* like. When I do this, it's easier the next time to do something I don't necessarily *feel* like doing. Discipline is hard, but I've found that not being disciplined in my health and wellness is much harder. Discipline is simply giving yourself a command and following it.

So yesterday, Brian wouldn't let me give up. He kept telling me, "Linda, you can do this. Fight through it." He didn't say, "Linda, let's do this another day when you feel better." You know why? Because he knows me, he has seen me work out, and he believes in me. When once in a while I'd throw a good right punch, he'd say, "Now that's the Linda I know." That helped me get through. Brian wouldn't let me quit yesterday. He knows I am no quitter.

Sometimes we need that. We need friends, we need coaches, we need that special someone to come beside us and bring out what's already inside of us. Every one of us has what it takes to do whatever it is we want to do in life. We just need that friend, that person who believes in us.

I believe that my clients always have the answer. Besides, if it isn't your choice in the end, it'll never work.

So many of my friends have partnered with me through this year to encourage me, motivate me, and not let me quit. I haven't always believed in myself or lived my life healthy and well. But because I had friends who saw something in me that I didn't see, and they loved me enough to believe in me and not let me quit, I'm healthy and well and always working on improving something else in my life . . . because we always have something we can improve upon. And we always need a friend to encourage us in our efforts to improve. Do your friends encourage you? Empower you? Lift you up? Well...if not...you need to change friends.

Define Yourself

———❦———

"Nothing can stop the person with the right mental attitude from achieving his or her goal. Nothing on earth can help the person with the wrong mental attitude." —Thomas Jefferson

Wow, how true is that. It's all about the mindset—our beliefs that have been formed, our perception of the world and of people. We color our world through this mindset, through our beliefs. Sometimes we just don't want to color it a different way because it's the way we've been coloring for years. Our perception is right . . . there is no other color to use. But maybe your perspective is wrong. Maybe another color could be used.

"It's in the struggle itself that you define yourself." —Pat Buchanan

I have found this to be so true. It's never in the easy places that I find out who I am or what I'm looking for in life. The easy can never define because . . . well . . . in the easy, you're conformed, not defined. You don't have to think. You don't have to stretch yourself beyond comfort. Maybe someone else is leading you in the easy because it's easier to say yes and please than risk saying no. Maybe you've allowed others to define you so you don't have to struggle to define yourself or to allow God to define you. Maybe it's easier to swim with the current than against it. Maybe it's easier to stay where you are in life than it is to struggle to reach that place you really want to be. Define yourself by challenging yourself to unlearn some old habits, some old belief systems that may not be working. Stretch . . . struggle . . . DEFINE.

Optimist

—∞∞—

"I am an optimist. It does not seem too much use being anything else."
—Winston Churchill

Wow . . . this is the truth. Whenever I let myself be anything but optimistic, it leads down that long, dark spiral of depression. It's amazing how quickly one pessimistic thought, if you allow it, can bring along with it a group of pessimistic thoughts; and before you know it, you just aren't smiling. You're mad at the world and mad at the person in front of you.

But the cool thing is, you have a choice. You can capture and change that thought. Optimist or pessimist? Is the glass half full or half empty or just flowing over? Mine is full and flowing over.

Live Your Dreams

—∞∞—

"When I was in high school, I went to my mom one day after school and said, 'Mom, I want to build an atom smasher. I want to build a 2.3

million electron-volt betatron in a garage.' And my mom sort of stared at me and said, 'Sure. Why not?'" —Michio Kaku

Don't let anyone tell you that you cannot live out your dreams.

I will never forget the time Robert had the dream to be another Michael Jordan. He ran into another parent and was telling her that he was going to be a professional basketball player. She looked at him and said, "Honey, that's nice, but you know you don't have a chance. The odds are just against you." I was appalled; I've always told Robert he could do whatever he wanted to do. Robert told me that it crushed him. He believed her, and he lost interest in basketball after that. He said what that parent had told him was in the back of his mind.

We need to be careful what we say to young children and be careful what we tell other people.

And if we're the ones with the dream, we can't listen to what others may say. We must follow our hearts and our passions, and never quit . . . because that dream is implanted in the depths of our hearts for a reason. Because they haven't yet reached their dreams and goals, some people think others can't reach their own goals. And they'll spout off all the reasons others can't . . . I call BS on that.

Dream, and dream big. Never stop following your passion. You're never too young or too old. God will show you, if you let him. He has bigger dreams for you than you can ever imagine. He's just waiting for you to overcome your fears and have faith that when you take that first step, He'll part the waters. Believe and live! It won't always be easy, but how sweet the results will be.

Sweet Strength is dreaming, planning, doing, and not stopping.

You Will Never Be Empty

———❦———

"God always gives his best to those who leave the choice with Him."
—*Jim Elliot*

God will never leave you empty; He will replace everything you lost. If He asks you to leave something behind, it's because He has something greater in front of you.

I know sometimes it seems when we lose something or someone, we'll never be the same . . . and we won't . . . but we can be better and we can be healed. And our lives can be even greater than before, in a different way, if we allow God to work in us and through us.

That means that our thought life, the way we think, has to be in complete sync with God's truth that He will not leave us empty and He will replace what is gone.

I don't understand why a lot of things happen. It's not my job to understand loss. It's my job to believe, trust, and keep my thoughts focused on God's promises—and to make my choices reflect that.

I do understand that I have to trust and believe there are greater things coming. I know that God loves us even when He takes from us the people and things that are so important and dear to our hearts. He is not going to leave us empty and lost. I also understand that He has given me His word, a mind, and a heart to guide me to this truth. I can choose to believe Him and His word or I can choose not to. I choose to believe that I will not be left empty, and I choose to believe that greater things are in store for me. I anticipate this good happening . . . I look for it every day. Expect it.

I often think of the story in Genesis—the great ancient text of Lot, who lost it all . . . everything . . . but God in His infinite wisdom and grace replaced everything. Not only did He replace everything . . . Lot received even more than he had before. I know some things and people cannot be replaced, and God understands that too. But replacing things doesn't mean what you lost was not valuable and special. It means you had a season of special gifts and love that you will always have memories of. I know it's hard to let go of seasons of love and gifts. But we need to understand that we were never promised eternity here on earth . . . just seasons . . . and when we can understand that this is not our home, it becomes easier to be thankful for the seasons and easier to let go of them when they're over. And it becomes easier to open our hearts and minds to next season of our life. Nothing last forever . . . but change.

If we trust and believe in our hearts and minds, He will give us many more seasons of even greater gifts and love than those we lost. He will keep giving us the best of the best until we reach the eternal life of our heavenly home with the ultimate gift of unconditional love and beauty like we have never ever known. The key is believing it and trusting what He says. Amazing grace . . . how sweet the sound.

God will never leave you empty. He will replace everything you've lost. If He asks you to put something down, it's because He wants you to pick up something even greater.

Dedication

———⊷⊷⊶———

"Dedication, absolute dedication, is what keeps one ahead—a sort of indomitable obsessive dedication and the realization that there is no end or limit to this because life is simply an ever-growing process, an ever-renewing process." —Bruce Lee

I was coaching a client about this yesterday. She has come so far and is changing her mindset, her weight, her nutritional habits, and even walking farther than she ever has . . . and she hit the wall. So last week and this week we talked about her strengths, mindset, motivation, what she has learned through all of this, and what's going to get her past this wall so she will become free . . . free to live this as a lifestyle, not another diet or exercise plan that fails . . . free to make choices that lead to health and wellness, not just physically, but in life satisfaction, stress management, and loving yourself so you can love others. You know, *take care* of yourself. She was taking care of everyone but herself.

Anyway, she said that her one word is "dedication." "I am so determined to continue to beat this once and for all. I have not come this far to go back. I am dedicated, Linda, to finishing this race. I feel better than I ever have. I am thinking clearer than I ever have. I am loving me for the first time in a long time. Yes, I am dedicated . . . determined. It feels too good to let it go."

In this life . . . in this ever-changing life . . . dedication truly is an ever-renewing process.

Missed Opportunities

"Our lives are defined by opportunities, even the ones we miss."
—Eric Roth

I enjoy looking for sharks' teeth on the beach. I walked along this afternoon, searching, looking with my head down . . . focused . . . looking for one thing . . . oblivious to my surroundings because I was on a mission . . . then I looked up and across the vast blue sea, and there, to my joy, just a few yards out was a school of dolphins playing, jumping, enjoying their habitat in kinship with each other. I thought, Wow. If I hadn't looked up, I would have missed the blessing that was right before me.

So I started thinking about how often we miss opportunities because we're so narrowly focused on what's in front of us. We have a limited perception of who we think we are or what we think we can accomplish because we can't see beyond who we are. We can't seem to bring into focus who we could really be . . . because all we see is who we are. We don't see that we are made in God's image, and the God who created us . . . He has no limits. We are His miracle. We are a unique creation. No other creation is made in His image. Wrap your mind around that!

That's pretty special . . . like a miracle, I would say. So how many of us are walking with our heads down, with our shoulders slumped, only seeing what's right in front of us . . . when opportunity, love, beauty, and miracles are all around us. All we have to do is lift our heads and look around.

Sweet Strength is believing there's a plan for your life . . . bigger than you can even dream. Jesus believed Peter could walk on water. Peter is the one who doubted.

Motivation and Desire

———❧———

"The bird is powered by it's own life and by it's motivation."
—*A.P.J. Abdul Kalam*

Motivation and desire . . . It's hard to understand, isn't it? I mean, what makes someone able to build something they never have before? To run a marathon or lose that fifty pounds? To skydive or scale that mountain or surf? To start exercising? To do something they want to do? There are incredible stories out there about people beating the odds to become who they've always dreamed of becoming: building that business they've always wanted, writing that book, beginning that new project, to starting a mission that will help others . . . the key is motivation and desire.

In coaching, we talk a lot about these two words. Action words, I call them, because they move you to action and keep you there. You see, without the motivation to begin and sustain, and without the inner desire, it will never happen. All the people in the world can tell you "should" quit smoking, you "should" lose that weight, you "should" start working out, you "should" run that marathon, you "should" write that book—even if it's your spouse, your doctor, your best friend . . . even you call tell yourself you "should" (I tell my clients: Don't should

all over yourself, because should is your enemy . . . not your motiva-
tor). You can listen to the best motivational tapes, read all the books
on what you want to accomplish, study and study, but until it comes
from within . . . until you find that motivation, that desire, that belief
. . . it isn't going to happen. Maybe in the beginning you'll be excited
because, hey, it's new . . . kind of like that new car. You wash it, clean
it on the inside, park sideways in the last parking space, tell everyone
they can't eat in it. Then, after a while, it just becomes something old
. . . no fun anymore.

    I tell my clients to look for that blowtorch motivation. Not the
candle—the blowtorch. If you don't have it, then when the challenges
come along and when life gets in the way of your goals—and challenges
will come and life *will* get in the way—you'll quit. You'll stop. I look
for the dynamite in my life to move me. If I think it's a firecracker, I'll
check it out, but if it isn't that dynamite stick for me, then I'll know
that I don't need to pursue it yet. The time just isn't right . . . or maybe
it doesn't lend itself to my strengths . . . or maybe I don't really want to
do it. Remember, it all begins with desire. What do you really…really
want and desire and what's your motivation to get there?

Reflection of Love

Love it happens when we least expect it. In a time and place that the
sun rises and reflects the new beginning through the lens of the eyes
and of the gaze. When the hearts collide as easily as the tide kisses the
shore. . ..in one single flashing, electromagnetic moment of life of love.
Wait for it. It can't be chased or forced or made to happen. True love

will find its way to you. .. .. ..as the new dawn and new day finds it way in the rhythm of the dance between the sun and the waves. Wait for it. Sweet Strength. Make It Sweet and Keep It Strong.

Morning Mantra

Good Morning! It's another new dawn…new day…new way…and it is indeed a beautiful day in the neighborhood. The sun has made its appearance repeating the mantra; it is a good day to be alive!

Happiest People

"The happiest people in the world are those who feel absolutely terrific about themselves, and this is the natural outgrowth of accepting total responsibility every part of their life." —Brian Tracy

Do know what the happiest day of my life was? It was when I discovered my world. A world that I could create who I chose to be. A world that suddenly looked different than before. It was my life and I was creating the world I wanted to be in. This was the happiest day. The day I took responsibility for my problems.

The day I stopped blaming the government, health care, my job, my money situation, my health, my so called bad relationships, my parents, the economy, my environment, my circumstances, (even those I didn't create) my teachers, and God.

The day I looked inside to see what beliefs weren't serving me. The beliefs I held, created by their thinking. I had never stopped to examine them. Where did they come from? The day I stopped and listened to the thoughts that were running around in my mind. The day I listened to the words that came out of my mouth . . . the day I made the choice to think about my thoughts and my words. The realization struck me like a lightning bolt . . . this is the results of my problems. I can change my problems by changing my beliefs that don't serve me or others in my life . . . my thoughts . . . my words . . . which result in my action . . . which result in creating the environment around me.

Yes, the happiest day of my life was discovering there was no one to blame . . . but myself.

Valentine's Date, Gym

My Valentine's date with Gym. He's always on time. He's always where he says he will be. Never leaves me disappointed. Gets my heart beating and sweat pouring. There's always variety in every date. He leaves me on an emotional high. The more I try to resist him the more he grows on me. He always leaves me feeling stronger and physically fit. Always makes me work hard for his attention, but gives me more attention than I could have ever hoped for . . . and the more I give to him the more he gives me. He teaches me so many lessons in life . . . like if I cheat on him, or ignore him, or don't love him . . . it just doesn't work . . . it never works . . . and it never will.

Because, just like in a marriage or relationship . . . it's a partnership. It's a commitment. It is a commitment to grow together and grow strong together.

Oxygen

"Encouragement is like oxygen to our spirits and our hearts. Don't forget you're carrying someone else's too. Encourage them and help them breathe" —— Linda McDandel

The rising of the sun softly over the beauty of the sea. It blossoms into another day of grace . . . springing up in life around us. Another day to encourage one another. Another day to lift one another up. Empower one of another to change. Love one another. Embrace one another. Embracing others for who they are not as we think they should be. It is indeed a beautiful day in the neighborhood.

Vulnerable

"Vulnerability is the birthplace of connection and the path to feeling worthiness. If it doesn't feel vulnerable, the sharing is probably not constructive." — Brene Brown

This is difficult isn't it? I mean if we want to be really vulnerable we are capable of being wounded. We are open to attack. Without a doubt vulnerability in itself, if we want to be honest with ourselves is well difficult. Who wants to be open to being wounded or attacked? I don't think there is a waiting line for either one of these? Do you? But, yet we all desire it in others. We want unconditional love and we want people to be vulnerable with us. But, we really don't want to give it to others. I mean, after all it's our heart.

Our guarded heart that beats with the mask of the day. It's our feelings of vulnerability that puts the shield up quickly (as if in war) if someone gets too close to our hearts with their interrogation of our souls . . . we put up our best shield . . . but, when do we let down the shield?

Love is Near

Valentines is near and love is always near. In fact, love is with us twenty-four hours if we allow it. It is offered to us today and eternally. Love and time is binding through thought, spirit and space. God is love and we are created in love, do you believe this?

I would like to leave you with the best words on love I have ever had the honor to read. Now, the question remains, can I live them? Imagine, if you can, if everyone lived them . . . how differently we would interact in our worlds . . . how differently we would live . . . how differently we would interact with others . . . others of opposing views . . . of beliefs. And those are my thoughts on this Friday night. I am just as conditioned in conditioned love as you.

*Love is patient and kind; love does not envy or boast; it is not arrogant or
rude. It does not insist on its own way; it is not irritable or resentful; it
does not rejoice at wrongdoing, but rejoices with the truth. Love bears all
things, believes all things, hopes all things, endures all things.
Love never ends. "— 1 Corinthians 13:4-8a*

Dead Conversation

What an incredibly moving sunrise this morning! It is a beautiful day
in the neighborhood. It's a good morning and it's a good day. How
are you going to spend it? In a great positive vibration or a negative
draining vibration. Because, which ever you choose you are planting a
seed for the same.

"Dead Conversation," What? That was her response. Let me repeat
myself, "Dead Conversation" That is what I say when gossip or
negativity about someone comes my way. It's simple really. You don't
have to partake. I don't live in negativity, because those aren't the seeds
that I want to plant. I don't want those seeds planted in me either. I
want to plant encouragement, hope, love, and support and that is what
I want planted in me. I want to build up, not tear down! I want people
to be happy, successful, and build their lives to match their dreams. It
is unfortunate that there are people out there that want to see others
fail, suffer and fall down. There are people who would rather gossip,
spit venom, tear down, than lift up. Why? Because that is how they feel
about themselves. Always remember, it is a reflection of them not you.

"Dead Conversation" That's what you will get from me if you have
anything negative to say about anyone. If you don't have anything

positive and uplifting to say about someone don't even bother to come my way. I don't want my seed to grow weeds and I am not going to let your bad seed plant weeds in my rose garden.

We rise by lifting others up. Strong People don't put others down they lift them up, weak people are just that weak. Therefore, encourage one another and build each other up.

And, that's all I got to say about that. It's time to plant some seeds of love and encouragement. Make your day great.

You Are Clothed in a Body... But Alive in Spirit...

Good Morning!!! What a great day to be alive!!! What a great day to tell your subconscious mind what you want to achieve, be, and do. So it can start producing the results. God in you . . . through you . . . and flowing out of you. Are you listening to the voice that screams in the silence of your gut, your soul, your very spirit?

You are an eternal being clothed, for your mission here on earth, you are not a being that is trying to find your spirit. You are spirit, you do not die. You simply take off your coat when your mission is over. However, you have to know who you are and who you are listening too.

And you can choose to get involved in the mission or walk away. Fear, doubt, indecision, poor attitude, failure, fear of what others will say, will keep you behind a prison door and away from your mission.

Until you get to know who you are and your mission. It will be difficult for you to change. The internal dialog will continue in cloudiness and confusion.

It's sad, I lived there in confusion the years I did. It breaks my heart that others live here today. I listen to what they feed themselves. I listen to what they speak to their subconscious and it always manifest exactly what they feed it. I listen to conversations. I observe people's actions . . . how they relate with others . . . I can read them just by listening to their words, eyes, and body language.

The sad thing is many people will take off the body . . . and never have had the satisfaction of the completed mission that was unique to them. Many people are in a prison. The door is closed but, it's not locked. Al they need to get out of their prison is to open the door and walk out.

We hold the key to all your problems and the key to all the solutions for those problems.

Why do we do this? Belief systems are strong. What's holding you back? What belief system is hiding in your sub-conscious that hinders the real you?

Weebles Wobble

"Challenges are gifts that force us to search for a new center of gravity. Don't fight them. Just find a different way to stand." —*Oprah Winfrey*

That's good, but I say: find a different way to balance—not just stand— in your search for a new center of gravity, to be flexible, to be ready at any moment to rebalance. Like those Weebles we had when I was a child: "Weebles wobble but they don't fall down!" Challenge comes not once, but sometimes, every day, in different ways. There are big challenges, life-changing challenges, but small challenges too. Every day, in every way, coming at you. Are you ready to balance?

If you don't learn how to stabilize yourself in an environment of constant instability, you'll never be able to balance or stand or get stronger when things are stable . . . not only in your physical body, but in your mind . . . in your spirit. Aware, strong, and learning to balance.

One afternoon, I asked Mark, my husband, if I could get my life coaching certification, and he said, "Linda, you can if you pay for it. I am not paying for any more certifications—you have enough." I was the perpetual self-learner, demolishing books and videos on thinking, mindset, working with people and anything associated with coaching, personal growth, spiritual growth, and training. So I signed up and was excited about getting another dose of experience and teaching. The program started the third week in January. Little did I know that before I could begin life coaching classes, my life would be in even more of an upheaval than it had been the last few years . . . that my life would never be the same, in any shape or form . . .

Anyway, I'm a certified fitness professional and wellness coach, life coach, and my fitness professional certification is through the National Academy of Sports Medicine. We have an integrated program design called the Optimum Performance Training™ model. It's a training concept that incorporates all forms of training as part of a progressive system. I train in flexibility, cardiorespiratory, core, balance, reactive, speed, agility, and resistance. It's based on the fact that in our society, we've never had more physical structural imbalances and susceptibilities to injury as we do now. It's a process that can systematically progresses any client to any goal. And the first place we start is always stabilization. You have to increase muscular endurance and stability while developing optimal communication between your nervous system and muscular system. So you have to learn stability and balance, and when you do, the body is forced to recruit more muscle. And what does more muscle mean? Stronger. Just like life—you become stronger when you learn to balance in an unstable environment. You can't skip the balance and stability, because if you do, you won't get the results you need to get stronger without injury.

Just like surfing. Now, I'm no expert on surfing . . . I just started last year at fifty-one, and this year at fifty-two, I plan on becoming a better surfer. But to do that, I need to learn balance, speed, endurance, and timing. That's what I've been working on this winter. You see, if I can't learn to balance on the board, sitting in the water or standing, I can't surf. I may as well give it up. But when I start learning to balance on my board in an unstable environment, then I've taken the first step to learning to enjoy surfing. You have to learn to balance in an unstable environment. Surfing is a lot like life. It's different every day. Every wave is different, and with each wave you have to learn when and where to catch it and how to balance on your board to stay with it. You have to learn to balance . . . to live in the moment . . . to feel what you're doing . . . to be able to change with each new challenge that comes your way. You have to learn to be flexible, to be aware, to live in the moment, to be aware of your surroundings (sharks, jellyfish, rip currents) . . . I can't even imagine going somewhere with bigger waves. Like life . . . you have to be able to balance, not just stand, in the midst of a world that will throw you new challenge each day. To handle the instability of life, you have to learn to balance, to stabilize.

It starts with movement, eating healthy, thinking positively, being thankful, forgetting the past, living in the present, giving the future to God, loving others, changing yourself, not trying to change the world or your neighbor. It starts with thinking about what you're thinking about, getting up and quitting the self-pity, doing something you've never done before, believing in yourself, loving yourself so you can love others. It starts today.

Time Allotted

"Dost thou love life? Then do not squander time; for that's the stuff life is made of." —Benjamin Franklin

Here I sit on the beach, after the river. Amazed, simply amazed by God's beauty. What a beautiful area we live in. The river and the beach in one day . . . God's grace always takes my breath away. Do we ever take the time to reflect—to stop, as they say, and smell the roses? To sit still in the middle of God's creation and take it in? It's so hard to take it all in, isn't it?

A picture never really captures the real thing. You just can't capture some things. Even a photograph doesn't quite capture the moment . . . the time . . . the view . . . no matter how hard you try. Kind of like time. You can never capture time, as hard as you may try. When I think about my days and time, I'm so thankful that we are even allowed days to enjoy, be thankful for, and live within—and thankful for all they have to offer. Time . . . it can be so elusive. Time . . . it can't be saved, bought, traded, or stalled, and you can't buy it back either. You can't bargain with the clock. It just ticks . . . tick . . . tock . . . But it can be enjoyed, if we really treasure it.

Time is so precious . . . and we never know how much time is allotted to us.

Interesting People

————∞∞∞————

This is why I like hanging on the beach until this time of night, after dark. You meet so many interesting people. I love people. We all have a connection. We wear the same mask . . . we take off the same mask. We all have stories and testimonies. We all live in this complicated, mysterious, beautiful world . . . together . . . alone . . . but we're here with stories, with heart, and with passion.

I met Andrea tonight, and we shared stories . . . standing there, looking over the ocean, sand between my toes, soul surfing with the rhythm of the waves . . . the centered sound of the rhythm of the waves.

Andrea, from Ohio, comes to visit her children and grandchildren in Conway often. She is a widow, twice over. Her first marriage was bliss for five years, and then, as life so suddenly pulls the rug of change from under you, she lost her husband in an accident. But as life would have it, through hope and grace she found another love for thirty-seven years. However, he succumbed to pancreatic cancer. Now, alone again at sixty-five, she puts her hope and love in her grandchildren and children. But the lure of companionship still lingers in the back of her heart. There's still room for love. She told me she hopes to find a friend to have dinners with, to converse with, to hug and hold. . . Don't we all? We shared laughter and hugs . . . stories of love and pain and loss. We had a bond.

People . . . I love them. We're all connected. God connects us. His grace connects us. His love connects us . . . if we want to be connected, that is. And hope is always, always in another sunrise. Sweet Strength . . . sweet dreams . . . hope . . . grace . . . in rhythm with your soul and the waves. Just let it wash over you!

Tears

—⟨⟨⟨⟨⟩⟩⟩⟩—

"Let the rain kiss you. Let the rain beat upon your head with silver liquid drops. Let the rain sing you a lullaby." —*Langston Hughes*

This morning, as I lay in bed not wanting to get up, I started thinking about everything and how thankful I am and how blessed I am. So I decided to jump off the fence and start running. What a great run I had. The rain hitting my face felt so good, because to be able to feel something so refreshing against your skin is good and it's good to *feel*. My heart was pumping hard, reminding me of how alive I am.

Each day is so different when you run on the beach. The elements change so much. It's never the same—like life, never the same from day to day.

As I ran, I thought about how rain refreshes and cleanses. The rain feeds our earth, replenishes our waters, feeds our precious animals, and so much more. I thought about tears; they do the same thing. Tears are another one of God's gifts to us. They renew us and cleanse us. Each tear shed contains so many emotions. Pain, loss, suffering, but joy and laughter too. And they also give us hope. Hope of a better day. It feels good to cry sometimes. Tears and rain are both healing, both bring pain and joy, both remind us that we are still very much alive. Our earth would not survive if it weren't for rain; somehow I think if it weren't for our tears, we wouldn't either.

I have to continue to run the race because I'm not the only one in the race; God has given us a world full of people to encourage, to love, to inspire. That is our purpose. Can I save the world? Heck no—tried that one time (not my job). Can I be all to everyone? No, of course not.

But it really doesn't' matter as long as you join the race and don't sit on the sidelines.

Strength

I love this quote from Martin Luther because it's true. *"It's all about what we can do, not what we can't do."*

In coaching, that's exactly what we work on with clients. We don't look at what's broken, but what's working, and go from there. If we focus on our weaknesses and try to make them stronger, I believe we'll lose the strengths we have. However, if we focus on our strengths, we'll become stronger in all areas, and weaknesses won't even interfere.

We all have weaknesses, and we all have strengths. If we continue to look at the problems, then we become weak and negative, but if we look at the solutions, we become strong and positive. When someone fails at something, the best remedy is to not look at why you failed, but to look at what you learned. You know, focus on what you did right, not what you did wrong.

This isn't to say that it will be easy to just focus on your strengths—it won't. There are challenges in getting stronger at something you're gifted at or love doing. But when you focus on your weaknesses, you just stay stuck. Don't get me wrong—there are times we have to do those things we may be weak at, but it shouldn't be your focus.

The Underdog

"I think that everything I do tends to root for the underdog."
—Judd Apatow

I wonder if other people ever feel like the underdog in life or that they just couldn't get it right no matter what they did or tried. I sure have and did for years, until about nine years ago, when I got serious about the long process of understanding my underdog mentality, which led me to realize it was a wonderful place to begin life. Because having a defeated or underdog attitude is a blessing in disguise. I love pulling for the underdog.

When I was younger, I never had self-confidence; I never believed in myself. I had a lot of fear and self-doubt. Even through the lack of self-confidence and the abundance of self-doubt, I still always, always, always picked myself up and got going again. However, even though I did that—picked myself up after I fell time and time again—I continued to set myself up for failure, consciously and subconsciously. And I was constantly looking for love, as the song goes, in all the wrong places. The constant thoughts reverberating in my mind were all about the negative: fear, self-doubt. Your thoughts can be your demise, your hell, or they can be your freedom to life, success, belief, and peace. Thoughts . . . the most important thing you can do is think about what you're thinking about. And that is how the underdog succeeds; he or she starts thinking about what he or she is thinking about and realizes that his or her own weakness is pure strength!

I believe every one of us struggles at some point in our lives with fear, doubt, and unbelief. It's just that some of us learn not to stay there. You can learn that there is good in every one of those detrimental words, which seem to have lives of their own when we allow them to hold precedence in our thought processes. It's a long journey to understand how you're thinking about your environment, society, and faith; it plays such a conspicuous part of your behavior, actions, and life lived out. Even when you're thinking about—or shall I say believing—your assumptions about what others are thinking, you can get that underdog mentality. Society will even label you that way, if you let it.

As I've worked on changing my thinking, looking at all the struggles as strengths, looking at all the failures as successes, looking at all the trials and pain as growth into a better way of life, looking at every bad thing that happens as good . . . well . . . it has and is still slowly helping me become the person I always dreamed of becoming. Sometimes when we get that slow start out of the gate, it just means that the rest of our lives will be sprints to the finish line. It means we're headed down that road of opportunity, looking forward and never going back! Yep, in everything there is opportunity!

I love my life. I am so thankful for all the hard times. I am so thankful to be able to begin again each time with a clean slate, to do whatever I dream of doing. I understand that I'm the only one capable of holding me back. I'm the only one who makes me feel like an underdog. I understand that I have to take responsibility for my choices, my life, and my feelings. I understand how powerful my thought process is, how powerful believing in myself is, how powerful passion and desire are. I understand the power of choice, the power of thinking about what you're thinking about, the power of love—unconditional love. For me, the unconditional love comes from my savior, Jesus Christ; without that love, I would have never understood any of this. I understand the power of empowering others to do the same in giving back what they've learned. I understand the power of eating right and taking care of your body. There are many things I don't understand; I just put those things in the hand of love and He handles them for me. Because the other thing I understand is that being anxious about anything means I don't trust God or His word.

I am no longer that underdog, but I am so thankful for what I learned as the underdog. Every failure has a seed of success in it.

Jesus chose the underdogs; they became some of the strongest, most courageous, most positive thinkers on earth.

Winning

We all like to win, but if we won all the time, how would we know what winning is like? We wouldn't. And if we won all the time, we couldn't learn, could we? Do we want to win? Absolutely. But let's first know what it is to learn to lose so we can be the victors . . . learn so when we win, we'll know what being a winner really is! Never give in, never quit. Remember you gotta love life with every ounce of passion you can muster up because you're a winner.

You live day to day as a victor, not a victim. Because winners and lessons learned are kind of like victors and victims. When you learn to not be the victim, you automatically become the victor. You become the learner. You become the winner! In the journey of life . . . of winning and learning . . . you can choose to play the victim or the victor.

There are times I really want to be the victim. Truth be known, I played the victim years ago during a divorce, and it felt good for the moment because I received a lot of sympathy—not empathy. But I suffered longer and didn't learn, and I certainly wasn't a winner in that circumstance. It took me down a long path of victimhood. When you're the victim, you can't and don't have power. You become powerless. You become locked in bondage. You're trapped. You can't think. You can't see outside the prison you've made for yourself. You can't see outside the people who love to keep you as the victim because it makes them the winners . . . because they see themselves as taking care of the victim. It can also make them feel like somehow they are stronger . . . better.

I think we all, at some time in our lives, have played the convenient and comforting victim. The victims of our health, our bodies, our minds, our relationships that have gone awry, our external circumstances . . . searching for that person who will agree with us. We seek that person to enable us to become victims . . . but we need to be victors and take responsibility for everything that happens to us because we want to be winners and learners. Victims don't have to take responsibility, and victims can complain and stay immobilized in their circumstances. They don't have to learn or become a winner. They can lean on other winners. We say, "I can't believe this is happening to me . . . even though I know I don't take care of myself—my body and my mind. Why am I sick? I can't believe that person did that to me. We say these things even though we know we live in a fallen world . . . a world where we know statistically that bad things happen. I think if we all learned to let go of the victim mentality, we would without a doubt know what it is to win.

Sweet Strength is being a victor and a learner . . . a winner.

Quitters Never Win

———— ∞∞ ————

I have this sticky, "Quitters never win and winners never quit," one of several affirmations, on my bathroom mirror. I look at it every day as a reminder of what I committed to. A reminder of a decision I made a while back. That I am going for those things my heart desires, and I am not quitting.

Believe me, it's easier to quit. I sure have wanted to at times, but I made a decision, a commitment that no matter how hard it got, no matter what it looked like on the outside, I would never ever quit. I would trust God with my life. I would trust the journey. He has given me a new story. He has given me the choice to live out my dream. That burning desire in my heart that I can't deny. That burning sensation in my gut that says I have to do it despite the odds.

In life, we can't wish it, we can't want it, we can't just think it, we can't just say it, we can't go back and change it, we can't predict the future—so we have to make the decision to just do it, no matter the circumstance, the challenge, the excuses, the heartache, the pain, the fear, or others' opinions. We simply have to make the *decision*, then the *commitment* not to quit. The race is not run until we reach the finish line.

Sweet Strength is crossing the finish line despite the hurdles.

Friendship

———❦———

"There is nothing on this earth more prized than true friendship."
——*Thomas Aquinas*

Today I was reflecting a lot on friends and friendship. I was thinking how important friendship is and how special it is to have people in your life that just bring that sunshine . . . the sunshine you need. Like that good ole vitamin D that's necessary for health. Friends are like that . . . part of our health. I mean, really, without friends, we would begin to atrophy in our bodies, souls, and minds. Friends are the very source of life-giving CPR.

I decided, after a weekend full of love and friendship that I needed to really ponder this bond called friendship and make it take root in the depths of my heart and my soul. Write about it, encourage others in it. But then it occurred to me that it's just another word in the dictionary . . . that you can't really express on paper or put into a seven-letter word exactly how a friend blesses a life, changes a life, gives life to life. Friends . . . can you really put it down on paper in a seven-letter word and think, Yep, that captures a friendship? No . . . you can't. I think the seven-letter word could maybe be captured better with images: a heart . . . two people embraced in a hug . . . a teardrop . . . the wind blowing beneath a wing . . . a cross . . . a kiss and the sunrise. . .

I think about how little I seem to love my friends . . . how little I do for them . . . how much more I want to care for them and tell them how much I love them. Yet, in the midst of living and taking care of my own life, I simply don't. I don't spend the time with them . . . give them the care I would like to . . . the gifts I would love to shower them with . . . the love I would love to walk with them in. It all seems to vanish in a time warp void that I can never get back.

If I could give my friends a life full of happiness all the time and no pain, I wouldn't. If I could give them success with no failure, I wouldn't. If I could give them joy and no tears, I wouldn't . . . because I love them. And if they never had pain, loss, tears, or failure, they wouldn't know what it was to have happiness, joy, success, and strength. They wouldn't know what it was to have peace. And because I love them, I want them to have strength, joy, peace, happiness, and success. But most of all, I want them to love life in the midst of pain.

I want them to know true love and friendship forgiveness and blessings. I want them to make the time to love . . . to feel . . . to be passionate about life . . . to experience . . . to ponder . . . to reflect . . . and to give this life all they have. All they dream about and all they hope for . . . I want it to come true for them. I want them to believe in themselves. I want them to believe in others.

I want them to know there is one who loves them more than they can ever comprehend . . . and who created them for a purpose. Even though we don't see it in completion or always understand it, He has our backs because He will be the best friend we ever had. I hope my friends will take the time to find out who this is. For me, it's God. I've found He is the way, the truth, and the life.

I want my friends to know that when they have doubt . . . when they're in pain . . . there is always a sun that will rise for them. That whatever they're worried about won't last forever. And that they have a home waiting for them when this life is said and done. I want them to know they're appreciated, valued, and loved by me . . . but more than that, they're loved, valued, appreciated by the one who created them.

I wish I could express it to them daily, how much I appreciate them . . . love them . . . and believe in them. But as life continues on a runner's track, I won't. I'll have good intentions, but they'll fall short.

But I hope they know that I carry each of them in my heart daily. And that I really care, even though there are times, I'm sure, that they wonder about that.

They know who they are. I talked with them . . . had breakfast or dinner with them . . . sweat with them . . . hugged them . . . worked out with them . . . worked in the same places as them . . . surfed with them. They worked me out . . . gave me a gift . . . danced with me . . . inspired me. I trained or coached them . . . kissed them . . . drank wine with them . . . rode home with them . . . listened to them . . . went to a concert with them . . . held hands with them . . . last week, this week, this weekend. . . And I will hopefully continue to be with them until I leave this earth.

Sweet Strength is having friends who love you when you aren't even lovable.

Outcasts

"Jesus loved the outcasts. He loves the ones the world just loves to hate."
—*Relient K*

I was thinking about this on my run this morning. I was thinking about my friends who confess they follow Jesus—and of course myself, too, because I follow Jesus. We talk about our enemies or people who rub us the wrong way . . . we judge . . . we hate. But as I recall, Jesus walked with his enemy Judas. He knew Judas was going to betray Him, but chose to love him and teach him as he did the other disciples. He treated all of them the same. He allowed Judas to make his own decisions, and He loved him even at the end.

"May the love of Jesus make you think before you judge." I pray for every day. That I will have Jesus's love, not my love, for my love is weak and inadequate and judging and self-centered, while Jesus's love is unconditional.

> *"Above all, keep loving one another earnestly, since love*
> *covers a multitude of sins"* —*1 Pet. 4:8*

Pearls

> *"Pearls lie not on the seashore. If thou desirest one thou must dive for it."*
> —*Chinese Proverb*

Love, love, love my new home. Wow . . . God sure is good and always supplies. It amazes me how He works. I'm always in awe.

It's like the little girl with the fake pearls and her daddy wants to give her the real pearls, but she has those fake pearls enclosed in that tight fist, not trusting that her daddy won't take them. Or she's not sure about what he's offering—after all, she loves those fake pearls. She's wondering, Is it real? Because these fake pearls. . . Well, they look good and feel good on me. I'm so attached to them.

The dad patiently waits until she decides to give him her fake pearls, which she does because she loves him so . . . and as she opens her hand to reveal the fake pearls, he gently takes them out and places the real pearls in her hand. Wow . . . what a gift it is to trust, to open your hand and receive. Receive the best, not just the good. Just think how many blessings will be offered to us if we take the risk . . . if we move outside our comfort zone . . . if we decide to soar, to believe, to hope. . .

Caged Birds

———⚬⚬⚬———

"Whether you're beaten or pampered, fed the best foods or starved, kept in filth or kept clean, a cage is still a cage." ——*Anne Bishop*

The power it takes to change in the midst of desire of the comfort to stay the same is the battle.

Man, sometimes I want so desperately to change certain things in my life. I hear desperation from my clients who want to change. We all really desire, yearn, hope, wish for change. We want to grow . . . to change these ingrained unhealthy habits, which have become like a well-worn pair of old jeans.

I really do want to change. I want to be different in so many areas. I mean, I think about it all the time. I know I want to change. . . Thus, the long, hard road of change begins . . . the battle between comfort and change. Between what you know and stepping into new territory. Kind of like taking a journey through the wilderness without a compass . . . without knowing where you're going and what destination this journey will take you to.

Why is change so hard? Why are old, tired habits so hard to shake? Because as unhealthy as some of our choices are in areas of health, relationships, and work, it's who we are, it's what we know, and it's a learned behavior that has become our alibi.

We find our freedom locked . . . our change frozen in fear of the unknown . . . because we like the known. We know the known. I don't think we can really have fear in something we don't know . . . but we can have the fear of losing what we know.

I was thinking about this the other day while looking at some beautiful caged pet birds that didn't have their wings clipped and could fly anytime they wanted. But they've been raised in cages. They're locked in their freedom . . . the freedom they don't even know is there . . . because they're so comfortable in the familiar.

We're like those birds when it comes to spreading our wings . . . trying something new . . . changing. We find safety in what we know. We dare not venture in that freedom outside our cages. Oh, we have our excuses. Why risk it? Why do it? Why try to fly away from here, from what we grew up in, what we know to be real? Why fly to places that may stretch me . . . challenge me . . . change me . . . make me reach those places I've dreamed about?

I know every inch of this cage, I know every mark. I know every toy I have. I know the distance between my perches. I know when the lights go down and I'm covered, I sleep. I have the same view every day. I know how far I can spread my wings. I'm fed some good food here. I don't even have to think about what I have to eat. I don't have to think about what I drink. I mean, I get talked to here . . . I get petted here . . . I'm safe here. Why would I leave the comfort of being taken care of? I'm happy. I don't have to learn anything new . . . don't have to . . .

Besides, if I were to fly out of this cage of mine . . . if I decided to spread these strong wings that have become weak . . . if I chose to leave what I know (or the perception of the known that I've learned), I might not find food. There might not be any other friendly birds out there. I might get tired flying long distances. I might not be able to find my way. I might get scared at night. Other birds might sing differently than me. Other birds might not think I'm special. What if my wings don't work right? What if I get lost on the way? And what if freedom comes with a price? No . . . I think I like it where I am. I like being fed, being taken care of, being in my cage, which I know every inch of. Maybe tomorrow I'll spread my wings and fly out of this cage. Maybe tomorrow . . . but today, I like this comfort.

Sweet Strength is flying into the journey of dreams with no fear.

Gray Skies

——— ⌘ ———

Foggy but beautiful morning. I've been out here since six fifteen . . . and no people, no noise but the breaking of the waves. Solitude is a friend in the dark before the dawn. And ah . . . even in the fog, the light comes in. It may not be the bright orange sun rising up in the blue sky over the blue water, but even in the gray hues of the water, sand, sandpipers, and seagulls—which all blend together on this Thursday morning—are separated through the artistry of white foam-topped waves, shells that lie broken on the shore, and the white feathers of the pipers and gulls. Gray skies hiding the reflection of the sun. The sun, which always paints color in the morning landscape. But the gray skies don't last forever. So enjoy the gift in the gray, foggy light because the color is coming. The light is coming and it will have magnificent, brilliant color.

Sweet Strength is peace in the gray.

Feels Good On The Inside

——— ⌘ ———

My heart and spirit seem as if they're in complete rhythm with the sights, the sounds and the feel of the morning delight . . . made alive by the sunrise, the crashing waves on the shore, the winter wind tantalizing my face. It makes you long for the beauty in the day. The opportunity. The life given. The gift of family and friends. To feel joy on the inside and peace in your spirit, not to just *look* like you have peace and happiness.

We have to learn to create a life that is good and feels good on the inside . . . not one that just looks good on the outside. We are so guilty of that in society. I listen to and see it all the time. People who look like they have it all; on the outside, they look happy. They look like they've achieved it all. But they're not feeling so good on the inside. They are miserable under the mask.

Don't get fooled into thinking the next thing will make you internally happy—the next car, the next relationship, the next house, more money, better grades, the next competition, losing weight, getting in shape. None of these things matter unless you can find the peace and the rhythm of your heart and spirit on the inside.

Bucket List

"What you get by achieving your goals is not as important as what you become by achieving your goals." — Zig Ziglar

Since moving to Mount Pleasant, South Carolina, there have been lots of changes. One is I hired a coach, Tres Bennett, to get me ready to enter my first National Physique Committee (NPC) Masters Figure Contest. It has been on my bucket list. I love stepping out of my comfort zone. It grows me, stretches me, and makes me stronger. I am looking forward to the challenge.

Working out with weights, eating healthy, and staying positive have empowered me to handle all of the changes that have occurred in my life. People ask me why I decided to do a contest at fifty-three. These are a few of the reasons:

1. I believe there is one purpose of my life: to maximize the gifts that God has given me. To inspire, encourage, empower, and challenge others to maximize their gifts so they can believe in themselves, love themselves so they can love others, and challenge themselves to never give up hope or settle.

2. I believe I can encourage women and men to take care of their bodies. To start moving their bodies and eating healthier. If I can inspire just one person by entering this contest at fifty-three, I have lived my purpose.

3. When I face my fears and challenges, when I give to others, when I take responsibility for my life and my attitude toward it, and when I get out of my comfort zone, I grow stronger, wiser, better, and can give to others on a higher level of awareness.

4. The contest keeps me accountable: to not only talk but live what I preach in my business.

5. If I'm strong mentally and physically, then when the rug gets pulled from under my feet, I am more apt to stand back up. If I'm not strong physically and mentally, when challenges happen, it's harder for me to get back up.

6. I believe it is our obligation to keep ourselves as strong as we can, both physically and mentally. If we don't take care of the one body, mind, and spirit we've been given . . . nothing else matters.

7. I believe that age doesn't matter. It's what you do with the time given to you. I believe that age is just a number. It's what is in your heart that matters. I believe there is no such thing as a limit because of age. I believe that whatever is in your heart—your desire, your dream—whether you are young or old, you need to go after it. If not now, when?

We take every day for granted. Mark went for a run in the after-noon, never suspecting it would be his last day on this earth. I certainly didn't think Mark would be gone that Monday afternoon. My sister-in-law didn't think it would be her last day either when she went to the cabin for the weekend, waiting on my brother to get there on Friday ... She never made it to Friday. Live each day as if it's your last. Love others and tell them how much you love them. I am optimistic, but I also know how real death is. Make sure when you say goodbye, you say, "I love you." Life is short. Just a breath . . . a heartbeat away. . . So live it to the fullest, in love. Move on, extend forgiveness, and share a hug, a smile, a word of encouragement.

Which is it Linda?

"Self-Pity is easily the most destructive of non-pharmaceutical narcotics it is addictive gives momentary pleasure and separates the victim from reality." —John W. Gardner

The other morning, I was feeling a little self-pity coming on from some stress I was experiencing from focusing on memories. What the heck? So I got out of the house for a little run.

Well, it was high tide, so my run was in the soft sand . . . a little resistance. A little harder run that morning. Sometimes we need some resistance in our lives to shake us back to reality. A hard run in the resistance of the sand was good for my self-pity. I had to work a little harder to get my feet up and had to watch my feet as I ran so I wouldn't twist my ankle on the uneven sandy path. But the harder I worked, the better I began to feel.

I started coaching myself, saying, "What are you feeling sorry for yourself for? What do you want from life? How badly do you want it? Are you willing to wallow in the past or grab the awesome future God has? Which is it, Linda? Where do you want to stay? Where would you be without these thoughts? What would you be doing differently? What in the world . . . look at where you are. Look at what you're able to do. Look at what you've accomplished. You didn't get here by self-pity . . . by looking back. Look what God has provided for you." Then the graciousness of life started creeping back in my heart. The thankfulness I have that I'm alive. That my health is great. That I'm able to breathe; run; walk; hear this ocean; see this ocean, this sunrise, this high tide, these birds. The thankfulness I feel for having a wonderful family and awesome friends who love me. For the work, Sweet Strength, which I love and have a passion for. For my ability to empower others. I am so grateful that I have a God who loves me so much that He offers me the opportunity to see, to feel, to hear, to know the love of people and nature. He gives me the gift of choosing to appreciate it and be thankful for it all. He gives me the freedom to choose my attitude about life. He allows me to choose to live life or to die in life.

Well, you just can't be grateful and have self-pity at the same time. And feeling sorry for myself has never gotten me to exercise more, eat better, have less stress and more peace, make one extra dollar more, make more friends, or be better able to give to others. Self-pity is the locked door of a prison cell, keeping you from the freedom of thankfulness and the love of life.

See Beyond

"Life is all about how we see things." —*Unknown*

Isn't this the truth? I sure have had to change my perspective on a lot in life. I mean, instead of rain and cold walking on the beach this morning, I see beauty and an opportunity to meditate. I have this beach all to myself except for a paddle boarder, who saw today as a great day to get in the water. Perspective. . . I've definitely had to make a choice to see the other side . . . to look beyond and climb over the walls I'd constructed. I had to understand that there was a way to climb over . . . that I wasn't confined by the imaginary walls I'd built. It was all about how I perceived it.

I've had to look beyond the mold that others placed me in. I had to understand that my mold was my own, not what others made for me. I learned I could shape my own mold to fit the unique person that God made me. It didn't have to be like others or look like others.

I've had to look at pain as growth. I've had to choose to see the rose instead of the thorn. I've had to look at death as life. Financial loss as gain. Failure as success. A shattered heart as one that can be whole again. I've had to see peace in the midst of turmoil. See fear as an opportunity to gain courage. Be able to find the positive in what others think is negative. I've had to come to peace with those painful experiences from my past and realize it was all part of the greater plan and purpose of my life: to help others through theirs.

Yep . . . perspective. . . Being able to see beyond my circumstances has given me the opportunity to embrace life in a whole new light.

Today is Your Day

This is the day you live in. Don't walk your life living in memories of the past . . . living in the what ifs. Are the same things happening right now that were happening yesterday or last month or last year? Nope . . . because it's the past. Can you change any of it? How about tomorrow . . . can you be absolutely sure of how tomorrow is going to turn out? No. So why be anxious for tomorrow? Today is your day.

Celebrating Jesus

—⊸⊷—

Celebrating Jesus today. I love Him. He is my Sweet Strength. Gosh I love that man.

My Jesus loves everyone; we don't—we have conditions to our love. So it's difficult for us to not project those conditions onto others because we only see through our eyes and hearts. Our hearts are broken, and our eyes can't see the whole picture. Yet, unconditional love comes from Him. Oh, how I long to love others like that! But I fall so short. His grace is difficult to understand because we don't understand how to live under its rule or give it to others.

Love and grace and the faith to believe in love and grace in a world that needs them both so desperately . . . that's Sweet Strength.

Beauty

—⊸⊷—

"Accept Yourself, Love Yourself." — *Chanel Iman*

Beauty . . . what is beauty? What is it to love yourself and your body? My passion is empowering women to love themselves as unique individuals and to help them see clearly through the muddy waters that have clouded their perceptions of who they are. When we start loving ourselves and our bodies, then and only then can we start the process of wellness and health. There are several factors that affect the presence of lack of self-love: environment, society, friends, and even family.

When I start a coaching session, I usually ask my client if she can name five things she loves about her body, five things she loves about herself, and five things she's most satisfied with in her life. Most of the time, they won't be able to name one thing—once in a while they'll name one or two things. It makes me so sad. In fact, it breaks my heart.

It's okay to love yourself. It's okay to like yourself. It's okay. In fact, that's how you'll get on the right track to wellness. It's okay to dream and dream big. It's okay to change your life and your thinking. And it's okay if others don't like you or the way you are. It's okay if others don't believe your dreams can happen. It's okay if they think you're crazy for doing something you've always wanted to do. We weren't created to be molded into someone else. We are all unique. I certainly don't fit a pattern, and I don't or won't mold myself into someone else's pattern. I'm not here to please anyone else; however, I am here to love and respect them.

No one really knows what another person needs. Only you know what you need. You just can't see it sometimes because you've allowed too many people, or society, to label you. You know . . . fat, thin, ugly, lazy, dumb, uneducated, etc.

Self-limiting beliefs are the worst beliefs a person can have. That thinking is your worst enemy. No one is better than you or smarter than you; they've just chosen to get rid of self-limiting beliefs. You can accomplish any goal you set your beliefs upon as long as you are motivated and willing to work hard. Willing to learn from any mistakes, willing to have a positive attitude—a can-do attitude.

The Face Plant

———⊶∞⊷———

We are going to fall, aren't we? I mean, we'll do and say some stupid things in our lives. Why, we can even sabotage our own sidewalk with holes. We let others place obstacles in our paths for us to trip over. When we do this, we let others define our fall. We will, at some point, fall on our faces. Life has a way of tripping us up sometimes and throwing us to the ground face-first. The old face-plant. It can be bad, that fall.

But the importance lies in how we handle our lives after the fall. Do we wallow in it? Do we replay it in our heads over and over—face down in the dirt? Do we let it defeat us? Do we stay with our faces planted in the ground so long that it becomes hard to distinguish between the imprint we made in the ground and us? What's the saying . . . fall down eight times and get up nine. Don't let the fall define you. It's your choice. Define the fall. Get up! Get up again and again and again. Brush the dirt off, learn from the fall, and then hold your head up high and get moving. Maybe next time the fall won't be so hard. Because you will get tripped up again in life, and you will fall. Until you decide and learn how to define the fall, the fall will define you.

Sweet Strength is defining my life as stronger, better, and wiser after the fall.

Starting Over

This morning, as I was getting ready for work, I was thinking about change. I was thinking about the opportunities we're given to change our lives around. How God gives us the choice to start over every day. It doesn't matter how old you are. It doesn't matter what you have or have not done. It doesn't matter if you feel trapped or stuck. You always have the opportunity to change your life. Even if you can't change your circumstance or your surroundings, you can change yourself in the midst of those circumstance or surroundings. You can change your mind—your attitude and perspective—about it.

Once a word is said, once you have eaten too much and unhealthy, once a wrong decision is made and followed through with, once an accident happens—a death, an illness, a natural disaster, whatever it is. . . It's in the past. We can't change it, no matter how badly we may want to. It's not going to happen . . . and sitting around thinking about it and wishing it were different doesn't change it or you. But the hope is that we can change ourselves and turn those past experiences into positive change, and start on the road to having a great life with a new us.

If change is not possible, if starting over each day is not possible, if changing who you are as a person is not possible, we may as well give up and quit life. I have wanted desperately to change so many of my circumstances. I've wanted to reverse so many bad decisions. I've wanted to change others. However, I found that I can change *me*; I can change my attitude about any situation. I can change my life and how I choose to live my life.

I think the most exciting thing God offers us is change. I think the most exhilarating hope we have is the opportunity to change ourselves and our lives at any given second, minute, hour, day . . . It's never too late.

Sweet Strength is always changing, always growing, and always thanking God for the ability to do so.

Make the Choice to Win

⸎

"Make the choice to win before you begin."
My friend Diane posted this online.

It was such an inspiration to me to know that she made the choice to win before she even stepped on that treadmill. She's writing her new story. I needed to see Sweet Strength from another perspective today . . . from a different story.

My business's name, Sweet Strength, has so many interpretations for me. The name itself has redirected any emotional thoughts to a story I can't change to a story I can change. A new story. Because, you see, if we're emotionally tied to an old story about who we were or where we were in that particular season of our lives, then we can't create a new story. The truth is, as long as we live in our old story, we'll never be able to see the vision that God has for our new story.

That name, Sweet Strength, has carried me and given me strength when I didn't have it. I have my struggles too, just like everyone else does. I've been in a bad place for the past week. I am optimistic, hopeful, strong, and I never quit. But sometimes, when I'm being emotionally pulled to the negative—to the old story—I need a reminder that it's about the new story. That our lives are about moving forward, expanding, and growing. Learning about how to write our own stories and how to avoid getting stuck in our old stories. Our lives are about how our stories develop into new ones. We are ever expanding and we are ever moving forward and our lives are forever changing. Let's change with them. Let's learn how to make ours the most interesting, adventurous, thrilling story we could ever read. Let's make our story so fulfilling that we don't want to put it down. It draws us back again and again. Each page takes us to a more adventurous place.

God always provides a reminder. Maybe He has put the reminder in front of us to say: What changes in our thinking, our attitudes, our moods, our environments, our choices must take place so we can walk into our new story? A reminder that we need to commit to win, to not staying in our old story, rereading the same pages again and again. No, let's commit to rewriting our new story . . . a bestseller!

Self-Image

"Low self-esteem is like driving through life with your hand break on."
— *Maxwell Maltz*

In my coaching and personal training, we talk a lot about how you view yourself. Your self-image.

I mean, you can go on diet after diet and lose that weight. You can be successful, loving, and giving. You can have the best physique you've ever had, but until you accept yourself as you are today or see yourself as beautiful, one of a kind, you'll never really enjoy what you've worked so hard to gain . . . because you will always, in your mind's view, think it's the great physique that makes you beautiful . . . the ten pounds lost that makes you beautiful . . . the success that makes you beautiful . . . the gorgeous body that makes you beautiful . . . the act of giving your heart away that makes you beautiful . . . the act of serving others that makes you beautiful . . .

You are beautiful because you are. You are beautiful because you were created to be unique . . . just as you are. You are beautiful if you've never accomplished any of the above. You are also loved by the Creator, just as you are. He knows you're beautiful. He sculpted you.

Anyway . . . in coaching, I always start with self-image . . . with loving your mind, body, and spirit just as you are today, where you are today. Because when you see yourself as beautiful . . . well . . . the weight loss, the strong physique, the success will come. They will be the fruits of knowing you are beautiful and that you don't have to strive to be like anyone else. Comparison is one of your worst enemies because you are you and there is no other. No one can take your place. Once you see yourself as beautiful, you will strive to take care of yourself and be your best . . . just as you would want for your beautiful best friend.

Find the Gold

It's a beautiful day in the neighborhood! Yes, we've been graced with the adventure of living another day.

May our adventures begin with looking for the treasure in this day instead of the trash. It's easier to see the trash than it is to see the gold in the day that's offered. That's why you have to train your mind to find the gold.

"Anyone can find the dirt in someone. Be the one that finds the gold" (Prov. 11:27).

Do Not Be Anxious

There aren't many things in my life that this morning sunrise, on this sandy beach, doesn't heal in my soul. It doesn't matter how anxious I may be about growing my business, preparing for my next contest, praying for someone, my clients' progress, my mom or my son, or the many other daily stresses that try to take over my mind. When I make it to this beach and I watch that magnificent sun rise over the beautiful sea, all is well with my soul.

You begin to understand the rhythm of life through the waves' ebb and flow on the shore. You begin to understand that being anxious about your life or others disrupts the rhythm. Because when we're anxious or feel distracted, stressed, overwhelmed, or fearful, we become our problem instead of our solution. We block ourselves. We limit ourselves. When we become anxious and stressed, we're unable to use one of our most fascinating gifts: our creativity. Creativity that leads to possibilities beyond the limits we have so easily placed in our minds and hearts.

So I stand here facing another day of anxious thoughts and limits, but the Creator reminds me through His creation of this beautiful sunrise, whispering ever so loudly, "Do not be anxious for anything, but through prayer, petition, and thanksgiving, give your request to me and I will give you a peace that transcends all comprehension. Now all is well with my soul.

Color Outside The Lines

It's kind of like coloring within the lines: living your life within the parameters of others' limitations of you . . . living with a past that is, well, past . . . black-and-white living, where gray isn't a part of the carton of Crayola crayons, because you only see two colors in the box. There's more than black and white in the spectrum of color. Nothing in life is written in stone . . . but everything in life is written on a chalkboard with one hand holding the giant eraser and chalk, ready to erase and rewrite your story again . . . and again.

Break the rules . . . not the law. Color outside the lines with every color. And keep the faith that your experiences can be rewritten again and again. Nope, nothing in this life is written in stone, so go and live out loud . . . outside of the stone, using the whole box of crayons. Color your world and let the big guy keep the eraser.

Off the Path

"I'm not sure who discovered water—but I'm quite sure it wasn't a fish." —Marshall McCluhan

It was a beautiful morning reflecting on this magnificent little place of peace for me. I really had some great wake-up moments. I just love it when something happens in my life that shakes me out of my comfortable illusion. I mean, at first you see it as pain, as something that's taking you off your path. But the reality is that the pain, the hurt, never took you off your path. It just cleared the way to what you really want in life. Sometimes we need to understand that the challenges and pain are just a wake-up call to say we're on the right path. It's just removing the obstacles that you couldn't or didn't want to see.

Stay on your path and believe that the difficult is really a clearing for your best, which is coming.

Stuck In Traffic

Okay . . . what do you do when you're stuck on the Ravenel Bridge trying to get to the gym, thinking, Oh no . . . I'm going to be late?

Well, you have a couple of choices. You can get mad and you can get stressed . . . or you can pop an inspirational CD in to get motivated for the day and learn something about patience.

How do we learn about patience anyway? We learn about patience when we're put in a situation where we have no other choice but to be patient. In life, there is no better way to grow, learn, get stronger, become better than to be in situations where you're given no choice but to get stronger and better. Unless you choose to get bitter and angry, and play the blame-everyone-and-everything game. The choice is always yours.

Choose to become better, take responsibility for your attitude and reactions. It makes life so much richer and sweeter.

Worry

"What worries you, masters you." —*Haddon W. Robinson*

What are you worrying about? Has your worrying ever . . . *ever* changed anything at all? Has it ever brought you the answer you desire? Has it ever given you hope? Has it ever made you healthier?

What can you actually change about what you're worrying about? Your thought process about it. You can't be thankful and worry at the same time.

I'm worry-free because I pray for what I am thankful for.

Story

"The world is not made of atoms. The world is made of stories."
—*Muriel Ruykeser*

Here's what I believe . . . every one of us has a story to tell . . . every one of us has a journey to share . . . every one of us can learn from anyone else Every one of our stories can help someone. Maybe not everyone, but someone and that someone needs to hear your story. God waste nothing not our struggles, our sufferings, our challenges, our joys, our triumphs, or our successes. We are what we share as human beings. . .we are really all the same in our individual unique diversity . . . we hurt . . .

we feel pain . . . we long for love and to be loved . . . we seek pleasure . . . we run from fear . . . we all die . . . and our stories . . . connect us . . . heart to heart. Our stories affect each and every one of us . . . whether you choose to write your story or live it. Because as long as we are in the same time in history . . . our stories . . . written or lived out . . . make the circle of life . . . continue around and around . . . as the stories of triumph and victory . . . heal the heart of another.

Open Your Hands

It's a great day to be alive. Captured my buddy, dolphin, playing this morning at sunrise. Love my morning on the beach. There's no other place I'd rather be. It's my piece of peace, my place to surrender all so I can receive all.

Open your hands to receive. Loosen your grip on the old . . . let it go . . . and you may be surprised what you'll be given. The gift of the giver is always more than you could possibly imagine. You just have to be willing to receive and believe it's possible.

Prayer. . . Strength

You certainly don't get stronger by easy. Nothing in life comes easily, and though we don't always want or desire those painful surprises in our lives, they are exactly what make us stronger. And whether they're caused by our own choices or uncontrollable circumstances, they are part of who we are and who we are becoming . . . part of our lives. God will use them to make you stronger. You just have to stop wanting the easy. Stop praying for easy and start praying for strength to get through the day . . . through the challenges . . . because we never know what a day will bring. If your perspective is clear, you'll be stronger by the end of the day . . . stronger than you were yesterday.

So Thankful

We love because He first loved us. So thankful.

Cheers to the unfathomable grace given each and every day. May we embrace its savoring beauty in the day of a new sunrise on the horizon.

You Are Not Alone

"The fact you feel alone means you are not alone; we all feel alone together sometimes." —— *Ken Poirot*

That early morning, before light, there were darkness, despair, defeat, and thoughts of death lingering in the hearts of the faithful. But then the sun began to rise. And with this new dawn . . . this new day . . . this new sunrise . . . came the best miracle of all: life and love that never ends. The darkness had turned into the bright grace of the new sunrise . . . the new day. Despair had become hope. Defeat was now victory. And the pending sting of death was gone. It lost its grip when life and love stood in the grace of that one *son* that rose.

You are not alone. And in the beauty of this sunrise . . . this new day . . . there is hope. It will get better if you believe. You are alive for a greater plan. You have a purpose. You are special . . . gifted and talented in ways others are not. You are beautiful and, most importantly, you are loved.

Nope Can't Earn It

"God's economy is: Grace is free. Sin is expensive. Love is priceless."[6]

Isn't this the truth. Wow . . . It's so hard to accept grace, isn't it? We want to work for it so hard because we know if we work hard for something, we'll attain it. But you can't earn it. We sure do want to earn it. I mean, if we can earn it, then we know how to get it. You can't work for it, but we try. You can't perform for it, but we like performance and to be measured by that performance. But grace doesn't have a measuring stick. You can't do enough good deeds for it, but we like good deeds because they make us feel and look good. You can't sin enough to destroy it, but we sure do want others' sins to keep them from receiving it . . . the grace of Jesus.

---

6 Sabiny Pierrevil, *Ten Powerful Secrets to Leading a Much Happier and Fulfilled Life* (Bloomington, IN: Xlibris, 2014),

It's hard to accept . . . hard to live by. I sure do struggle with it, and somehow I don't think I'm alone in that. We Americans . . . if we could only accept His grace, then maybe we could learn how to give it and live it.

Hearts of Understanding

"It's always in the reflection of the sun that we find the reflection of ourselves. The light lives in us and the light reflects from us when we embrace the rising of the sun." —Linda McDandel, Sweet Strength

And the sun rose again in the hearts of those looking for a new understanding of who they are and who they could become. The longing for a better way is always found in the grace of the sun peaking over the horizon shouting it's a new dawn, it's a new day, and it's a new way. Its glory echoing the confidence of faith of those dreams not yet seen.

I am happy and grateful for the peace, reflection, and beauty that another day. Here on this piece of paradise that God hands us This is where opportunity and hope live in another day of a heartbeat. The heart beat that beats in sync with the pulse of life. Let us rejoice we are alive to seize the day.

Roller Coaster

———✦———

"Sometimes it's good to get off the merry-go-round and get on the roller coaster instead." ——*Gareth Pugh*

I just booked our ride on the roller coaster. That's where our stories will come alive.

Why Not?

———✦———

You hold the pen to your story. Don't live life in the unconscious comfortable habits or the repetitive thought pattern of "what if." Instead, live life with intentional choices that make a difference and the thought pattern of "why not?" Why not make a change for the better? Why not start today with a new perspective? *Why not?*

Try One More Time

———✦———

It's warm today. The clouds gave in to the sun . . . and it is absolutely without a shadow of a doubt wonderful to be alive.

It never ceases to amaze me how quickly the sun rises and sky, within minutes, changes to create different scenery over the magnetic ocean, which draws me into its beauty. I love how the sun has this indomitable will to shine through the clouds, and today it won. It keeps trying one more time.

What does it take for a person to win? The will? The desire? The passion? Determination? What value . . . what quality . . . what strength do people have as resources to help them win? Could it be simply trying one more time, because you can?

Fitted Lens

To see through my eyes . . . to see through a loved one's eyes . . . to see through our animals' eyes. . .

But I'll never see through another's eyes. My perspective on life opened this morning . . . the gifts of my specially fitted lens on the world opened.

I wonder what my view will be today.

Personal Responsibility

"I have come to believe that caring for myself is not self indulgent. Caring for myself is an act of survival." —*Audre Lorde*

I've known what it's like to not care for myself, and the roller coaster ride associated with that. I understand now what it's like to care for myself, and it certainly has a better outcome all around.

One result was it launched my career of empowering others to take care of themselves. That's what positive experiences do. They lead us to want to share with others what we experienced.

Is that to say I wake up every day excited to work out or optimistic or strong? No, but it does mean I can handle those difficult times much better, and I recover faster.

I care about myself and others in my life, and if I take and make the time to care for myself, then I can take and make the time to love others a little better. An investment that reaps lots of dividends.

Not only do I see self-care as survival . . . I see it as my personal responsibility.

Be Like Water

"Be like water making its way through cracks. Do not be assertive, but adjust to the object, and you shall find a way around or through it. If nothing within you stays rigid, outward things will disclose themselves."
—*Bruce Lee*

I like that quote. It's so true . . . in sports . . . in life . . . in relationships. If you adjust and not fight through, you'll find that it's much easier to learn and grow. It's like Brian was teaching me in boxing yesterday. You can be powerful—in fact, more powerful—if you're not rigid. Breathe and feel it. The same with surfing: go with it. Get the feel of it. Let your body move naturally with the waves. The more you fight things, the tenser you are and the harder they become. It's the same in relationships and in life.

Become like water . . . adjust . . . flow. I like that . . . because when you can be fluid, everything else changes around you and suddenly you can see more clearly.

Discovery

"The greatest obstacle to discovery is not ignorance it is the illusion of knowledge." — Daniel J. Boorstin

Made it home in time to share dinner with another friend and witness this magnificent sunset.

You know . . . life is ever-changing, and learning to change with it makes for an incredible and unforgettable journey. I love my friends. I love the uniqueness and the beauty, the talents, and the gifts each one offers to the world. As I have changed and grown through my life experiences, I've come to embrace the vulnerability that comes with the special gift of friendship. I believe that everyone we meet—whether for a moment, a season, or a lifetime—are in our lives for a purpose bigger than we will ever realize while on earth. I thank God for the gift of friendship.

I also thank God for the ability to embrace change no matter the circumstances. I was talking to my son tonight about this. I was thinking about those moments in life that change you. The moments that you know in your gut that things will never be the same. That *you* will never be the same. And you know that in your heart and soul, you understand that all is well with it and that somehow you'll become better because of it. You'll discover things about yourself that you never knew.

For instance, I didn't realize how much I enjoy traveling by my-self—getting in the car and driving or on a plane and flying—because I'd never done it. I'd always had a companion. But until life forces you in those unknown places . . . until you embrace the change . . . until you decide to grow in it . . . you'll never know how God will work and bless you through the pain. Joy always comes when you allow it. Joy comes with discovery.

Discovery . . . take the time to know who you are, what you love, and what you have the capacity to become. God works through your tangled thread of cross-stitch to create a beautiful needlepoint master-piece of your purpose, passion, and dreams. Don't get tangled up in the threads and lose perspective of the completed masterpiece. Let the different colored threads and needle weave through the canvas cloth of the unknown to produce the Creator's view of the known . . . because he sees the completed mastery . . . the journey where the story begins with needle and the tangled web of different threads beneath. But when viewed from the top, it's a beautiful needlepoint masterpiece.

Clouds

Some broken clouds over Sullivan's Island this morning. I captured some pictures during my walk as I took a journey through my thoughts. I noticed afterward that one formation looked like a shark in the clouds. Mark the Shark, with me this morning. It made me smile.

Friday I'll head to Columbia for my figure competition at the Palmetto Classic. It's nice to know I'll have the Shark pulling for me.

My thoughts take me to hard places . . . easy places . . . truthful places . . . and some places that are broken like the clouds, but are always waiting and longing for the sun. Because in the midst of the cloudy thoughts comes clarity if you ask yourself the right questions. Solutions are always in the questions. The sun is always shining through the questions.

Instead of waiting for the right answer, seek the right question.

Emotions

─────❊❊❊─────

"All emotions are pure which gather you and lift you up; that emotion is impure which seizes only one side of your being and so distorts you."
——Rainer Maria Rilk)

I was thinking this morning about emotions and the impact they have on our decisions. Especially when we let them dominate us. Rule over us. Imprison us. You know . . . confine us.

I like to remind my clients that emotions are like visitors, which come and go. Some stay longer than others. Some are lots of fun and give us energy. Some drain our energy. Some aren't welcome, but come anyway. Some are a surprise, unexpected. But there's one visitor that can be dangerous and forceful . . .

There is a visitor, a force that plays inside and is bigger and more dangerous than the rest. In fact, it sways our hearts and every decision. Our decisions of how we treat one another. How we view the world.

How we view ourselves and how we decide to live our lives. It has a name and a strong presence. It is called fear.

Fear causes us to run . . . to hate . . . to contest . . . to fight . . . to retreat . . . to lose . . . to become dogmatic . . . to become judgmental . . . to become unfocused or intensely focused on the wrong things . . . to deny our own beauty . . . to sabotage our own lives . . . to become prideful, angry, hateful, unforgiving. I have found fear to be the great enemy of my life.

Fear sends us to the hospital. Fear kills dreams and hope. The fear of death . . . of the unknown . . . not understanding life. The fear of love . . . of pain . . . of who we may become or who we will never become. The fear of aging . . . of loss . . . of not doing what's right . . . of not holding tradition. The fear of monsters and the dark.

I've experienced fear. I hate fear because I understand it is an enemy, and it rears its ugly head more than I desire.

But fear is an indicator that something is not quite right. It's a natural response to both real and imagined danger. It's an important survival mechanism. The problem is when we let the visitor become dangerous in our imagination. When our imagination runs away from us, showing us all the disastrous things that could happen, we give all our energy and power to the fear.

But we are told perfect love drives out fear.

My hope is that we will experience and open the door to perfect love and understand that FEAR is False Evidence Appearing Real.

Circle of Life

———∞∞∞———

"Only by giving are you able to receive more than you already have."
—*Jim Rohn*

My night was just made. A friend stopped by with cut flowers. I love fresh flowers . . . fresh flowers . . . did I mention I love fresh flowers.

You know what's wild, I was at the store earlier buying flowers for a friend who is in the hospital and the cashier was remarking how pretty the flowers were.

She said, I see you are buying yourself some flowers, and I said actually taking them to a friend. We both said how much we love getting flowers. I said, I love them, but I haven't gotten them in a long time. So, a friend came by and surprised me with flowers just now.

And that's how it works. You give and receive . . . give and receive . . . the circle of life. Gotta love living and giving.

God never ceases to amaze me with His love. He always knows our hearts desires. And that's how He works.

Persistence

———∞∞∞———

"Energy and persistence conquer all things."
—*Benjamin Franklin*

Good Saturday Morning! What a great sunrise this morning. I just cannot express into words the happiness that fills my heart when I watch the morning dusk turn to dawn and then into day. The progression is like watching a morning glory opening in its nature induced time to drink in the day. Its grace rising in our soul with purpose pumping life through our veins with each heart beat we feel. We are alive. We are co-creators in the day with the one who created us in His image. There is work to be done. There is a streaming persistence that lies beneath the rocky circumstances that would try to muddy the vison of our dreams. This persistence gives fire to the passion that would be otherwise smothered by failure and loss. Persistence is a character enhanced fuel that guide the senses through the dark tunnel of indecision, doubt and fear. Persistence will carry you over the threshold of comfortable into the knowledge of faith. Persistence.

Show Up

"Show up in every single moment like you are meant to be there."
—*Marie Forleo*

I just keep showing up every single day. Someone said to me, you take awesome pictures, you should be a photographer. But, you see. It's not that I am a good photographer, the picture is always there. The sunrises every day. I just simply show up every day to wait for it. Some days its hidden, some days are cold, some days it's raining, some days its high tide, some days' low tide … just like life . . . but, I show up anyway…because the benefits out way the excuses not to. Anyone could take the pictures I take. I take them with my phone. All they have to do is show up and wait and God does the rest.

Calmness of Mind

"Calmness of mind is one of the beautiful jewels of wisdom. It is the result of long and patient effort in self-control. Its presence is an indication of ripened experience, and of a more than ordinary knowledge of the laws and operations of thought." —— James Allen

Calmness and peace, I find, is found within the spirit of thought that echo's in the depth of the soul. Peace we long for peace. We long to find the calm within the storm. The ocean this morning resonated these very sentiments that I was meditating on. The ocean was like soft moving water pouring gently on the shore. Now we both know how quickly that can change. The ocean can become rough and treacherous. But deep beneath the ocean is always a calm. A steadiness. A strong and steady current of calm. Calm in the midst of the storm.

You can have it. You can have peace in the center of chaos. You just have to see beyond your circumstances into the strength that you have been given through the spirit of your thoughts.

Beyond The Reality That Limits

———— ∞∞∞ ————

"There is no planet, sun, or star that could hold you, but you knew what you are." —*Ralph Waldo Emerson*

Well Good Morning! It is indeed a beautiful morning in the neighborhood. I was so elated to see the sun this morning. I headed down quickly after my am cardio with my jacket bundled up tightly around me, my sweat drenched body from the gym drying underneath the thermal shirt I had donned this morning as I ran out the door. What the cardio does to get the feel good endorphins running around in my mind the beach at sunrise does to my soul. It makes me feel alive and hopeful. It helps me to understand my purpose in a world that tends to regulate your purpose. As, I sip on my heated coffee writing, praying, and listening. My thoughts of worry and doubt disappearing with each written word of thanksgiving and each sip of coffee warming my breath. I understand that the way to dispel circumstances beyond my control is to be thankful for those things in which I can control . . . my prayer life, my thoughts, and how I act upon them. I understand that God has given me everything I need to uncover my purpose in this life. I understand that God has also given me a mind, a body, others in community to help me become successful. That he has given me responsibility to become a victor instead of a victim of my circumstances. I understand that there is a world that I cannot see that is so much more infinite and mysterious than the world I place my senses around. I understand on that piece of sand beneath my feet that there is more to me to you than we will ever comprehend in the reality of our environment. We have to learn to get beyond the reality that limits our imagination and we have to see beyond our environment in order to live the life we have been given. We can't get wrapped up in the challenges and circumstances we cannot control, but we need to open ourselves to those infinite possibilities that we cannot see. We are given everything we need to be everything we need to be. How we choose to use it is up to us. We just have to listen to that small still voice that is guiding us and use the strength within to get us there.

Seasons

'When seasons shift, even the subtle beginning, the scent of a promised change, I feel something stir inside me. Hopefulness? Gratitude? Openness? Whatever it is it's welcome." —Kristian Armstrong

It's rainy here in my neighborhood, Mount Pleasant. My little friends in the picture are ready to see summer fun.

Another new season is almost upon us. It seems the seasons pass so quickly . . . except those for which we only feel apathy or dislike!

Some enjoy winter more . . . even though I can't imagine that at all. Some favor spring, some opt for fall, and like me, some thrive and survive in the summer months. It's what gets me through the other seasons.

There are some places I could live that would give me a summer feel year-round . . . all day . . . and I may move to one of those places one day. But for now I have to walk through the seasons.

It's like our lives. We have seasons that feel like the season we long to rush by, and our hearts long for our favorite season. But we can't hurry it. We must walk through it to be able to enjoy the next season in our lives. And one thing I've learned is that the seasons pass and new ones always come.

It's coming . . . your season to bloom. It's just that your body and your mind have to learn how to adjust to your new life so you can be more beautiful, stronger, wiser than the last season.

Aging . . . getting more mature, wiser, and aging through the seasons of your life can actually be the thing that keeps you young.

Sunrise

"The eyes of the beholder can see the artistry of the divine, in the intimacy of her thoughts. She sees through the senses that penetrate her eternal soul . . . right there on the wave kissed sand by the magnificent sea . . . as the first appearance of sunlight arises in her hope of the knowledge of her faith in a brand new day."
—Linda McDandel, Sweet Strength)

Treasure

———— ∞∞ ————

*"Where your treasure lies, there your heart will be slain open and laid
bare. Be sure the treasures you store up are worthy of the nakedness."*
— *Linda McDandel, Sweet Strength*

This early morning as I laid on the sand to take a picture through a
magnifying lens of my camera phone. . . up close of the shells as I
focused through the lens of my eyes. The gold sparkles reminded me
of treasure. Treasures in life. Treasures in love. Treasures that I have
kept and given. Treasures I long for and Treasures of wisdom and
love that I seek. As I talked with God on the sandy beach floor . . . I
became keenly aware of the allure of treasures of the heart and soul
and personal thoughts resonated with the reflection of the liquid gold
that rose this morning on these seashells by the shore.

Because we really don't own anything, but we recycle everything.
To understand our treasures, we have to be free to give every piece
away . . . cheerfully and in full expectation that more will be given.

If we can't let something go, it owns us, it becomes our master
and therefore . . . we are its slave. And the beauty of the naked heart
slain and laid bare . . . will become callous, depleted, and parched as if
drying in the desert sun. The lure of the naked beauty now is repelling
the very thing that was once drawn to it.

The unfolding of another day of abundance and grace . . . where
are you going to recycle yours?

Spreading Light

———∞∞∞———

*"There are two ways of spreading light: to be the candle
or the mirror that reflects it."* —*Edith Wharton*

Some days are just tougher than others, aren't they? Remember that as you go out and start your day—that it may be a tough day for someone. I can say with 100 percent certainty that there's someone today who needs a kind word, a hug, a kiss, encouragement, love, maybe some financial help, and always a smile. Life if short. You're here for a reason: to live it.

If You Hurt

———∞∞∞———

*"If you love and get hurt, love more. If you love more and hurt more,
love even more. If you love even more and get hurt even more, love some
more until it hurts no more. . ."* —*William Shakespeare*

I was reading this quote earlier about whatever pain you feel, make sure you don't ever inflict that pain on anyone else. Think about that. We sure wouldn't want another to feel the pain we feel when we've gotten hurt.

It's hard, isn't it? To love, get hurt, and not hurt back. Pain begets pain. Unforgiveness begets unforgiveness. Love is the answer to pain . . . to hurt . . . to fear . . . to forgiveness . . . to hate. But rejection, pain, loss, and fear make us do non-loving things. However, this is never the answer. Loving more is. May we all learn how to beget love through the pain so it will have a ripple effect on our own souls and others.

We all fall so very short . . . but may the grace that we've been given today give us the strength to love in the hurt.

Unlearn

"The most useful piece of learning for the uses of life is to unlearn what is untrue." —Antisthenes

It's a beautiful day in the neighborhood! A new day to wake up and to unlearn—that's right, unlearn—old ways. It's harder to unlearn a belief, a habit, or an old pattern than it is to want a change or learn a new one. But you have to unlearn first.

We want to cling to old habits and old beliefs because it's what we know, and it's comfortable. It's our sense of security. We know consciously or unconsciously what the outcome will always be, regardless of the circumstances because it's our belief system, and we have it ingrained in us so deeply. Circumstances change all the time, but inside is where the change is hard to come by.

But we have to have a willingness, an openness, to let go and discover something new if we want to change ourselves, our happiness, or our life satisfaction. I bet I'm not the only one who would like to find more happiness or life satisfaction or change a unhealthy habit or pattern. I need to unlearn some things that hinder me.

Sometimes I think we listen for answers to confirm what we already think. We ask for help to confirm. We hear the answer in what we want to hear, not what is really said, but what we already think . . . our belief about it. We seek change and help because we want relief, not truth.

Do we really want to discover what's new? Do we really want to know the truth, no matter the consequences?

To unlearn a belief system that's hurting you is to listen to the truth, no matter where it may lead us. And that becomes faith—not belief, but faith. Truth gives us the ability to have faith . . . to unlearn those habits, beliefs, and patterns that no longer serve us or bring us happiness.

There are some things I need to unlearn so I can be free to new opportunities and open to faith, wherever it may lead me.

Eagle

From sunrise to sunset, and all life in between. . . It is indeed a beautiful day in the neighborhood! Grace has embraced us once again.

> *"It's not what you are that holds you back, it's what you think you are not."* —*Denis Waitley*

"A man found an eagle's egg and put it in a nest of a barnyard hen. The eaglet hatched with the brood of chicks and grew up with them.

All his life the eagle did what the barnyard chicks did, thinking he was a barnyard chicken.

"Years passed and the eagle grew old. One day he saw a magnificent bird above him in the cloudless sky. The old eagle looked up in awe. 'Who's that?'

"'That's the eagle, the king of the birds,' said his neighbor.

"'He belongs to the sky. We belong to the earth; we're chickens.'

"So the eagle lived and died as a chicken, for that's what he thought he was."[7]

Unfamiliar

*"Faith is the confidence of things hoped for,
the evidence of things not seen" —Hebrews 11:1*

I hope today is a day not of running away, but of taking a breath to believe in the hope of the unfamiliar. The unfamiliar that has become my journey.

I was welcoming the sunrise this morning and pondering the realization that our lives are always changing, despite the illusion of the familiar . . . of the known.

For me to embrace all the change and loss I've experienced, I must come to the place of truth without running. I must be willing to "wake up" to see. But sometimes I don't want to wake up. It takes work to face a different reality and to become a different person. But if you don't become a different person in your ever-changing reality, you'll have no

7 Anthony De Mello, *The Song of the Bird (Colorado Springs: Image, 1984).*

choice but to run . . . and if you run, you'll be running forever. I want to run, and I have run, but when I stop and breathe, I begin to understand that I'm waking up. I'm waking up to the unknown.

How much truth can we take without running away? How much of everything we love . . . that we hold on to and that we know as our reality . . . are we ready to have shattered, to have taken away, to lose without running away? How ready are we to face the unfamiliar—the unknown?

It brings fear. That's our reaction. I used to think it was fear of the unknown that made me run . . . the fear of not knowing the outcome of my future . . . the fear of wondering who I am, now that my life is not the same. No . . . I've come to understand that it's not fear of the unknown. What I really fear and run from is the loss of the known.

Today may we embrace and face and learn to grow in the unfamiliar . . . the loss of the known.

Debris Flying

"After every storm the sun will smile: for every problem there is a solution, and the soul indefeasible duty is to be of good cheer."
—William R. Alger

It's hard to stay calm in the storm, isn't it? I mean, it's a storm. There's debris flying all around and lightning flashing to the ground. You don't know where to run. It's another storm and you're in the midst of it. Storms, they come and they go. Sometimes you wonder where the storm came from. It was, after all, sunny just a few minutes ago and you were basking in the sunshine and having fun. Now you're just wondering where to run. Where is the shelter from the storm? But the sun will come again and the storm will come again too. Unexpectedly and you will get caught in the rain, wind, and debris . . . but when the rain loses its flow to the sun, the wind subsides, and debris is picked up and thrown away, you'll know that the way to the sun and blue sky has been yours all along. The shelter and the calm from the storm were always there. They were in the choices of thoughts and beliefs that run consistently in your mind.

Plunge into the heat of the storm, but keep your heart in the palm of the Savior.

Courage Will Awaken

Is strength our only option? What other choice do we have? What choice are we going to make? Remember that in our weakest moment is the golden opportunity to become stronger than we were before. Courage will awaken.

Resistance

It's peaceful, this morning. I'm becoming aware. Waking up. Becoming aware of my inner dialogue. Of my surroundings. Of the resistance in my life.

When we set out to change anything in our lives, we have to expect resistance. We have to understand resistance in our lives will come as we become better . . . as we get closer to our dreams.

The harder you try to change or reach dreams, the worse it can get. Resistance steps in and tries to overpower and stop you. The more you resist something, the more power you give it. You always empower the challenges that you fight.

Change Your Thinking and You will Change Your Life

If you have a challenge or a difficult circumstance stopping you from moving forward or living life to the fullest, it's because you're using an old mindset. You'll never grow through or get over challenging situations or hard circumstances until you adjust to a new way of thinking about it.

You cannot remain the person you were before the challenge and expect to move forward or get through difficulty. Change your thinking and change your life. Challenge your old ways of dealing with life, and you might be surprised with the outcome.

Greatness

The rough times are going to come, but the good news is they haven't come to stay. They have come to pass. And attaining greatness is not some wonderful, great, moment that we will not accomplish and that only the special among us will ever taste. No . . . it is something that truly exists in every one of us, not because we say so, but because God says so.

Too often, we settle. We settle with who we are at the moment. We settle in a relationship. We settle in life. Why? Because we don't believe we have inside of us what it takes to attain greatness and have a great life.

It's important that we believe we're important . . . that our lives and what we do with our lives makes a difference in this world.

Knowing the Story

Everyone has a story; everyone has something they don't want others to know. It's just life. You don't have to share everything. You just have to understand and know that everyone has something they don't want to share. We are more alike than different when it comes to our experiences.

Everyone doesn't have to look like you, think like you, or do things the same way. It's okay . . . it really is. What a boring world we would live in if everyone agreed and did things the same way, like we thought they should. Remember: you can't judge and love at the same time . . . and judging is really nothing more than not knowing the story.

Choices

————⟨∞⟩————

"You are always one choice away from changing your life."
—Marcy Blockowiak

I write about choice a lot. Well, mainly because every day we make choices; hopefully most of them are conscious decisions, but we're on automatic pilot for others. I just like to remind people that they have choices. I mean, we forget, don't we? We'll say things like, "I really don't have a choice; I have to work these two jobs." "I really don't have a choice; my time is all used up. I have no extra time to exercise, play, or relax." "I don't have a choice; I had to eat what was in front of me at that party." "I had to eat at the fast food place, I was on the road." "I have to . . . I should . . . there's no other choice." Really?

Autonomy, what a wonderful gift. We always have a choice. We may not like the consequences, we may not want to change because we're comfortable, or we may not think we have a choice—but we always have a choice. We may want to work the two jobs because we want to provide certain things for our family or even ourselves, but we have a choice to work those two jobs or not. We have a choice how our twenty-four hours are spent each day. We may have to change some things around to be able to take care of ourselves and our health, but we certainly have a choice. The minute you realize you're free to choose in any and all circumstances, you become free to make good choices. Even if it relates to circumstances beyond your control—accidents, deaths, imprisonment—you still have a choice regarding how to respond to those circumstances.

Choice . . . the freedom to choose those things that are good for you or those that aren't. It really is totally up to you!

No Easy

———— ∞ ————

We always want easy . . . there is no easy. We always want fast . . . there is no fast. We want the sure thing . . . there is no sure thing. There is no secure and safe way. We always want good . . . how about wanting the best?

How about not settling for good, for easy, for fast? How about doing the time it will take to have and be the best? How about giving it enough time, dedication, persistence, fortitude, willpower, desire, faith, and enough of a positive mindset instead of looking for the easy, the fast, the secure? And when you reach that vision, that goal, it will be worth it!

Sweet Strength is dedication to your goals.

Trail and Correction

———⚬❀⚬———

"We learn from failure, not from success!" —*Bram Stoker*8

Failure . . . lessons . . . that's how we learn. If we want to succeed, we will fail . . . sometimes many times before we succeed. And we won't succeed unless we fail. That's how you learn to do things differently— through failure . . . trial and correction. That's what I tell my clients: not trial and error, but trial and correction. Doing things differently than you did them last time. It's not an error. It's not failure. We've just learned what not to do and have been given the opportunity to do it another way . . . a better way. Stepping out of your fear of failure is how you become your best friend and a winner at life.

If we want to win at life, we risk failure. In other words, if we have life satisfaction, we've learned to let go of our fear of failure.

The enemy is within. And an old African proverb says: "If we don't have an enemy within, then we won't have an enemy without." Our failures, circumstances, and others' opinions won't keep us from success because we will have become our own best friend. We will have grown to understand the valuable lesson that our failures actually lead to our success.

---

8 Bram Stoker, *Dracula (Mineola, NY: Dover Publications, 2000).*

Nothing to Lose and Everything to Gain.

———— ∞ ————

"Remembering that you are going to die is the best way I know to avoid the trap of thinking you have something to lose. You are already naked. There is no reason not to follow your heart." —Steve Jobs

Nothing to lose and everything to gain. You come into this world with nothing, and you'll leave with nothing. What counts is what you do with those precious moments in between. Follow your heart. Follow your passion. Make your own path just for your dash . . . the between-your-birth-and-death dash . . . because that's how fast our lives go by—in a dash. Make the moments count. Live out loud. Face your fears of failure. Face your fears of getting your heart broken and love again and again until it doesn't break anymore. Make a journey that counts. Stretch yourself. Challenge yourself. Love yourself. Love others. Encourage and inspire others. Be grateful. Stay hopeful and optimistic. Fight for your mindset. Fight for your health. Never, ever give up.

Follow your heart . . . it knows what to do. Change is on the horizon, and I can't wait to continue to fill those moments of my dash with life! How can you fill those moments between the dash?

My World

———∞———

Good Morning! My world this morning. Immersed in the beauty of nature. Thoughts warmly wrapped up in my mind of the mystery of God. Always puts a smile on my face. The mystique of the complexity of this world and the people who are created in the image of a elusive, but clearly seen God. An infinite God that our finite minds will never see clearly nor grasp. We have been trying for millions of years. Millions of years of telling stories about and writing about the human experience with the unknowing. Because it is only through your soul, your spirit, your heart that you can begin to have peace, faith, and hope in the one you were created and designed by. And some people will disagree with this. I know. I talk with people of different faiths, and those who question his existence. And God loves all of his creation. No one is a replica of another. . . not even the snowflake. . . It's always been that way . . . since the beginning of time. Answers bringing more questions. Questions are the answers to your peace. May this day you find the truth . . .through the words engraved and tattooed on your heart and soul. It always starts from the inside out, not the outside in. May you come to know who you are. Who you would like to become . . . and where your faith dwells.

I am Ready To Start This Day

———∞———

It's a beautiful day. Another day to fulfill my purpose in life. Another day of opportunities. Another day to live out the potential that resides within my heart and soul. Another day to love. I'm ready to start this day!

When God created us, He endowed us with only one thing that we have absolute control over. We really have no control over anything or anyone else. That one thing is our thoughts. This is how you change your life. This is the only way anything will ever change for you. It doesn't matter what circumstances you're in the midst of . . . your thoughts will literally change the perception and reality of the situation.

At some point, we all want something in our lives to change. We want others to change. Heck, we even want our world to change. But if we want someone or some situation to change or improve, we have to begin with ourselves. Changing ourselves. Changing our thoughts. What holds us back from becoming all we're meant to be is our thoughts. The way we think about things.

Don't Complain

"Shoot for the moon. Even if you miss, you'll land among the stars."
—*Norman Vincent Peale*

What an awesome day to begin again . . . to be someone's encouragement . . . to tell someone that they have abilities and talents and potential that need to be used. Encourage, lift up, and appreciate those in your life.

Don't criticize, condemn, or complain about anyone today. Don't complain about anything in your life today. I mean, really, how's that working for you anyway? Criticizing, complaining, and condemning—

they never work for me. How many times have criticizing and complaining made you feel better . . . made you a better person . . . made your relationships better?

Change those negative thoughts into gratefulness, appreciate and love those around you, and be sure to tell them. It just works better.

What Are We Expecting?

It's great to feel our hearts beating to the rhythm of purpose.

What are we expecting from our lives? What are we doing to give and receive the most from our lives? Let's not let our lives go by without making our dreams come alive.

The following poem, "The Wage," is one I like to think about.

I bargained with Life for a penny,
And Life would pay no more,
However I begged at evening
When I counted my scanty store;
For Life is a just employer,
He gives you what you ask,
But once you have set the wages,
Why, you must bear the task.
I worked for a menial's hire,
Only to learn, dismayed,
That any wage I had asked of Life,
Life would have paid.[9]

---

9 Jessie B. Rittenhouse, *The Door of Dreams* (Boston and New York: Houghton Mifflin Company, 1918).

Grace Given

*Rain is grace; rain is the sky descending to the earth;
without rain, there would be no life.* —*John Upkike*

Another day given to us to adapt to this life of constant change. Another day to live our lives with hope and dreams. Another day of grace.

I say grace because we cannot control whether we get another day to live. I think if we would all look at our days as given to us in grace, we would live differently. But a lot of times we don't want to think in those terms. We want to think a day of grace will be given tomorrow and the next day and the next. . . And we begin to take days for granted. We begin to take others for granted—their days of grace, that is.

We begin to think our lives will always be the same. We get comfortable. We forget to be thankful for the day that was given to us by grace . . . the opportunity to live a life of great satisfaction . . . of joy . . . of appreciation . . . of love.

Every morning I try to be on the beach before the sun rises so I can watch the beginning of a new day . . . so I feel the hope, love, and grace in another sunrise. It's here where my heart heals from yesterday's mistakes and gets another day to become better . . . to improve. My heart grows and succumbs to another miracle created in a new sunrise, which my eyes and my soul are so grateful to experience.

I know and understand that with this day will come change. We create some change, and some change will be out of our control . . . and it's how we adapt to that change that will either make our lives full of meaning, purpose, love, peace, and joy . . . or that will make our lives miserable.

It doesn't matter how strong, persistent, determined, or dedicated we are . . . we will not win at life or have life satisfaction until we become grateful for the day of grace that's given to us and until we become adaptable in the consistency of daily change.

God's Work

God never ceases to amaze me. I met this gentleman on the beach about three weeks ago. It was early in the morning and he stopped me to ask what my Sweet Strength logo on my shirt meant. I was excited to tell him. We shared stories. He's a chiropractor in the area and had such an encouraging spirit.

Well, this morning on my walk/run/pushup beach trek, I ran into him again. He said, "I knew I was going to see you this morning. God woke me up last night to pray for you." He said he'd been praying for me since the day we shared stories. I asked, "What did you pray for me?" He told me and I was like, "Wow. . ." It was what I prayed last night before I went to bed and this morning before I went to beach.

God always, always brings people in your path at the right time. Here is this stranger, friend now, who took the time to pray for someone he doesn't even know well. God, prayer, and love of others are why we're here. You just never know how much it means to have people pray for you. Nothing else can replace it.

Movement of Life

We are responsible for ourselves . . . for every aspect of ourselves. No one else can be responsible for us, our lives, or our decisions. If we're stuck in our own lives, it's because of our own actions.

Life is movement . . . a constant flow of movement and change. We have to flow with the movement of life in order to change. It doesn't stop because we do . . . and the action we take in the flow of life is what gives our lives meaning through the changes. We are responsible for how we flow with life.

Are we taking care of our bodies and our minds? Are we giving our lives meaning and purpose? The only person who can give your life meaning and who can discover your life's purpose in the movement of life is you!

Liquid Gold

The beach and this liquid gold array of sunshine was waiting on me to start my day! Wow . . .

If you smile right now . . . right where you are . . . the feelings of thankfulness will come. The expression on our face is so much more important than what clothes we put on. It reveals what's on our mind and what's in our hearts.

In life, it isn't what you have, where you are, how successful you are, or who you're with that makes you happy or unhappy. It's what you think about . . . your attitude in life.

Two people may be in the same place doing the same thing, have the same amount of money and prestige, and yet one is miserable and the other is happy. It's all in our attitude . . . our smile.

As Dale Carnegie said, "Charles Schwab told me his smile had been worth a million dollars."[10]

If you share that smile, you'll find not that it's worth a million bucks . . . but that it's simply priceless.

"A man without a smiling face must not open a shop." —Chinese Proverb

Little Fears

The sun came up again. . . We have work to do. We have to change the world, right? We have to make things right, right?

Well, we'd better start working on ourselves first, before we work on changing the world.

This morning I went to another Toastmasters meeting. I'm trying a couple before I make the decision as to which one to join. Facing fears. A new environment and people who know more about public speaking than I do. However, I so desperately want to improve my speaking

---

10 Dale Carnegie, *How to Win Friends & Influence People (New York City: Pocket Books, 1998).*

and writing skills that I'm willing to do whatever it takes to get out of my comfort zone to become more proficient and efficient at speaking. Because I have some big dreams that I will not reach without being able to speak and communicate effectively. Like changing the world . . . just kidding.

Well, this group asked me if I would like to do an impromptu speech, where they provide a topic to a few people who then speak on it for a minute and a half. Then they pick a winner. I thought to myself, No, but "yes" came out because the only way to grow is to do those things with which you're uncomfortable. So I gave my little impromptu speech on an apple. That was the topic they chose for me, and I won! I was so glad I said yes.

Sometimes it's the little fears in life that hold you back. Facing those little fears will propel us to greater things.

You Cannot Ignore Health

I write about this all the time because it's a passion and a fire that burns within—to empower people to take control of their health and wellness.

We are a nation that is overweight, stressed-out, drug dependent (legal and illegal), and saturated in negativity driven by the media.

We have one body and one mind and one life to get it right. The only way we can reach out, make a difference, and be a part of our surroundings is through our body and our mind.

If you aren't feeling your best and taking care of the one body and mind you have, then you can't expect to give your best or be the best for those around you.

People say they're too busy to exercise and too much in a hurry to eat whole, nutritious foods, but the challenge with that is every day you're either healing your body and mind or killing your body and mind. You can't have it both ways.

You cannot continue to ignore health and wellness and think that you'll be fine.

Take the time to exercise and eat healthy and rest. Take the time to be thankful, pray, and read positive and uplifting books. Turn off the TV. Surround yourself with positive people. When you do this, you can do what you love doing for so much longer.

Perfect Love

Reminding myself that perfect love drives out fear.

Dietrich Bonhoeffer's *Life Together* is one of my favorite books. One of those books I pick up and read again and again, trying to live it out . . . and I fall so short. I write this in recognition of our lives being both complex and simple. . . We choose.

Where the discipline of the tongue is practiced right from the beginning, each individual will make a matchless discovery. He will be able to cease from constantly scrutinizing the other person, judging him, condemning him, putting him in his particular place where he can gain ascendancy over him and thus doing violence to him as a person. Now he can allow the brother to exist as a completely free person, as God made him to be. His view expands and, to his amazement, for the first time he sees, shining above his brother, the richness of God's creative glory. God did not make this person as I would have made him. He did not give him to me as a brother for me to dominate and control, but in order that I might find above him the creator. Now the other person, in the freedom in which he was created, becomes the occasion of joy, whereas before he was only a nuisance and an affliction. God does not will that I should fashion the other person according to the image that seems good to me, that is, in my own image; rather in his very freedom from me God made this person in His image. I can never know beforehand how God's image should appear in others. That image always manifests a completely new and unique form that comes solely from God's free and sovereign creation. To me the sight may be strange, even ungodly, but God creates every man in the likeness of His son, the crucified. After all, that image certainly looked strange and ungodly to me before I grasped it.[11]

Don't Indulge

I've had enough pain, loss, and tears in my life. Negativity is all around if you want to indulge. It's right there at your fingertips. It's so easy to cause pain and plant negative seeds . . . so I have no desire to welcome more into my life or create it. Pain and struggle will come on its own. We don't have to be a part of creating it.

I sure like feelings of joy, hope, optimism, peace, and love better. I have found that life is richer, fuller, and more beautiful if you lean toward the good and not the bad. . . It just works. And it takes a lot

11 Dietrich Bonhoeffer, *Life Together* (New York City: HarperOne, 2009).

of work. We're bent toward the negative. It's our nature, but we can change it. But it's work. I work at it every day. And as I do, my heart sings, "Every little thing gonna be all right."[12]

One of my continuous goals is to be the most positive, loving person I can . . . because there's just enough of the other. Those loved ones that have gone before us and are in complete paradise would tell us too that everything is gonna be all right.

Words

Ralph Waldo Emerson said, "Use what language you will, but you can never say anything but what you are."

That's powerful.

Words, perception, reality, belief, interpretation, freedom, empowerment, and decisions. What do these words have in common? Well, I believe that we will find life satisfaction, freedom, joy, peace, hope, and empowerment when we understand . . . when we wake up and realize that we, not our situations or circumstances, are in complete control of our thoughts, our attitudes, our perspectives, and our choices.

Yes, we get to choose our perceptions, attitudes, and actions! Wow. Our attitudes and actions have a direct impact on the choices we make in life. These choices result in who we become and determine our future. Our freedom to live life fully, happy and satisfied.

---

12   Bob Marley & the Wailers, "Three Little Birds," *Exodus, Island Records B000001FY5, 1977, compact disc.*

July 1, 2015

Anything is possible. It really is.

My passion is helping others, empowering others to reach their dreams . . . to be healthy and happy . . . to have life satisfaction. And nutrition is a big part of that. In fact, millions of people will die early deaths because of what they eat. They will get all kinds of inflammatory diseases from eating poorly. But, through my coaching experiences I have come to understand that most people seem to be dying not from their foods, but from their thought process. They have given up on their dreams. They have lost hope and purpose. They see their lives as over, instead of beginning.

Don't let your dreams die because of a mindset that you have or others want you to have. Don't live your life with regret and only half a heart. It's possible. You're the only one who can make it happen. Your dream may just help others' lives become better. Don't let it die with you. Don't be transformed by others . . . instead, be transformed by the renewal of your mind. Change your mindset to "It's possible!" Now let's open our eyes and hearts to "It's possible!"

Rainbow

It's a beautiful day in the neighborhood! A rainbow greeted me this morning on the beach! Seek and you will find. Life is so rich! Full of color . . . full of beauty . . . full of variety . . . full of adventure . . . full of sound. And for those who can see the rainbow and embrace all the possibilities that life offers—the goodness, the heartbeat, the rhythm, the music—there is a pot of gold waiting at the end of your rainbow. You just have to see it. Open your eyes . . . reach into your heart . . . it's there.

Smile. It makes you beautiful, and you might just start to feel some happiness creeping in and see the rainbow . . . and then you can spread that happiness to others.

Creating Life

———∞∞∞———

Are we creating life or are we trying to find life? There's a big difference. You know, life happens. Life goes on, as I always imply. But I'm simply saying the truth. Tick tock.

We need to be intentional in what we want for our lives, for our family, for our friends, and for those we haven't even met yet. If we're constantly trying to find ourselves, whatever that may look like, how can we ever create who we are to become, when we don't even know where to look?

God is our Creator. He creates. We are made in His image; so therefore we create. We don't find . . . we create our lives in accordance to our hopes and dreams.

A great friend of mine asked me last night what "make it sweet, keep it strong" meant. I replied, "Life is sweet. Keep it that way. Stay sweet and keep your body, mind, soul, and spirit strong."

You can create your life, any way you want . . . and it will be sweet and strong.

Inner Core

If you have the core strength to believe it, all days are made just as you make them.

"My strength comes from the abdomen. It's the center of gravity and the source of power." —Bruce Lee

Not only is it important to build your core on the outside, it's imperative to build your inner core. It's the basis of your physical strength and your inner strength.

Adversities Within

"When there is no enemy within, the enemies outside cannot hurt you."
— Winston Churchill

There are always going to be people who are stronger, wiser, faster, better than you. Their circumstances are always going to seem like they're easier than yours, better than yours, more adventurous than yours, more financially secure than yours. Of course there will always be those who are weaker, slower, poorer than you, and their circumstances are much worse than yours.

But I think our real adversities come from within us. Something tells me that if you beat the opponent and the adversary within, then you'll win the race . . . the prize . . . the freedom to choose strength over weakness, wisdom over foolishness, better over worse, adventure over boredom, peace over anxiety, friends over enemies, love over hate, living over dying. Here's what I believe . . . when you don't have an opponent within you, then you won't have one to beat, because you will have already won.

Best is Yet to Come

It's a beautiful day in the neighborhood because if you're alive, that means you have purpose left. Do you doubt that? Do you believe the best is yet to come, or do you look around and think, this is the way it will always be?

"A person who doubts himself is like a man who would enlist in the ranks of his enemies and bear arms against himself." —Alexandre Dumas

The quote above is sobering. Sometimes we just need to sober up, don't we?

The journey of self-doubt is full of despair and self-destruction. We will sabotage the best of well-laid plans . . . sabotage our freedom and our success . . . by doubt.

But we don't want to look in the mirror and see the truth in the re-flection . . . the reflection that pierces the heart and speaks to us, saying so gently with force, "You are the one sabotaging your journey. Yes, the person looking back at you is the enemy."

The person looking back at you could become your best friend. It's your choice because it's your thoughts that make it so.

Mind is the Master

"Mind is the Master power that molds and makes, and Man is Mind, and evermore he takes the tool of Thought, and, shaping what he wills, brings forth a thousand joys, a thousand ills: He thinks in secret, and it comes to pass: Environment is but his looking glass." —*James Allen*

Well now . . . it was great to set my eyes on this God-spoken sunrise in this life-giving Tuesday morning. As Mark and Mr. Rogers always said . . . "It's a beautiful day in the neighborhood!"

Watch your words, because your words create. What are you think-ing and speaking?

Make your thoughts and words reflect your looking glass.

If we want success, we must talk about it . . . think about it. If we want love, we must talk about it and think about it. If we want health, we must talk about it and think about it. Whatever we desire, we have to start thinking about it and talking about it . . . then we'll start doing it and living by putting it into action.

If we talk about others and gossip . . . if we think and talk about those things we're angry about and hate . . . if we think about others negatively or talk and think about failure all day, that's exactly what our world will reflect.

What Are You Going to Do About Your Life?

———⚬⚭⚬———

"If you want to keep getting what you're getting, keep doing what you're doing." ——Les Brown

You have to say yes to your dreams. Don't talk about how bad your life is and how bad everything is. What are you going to do about it? It's up to you.

Your Unique Dream

———⚬⚭⚬———

The day is full of hope and possibility and our journeys are not complete if we're breathing and our hearts are still beating this morning.

This morning I was thinking about how easy it is to abandon our paths. Abandon our goals. Abandon our dreams. Especially when they seem so out of reach or impossible to others and ourselves. When we feel a little different than the rest of the crowd because of them. Like we don't quite fit in.

We get easily distracted by wanting to fit into a certain group or get approval for what we want to accomplish in life. Our dreams. We want to be like everyone else . . . it's more comfortable that way. We like people to like us . . . we are, after all, people who need people. We need relationships and love. That's what makes the world go around.

However, we need to be careful that we aren't sacrificing a dream because we're worried we may not be liked or we may not fit in, because truth be known, if you are truly living out your passion . . . if you are truly learning and growing into who you are to become, then you'll realize you're different from everyone else and God gave you a certain vision, a purpose, and a dream that's yours and no one else's.

So when we try to be like others . . . when we try to fit in . . . we lose the very person we are created to be.

"Stop and think about yourself. In all of the history of the world, there was never anyone else exactly like you, and in all the infinity of time to come, there will never be another." —Amram Scheinfeld

Celebrate who you are and the gifts you've been given, and make the decision to give those gifts to others with all the passion that burns within you. Live out the dream that's planted within you with no reservations about what others think or say about it . . . with no reservations about the challenges you'll face in reaching it. Don't worry about the how. Just know it was given to you, and only in your uniqueness will that dream ever come alive. Just believe. Believe in the dream, no matter how foolish it seems. Believe in yourself.

Columbus believed the world was round when all others thought it to be flat. Edison believed in his invention after failing thousands of times. The Wright brothers believed they could fly. Everything starts as a dream . . . a thought that was given to them. What if they had dismissed it because of what others thought or said?

Don't let your dream go to the grave with you. Share your uniqueness . . . your beauty . . . your gifts with others. The world needs you.

Power Of The Moment

What I would give to live right here on this beach. I'm so thankful I can be in this moment here, now. These small moments that bring to life a new day in the magnificent beauty of a sunrise can't be captured for long, but they can be savored in the moment . . . this moment . . . now. . .

We make our moments, just like the sunrise makes his. The sunrise, in all its grace, creeps' moment by moment in the sky, laying the foundation for the day.

Our moments count because they are the path our feet walk on as our journey here continues to unfold. This moment counts . . . right now . . . not the moment before. The moment before this one has already said its goodbyes. It won't return, no matter how hard we try. A thought, a word, an action, an experience gone . . .the next moment will come in accordance with the moment we're having now—in thought, action, and experience—creating the future of who we'll become and what we'll do.

Never underestimate the power in the moment. You're shaping your future. Make sure your moments are powerfully optimistic, hopeful, and full of love and life.

Life and death are set in front of us each day. In each moment, they are given to us. . . Choose life.

***

For the second evening in a row, I'm at my favorite place. I needed to come and be with my thoughts. I love this place. Charleston . . . Mount Pleasant—it was named that for a reason! I moved here on faith . . . on that little gut intuition that, when I listen, guides me to where I need to be.

Faith . . . the beauty of stepping before you know where the next step is. But you know it's worth the step. Not knowing, but trusting.

I just had an incredible meeting with an incredible person. In the short time we were together, I knew the next step in my journey was there. I'm so excited about my next business adventure.

Part of growing, stretching, and reaching your dreams is stepping out on faith . . . listening to that small, still voice in the silence of the night and trusting that you're making the right decision—not because you know the how, but because you know you've been given a dream. And you have to believe and trust and have faith that the dream is manifesting through that gut feeling, which goes before and sees the plan already laid out before you . . . because you believe in something bigger than yourself, and you believe that bigger something gave you that dream.

Step by step . . . day by day . . . moment by moment. . . Just stay the path.

Imagination

"The most beautiful world is always entered through imagination."
—*Helen Keller*

I can stand on this piece of paradise and breathe in the grace with each unconscious breath. Each morning I allow my imagination to grow in the allurement and artistry of the sunrise that paints the sky before me.

"Imagination should be used, not to escape reality but to create it." —Colin Wilson

"Imagination is the greatest nation in the world!" —Bob Proctor

Imagine what your life could be . . . what you could do or create . . . what you could offer others. Imagination will take you where you want to go. Old belief systems will tell you can't.

Everything that has been made began in someone's imagination. Someone decided to act on their imagination's whim, and all those things acted upon have given to us many comforts: cars, electricity, refrigeration, architecture, bridges, boats, surfboards, planes, computers, etc.

As a coach, the first thing I help my clients go through is a vision casting session. It's powerful and asks the question: What do you want your life to look like?

Imagination will take you where you want to go. God gave you a powerful tool when He gave you an imagination. It's there for a purpose: to help you and others.

"The world is but a canvas to the imagination." —Henry David Thoreau

The Race

We are so often our own enemies in the race of life. We run for the wrong reasons. We get in the wrong races. We focus on the wrong competitions. We quit before we reach the finish line. Sometimes we quit before we even begin.

We fail to understand that the real race in life comes not from how fast we run. We fail to understand that the race of life really isn't about the other competitors. They aren't our true competition. The hurdles that have been placed in the path to the finish line are not what cause us to stumble. No . . . what causes us to not finish is the false belief that our success or failure lies with the hurdles and is because others are faster and luckier or slower and unluckier than us. What we fail to grasp is that this race is never against our hurdles or others . . . it's always against ourselves.

Make the decision to draw a map of the race you want to join. Find the path that is right in front of you, marked out for you on that map. Take a breath, and take the responsibility to run your own race . . . and be a victor, not of victim of the race. And remember that your finish line is just the beginning of a new race.

Attitude

———⊗⊗⊗———

"I don't think of all the misery, but of the beauty that still remains."
—*Anne Frank*[13]

Clouds and sun. They produce pretty opposite feelings and attitudes, if you let them. It's all about what you're looking for. If you look for the clouds, you'll find them, whether it's cloudy or not. If you look for the sun, you'll find it, whether it's sunny or not. It's how you view it.

If my attitude toward life is fearful and hopeless and boring . . . well . . . that's what it will become. If my attitude toward life is adventurous, full of opportunities, hopeful, and awesome . . . that's exactly what it will become.

Our attitudes will determine our lives. If we want to change others and others' attitudes, we need to change ours first. Don't expect them to change—*you* change.

I tell my single friends (and it can really apply to anyone in a relationship): become the person you want in a person, and watch the magic begin. If you want to draw to you that person who has the attributes you desire in a companion, you better start becoming that person you desire.

It's no easy feat to change a lifelong attitude toward others and the world around you, but it can be done. You can change your life any time you choose. Make the decision and begin.

---

13 Anne Frank, *The Diary of a Young Girl (New York City: Bantam, 1993)*.

Expect the Beauty

I just got back from a beautiful run on the beach listening to Eva Cassidy and a line from the song Down by the River, she sang, Going to the river for my rainbow today. As I was thinking about this song and the beauty of the dreams we've been given, it brought a smile to my heart. Dreams are just dreams unless we act upon them. Everyone has dreams, and everyone needs to have hope that one day their dreams will come true.

I know life is tough and we're all subjected to heartache, pain, disappointment, illness, setbacks, stress . . . and I know there are horrific evils in this world, but there is such beauty all around us . . . and dreams help us see the beauty. The beauty of what can be and the hope of what's to come.

If you just look for the beauty, you'll find it. You just have to look for it and expect it. Yes . . . expect to see the beauty, just as there is beauty in your dreams. Because it's your dream and it's special. You've been given that dream. Life is short. I believe that dreams are given to us so we can find the beauty and hope in living and sharing our hearts with others . . . sharing beauty and love. . .

I believe you have been given that dream for a reason. I believe that when you begin to turn your dream into reality, you'll find the reason. Dreams—we are so blessed to have them. Dreams give us hope . . . and without hope, there is no beauty.

Moments That Change

⸺⚬⚬⚬⸺

Sometimes we let life get in the way of the very experiences that give us life.

I decided. I made a deliberate choice that I would not let the stresses of life, time, or others run me anymore. I decided and made the choice to step into different water . . . a different current.

There are painful moments in life that change us . . . that wake us up and cause us to become aware of the life we're living. It's an awareness so clear that you no longer need glasses to see. Everything is brighter and more beautiful and sharper. It's a good wake-up call. I mean, who wants to sleep walk through life?

How we want to live is always our choice. It's hard to admit this. We all want something or someone to blame. It's easier than learning how to work on ourselves. It's easier than having to learn to change our attitudes and perspectives.

But at the end of day, it is our reactions, our choices, our attitudes that determine our journeys. We always have a choice. We may not like the consequences of that choice or we may love the consequences of that choice . . . but we always have a choice.

Mindset . . . your freedom to paradise or your prison in hell.

Today is a good day, today is a great day to be alive, today is a new day, and it is a very good day. It's never too late to change what you want because it's your choice. Today is a very good day.

August 15, 2015

"I'm always thinking about creating. My future starts when I wake up in the morning and see the light." —*Miles Davis*

As I was taking in the beauty God's creation in another sunrise—God, the master Creator, who created us and gave us the gift of creating— and walking on the beach, I stumbled upon this one-of-a-kind sand-castle. It started me thinking about the person, or people, who created it. It made me feel good to see creation in the sand. It made me smile, just thinking about how they'd imagined their castle, every detail of that castle, then about how good it felt to build it . . . how good the sun would feel while in the sand . . . digging, laughing, creating, imagining . . . So they began building with their imagination their sandcastle world . . . and then their creation became inevitable. Right in front of them . . . all from an idea.

God's creation is right in front of us. It's inevitable. When we create, we have glimpses of the divine.

There is a gift you've been given to create the world around you. Use it for good and let your creativity flow into life so others can enjoy the gift you've been given.

There is much excitement in creating your life . . . a new life . . . if you are not excited about the one you are living.

You have a great creation to offer, and it's waiting to be seen in the physical world. It's waiting to come alive and be part of your world. It's ready to get out of its cocoon and fly. Free it and let it fly. Learn to create your world.

"True happiness comes from the joy of deeds well done, the zest of creating new things." —Antoine de Saint-Exupéry

Miracle of Life

"I've found that if you love life, life will love you back."
—Arthur Rubinstein

I've been here this morning—reading, praying, and studying—in an environment of beauty and consistency, but also of continual change. What a great place to grow in thought and spirit. I love God and His wisdom and the different avenues in which He teaches me His word, inside and outside. Through nature, through others, through a variety of authors, through music, through experiences, through every aspect of my life. Most importantly, He does this through my ability to think and then process life experiences. The mind . . . a powerful force. A miracle.

"As a man thinks in his heart, so is he" (Prov. 23:7).

He is always teaching and showing me His world and the love He has for His world. Miracle by miracle. Everyone you meet is a miracle. Everything you see and experience is a miracle. You are alive this day because you are a miracle. It's not by coincidence that you are here at this time and this place.

Love yourself enough to believe in the miracle. Value yourself enough to make decisions that will give you life, not just existence. Make the decision to study the miracle of life. Slow down enough to learn about yourself. Make the time to be alone with your thoughts. Make the time to slow down and think about the miracle of thought.

"Education is not the learning of facts, but training of the mind."
—*Albert Einstein*

We Will Be Challenged

This morning, the sky was painted by the master artist with magnificent and breathtaking beauty. This small piece of morning paradise, where eternal life connects to the physical life. I never want to leave. I want to be in this moment of peace forever . . . so I need to continually recall what peace feels like.

In the life events that I will face today, I have to make sure to imprint that feeling—that moment, that sight, the sound of the waves— in the recesses of my mind. I need to make sure before I leave to imprint every experienced feeling . . . all the peaceful, joyful, thankful, hopeful emotions I felt there.

Why bother? Because I will be challenged in some way today to give up joy, hope, or peace. So when something or someone challenges my sense of wellbeing and my happiness in this day, I have a place to turn that's calm and familiar . . . good feelings I can focus on. So when a situation rocks that today, I can be proactive instead of reactive. I can know that I have calm and joy inside of me to tap into. Because if we don't master our emotions, our emotions will master us . . . and we'll react to everything and everyone around us—and it probably won't be with love and calmness.

It is to learn to practice to see things the way they are . . . not worse than they are. We tend to make it worse. It takes more courage to make it better. It takes more courage to challenge your emotions than it does to follow every emotion. When you're on the edge of that emotional cliff, you're the one who decides whether to jump off, turn around, or spread your wings and fly to higher heights.

The Treasure Map

It's a beautiful day in the neighborhood. It's a very good day. It's a new day in your new life. But sometimes you don't feel like it's a good day, do you?

I promise, if you look hard enough, there's treasure in this day. There can be treasure every day. First you have to follow the map that leads to the treasure . . . the map you never looked at before because you weren't sure you believed in treasure maps (even though it was given to you at birth). And that map may just take you through some treacherous terrain . . . so you'll need to take the right tools with you: hope, optimism, a positive mental attitude, a new perspective on difficult terrain. Then, when you make your way to the "X" on the map and you start digging, you may just have to dig a little deeper than you first believed to find the treasure. You may have to use more substantial, solid tools—like not quitting, not stopping, belief, persistence, determination, purpose, passion, and desire. But the treasure's there, in the day. In your tomorrows. It's there . . . and when you reach it, you'll open it with the key and you'll suddenly realize that you've always had the map and the key to the treasure . . . all along. You just never believed in treasure maps . . . until you started looking for the treasure.

I Love You, As You Are

"Love says, 'I love you no matter what.' Love says,
'You are fine the way you are.'"—Byron Katie

"I am always what I judge you to be in the moment. There's no
exception. I am my own pain. I am my own happiness." —Byron Katie

If we think someone needs to be different than they are, then we don't love them.

We expect relationships will make us happy, but we can't get happiness from another person.

We put expectations on others, and when they don't live up to those expectations, we experience pain. They may not want to live up to our expectations. They may be happy the way they are. I know I won't ever be able to live up to others' expectations of me. . .

When we begin to desire love, approval, or appreciation, we'll begin to feel pain. We must first learn to be happy in our aloneness, completely at peace with who we are as an individual. We have to be the source of our own approval, love, and appreciation. We must learn to love our own company. We must learn that we are complete as we are. No one else completes us. When we begin to love ourselves, we love the person we're always with.

When we can learn to love ourselves, then we can love another . . . then we can be happy with someone as they are, not as we think they need to be . . . then everyone completes and complements each other.

It's a long journey to loving and seeing yourself as God loves and sees you: as beautiful and complete. And speaking from experience, it's worth the pain to get there . . . and the continued growth. If you want to find the love of your life, all you have to do is look in the mirror. You'll find God's image looking back at you.

Habits

⊶

Habits . . . they create us. They are what drives us. There are unhealthy and healthy habits. Our lives are driven by them. Some habits are so ingrained that we do them unconsciously . . . it really doesn't matter if they're good or bad for us. They're ingrained in our subconscious.

One of my habits is going to the beach at sunrise. If I miss it, I feel disappointed . . . a little disoriented for some time, and I have to regroup. Like this morning—my alarm went off . . . but no sound?!

So I didn't get to the beach until seven o'clock, just in time to see the turtles. I had to laugh at myself about how disappointed I was that I missed the sunrise and that my whole routine was messed up. So I just regrouped and made a different agenda. It's life . . . little things . . . big things. Our habits make our life healthy or not. They compel us forward or drag us backward or, worse, make us stay where we are.

I started the habit of going to the beach and watching the sunrise after my husband died. I needed to know that the sun was going to shine again. I needed to get out of the house before grief had its way with me . . . before I let its darkness overtake me . . . so I developed and made a choice to get up and watch God's hope come up in that sunrise over the ocean. My healing came from forming a new habit. It's still my place to meditate, learn, grow, and renew in grace for the day.

Passenger or Pilot?

Are you a passenger or pilot of your life? Some people would say, "God is my pilot." But God is my air traffic controller; He wants me to learn how to fly. He has a clearer view than I do . . . besides that, He designed my plane.

Heart of A Cloud

This morning's sunrise was a heart-filled one. Love was in the clouds. Our Creator always makes me smile.

I've had a few people ask me how I get up so early every morning for sunrise. I tell them it's simple: I like the experience it gives me—the energy, aliveness, renewal, peace, and strength—more than I like sleeping in.

***

Embrace your inner superhero. You can fly, and you didn't even realize it because you've been looking for another superhero to fly you there. Whatever you believe about yourself on the inside will manifest on the outside.

280

Formation of the Dawn

───❀❀❀───

It's a beautiful day in the neighborhood. What a great day to feel the experience of life through the senses and the soul. Grace in its formation through the dawn of a new life and a new beginning. Grace that ravished my heart this morning, awaking my spirit to the music that resides within the rhythm of each beat of purpose that resonates with my every step forward on the path laid before me . . . the journey. It's amazing to be alive at this time and in this place.

> *"In the ocean of life the isles of Blessedness are smiling, and the sunny shore of your ideal awaits your coming. Keep your hand firmly upon the helm of thought. In the bark of your soul resides the commanding Master; He does but sleep: wake Him. Self-control is strength; Right Thought is mastery; Calmness is power. Say unto your heart, 'Peace, be still!'"*
> ——James Allen[14]

Rain On My Skin

───❀❀❀───

It's a beautiful, rainy, sweet day in the neighborhood. I was hanging on the beach this morning with a bird, feeling the rain . . . and it feels good to feel . . . to be alive. What an amazing walk on the beach this morning . . . wrapped up in my thoughts of experience . . . experiencing

---

14   James Allen, *As a Man Thinketh (New York City: Cosimo Classics, 2005), 82.*

the feel of the rain on my skin . . . the cleansing and renewal in each drop of grace and love pelting down in the form of rain from above.

I love the sun. I love summer. I love brightness, blue sky, and the sea . . . but this morning I loved dancing in the rain. Because sometimes in life you just have to show up, no matter what the weather, and feel the life in the pulse of dancing in the rain.

Get rid of your umbrella and feel the rain. It's time to live and dance.

Headed for my weekly check-in to see if my diet is working for the contest. My coach is awesome. He is so smart. He can look at me and suggest a diet plan immediately for the week. And as we get closer to the contest, I may go three times a week. It amazes me—our bodies and how much food and exercise can shape them, making us stronger. Such a science to it. Our bodies . . . such a gift from God.

What Stop?

I just finished my run on my lunch break. Before heading back to the gym, I was thinking of something someone said to me: that I needed to slow down and stop once in a while. I told them that I do rest. Heck, my wellness coaching incorporates rest because without it, you'll stop—whether you want to or not.

But to just STOP . . . ha! This is what STOP means to me:

Stay steadfast with a smile.

Touch someone with love.

Open to change at a minute's notice, without grumbling.

Put the pedal to the metal and drive that thing forward with a positive mindset.

But dang . . . never stop!

The "S" in "STOP" is so important. SMILE.

A friend and I were texting last week, and I was sad about something, so I sent them a sad face—you know, an upside-down smile.

Anyway, this friend texted me back: "Be happy. It's your nature. SMILE." In my nature? I thought about that, and maybe it is in our nature to smile and to be happy. I do love to smile. I know that smiling is a gift God gives us.

Some say that if we're down and we make ourselves smile, we'll start feeling better. It works—I've done it.

People need smiles, too. There are way too many sad, serious faces. A smile can be really powerful; if you smile at someone, it's usually hard for them not to smile in return.

Now off to my clients to smile and encourage them on their way to wellness.

Escalator

I was thinking about how we go about our days, sometimes carried by our environment or others. The escalator of life . . . you just hop on and let it take you where it may. And then we complain because it didn't take us where we wanted to go. But we don't stop and think, Slow down! And we didn't ask ourselves, what do I really, really want?

We don't want to take the stairs . . . too much effort. Besides, where do they lead?

Do we stop and ask ourselves, where do we sense God is leading me? Right now am I being the person I want to be? The leader I want to be?

"Live your questions now, and perhaps even without knowing it, you will live along some distant day into your answers." —Rainer Maria Rilke

Do we stop and ask ourselves why we react the way we do toward life, toward our circumstances, toward others? Or do we let the current of the waters carry us to the falls?

I'll leave off with this poem by Portia Nelson:

I walk down the street.
There is a deep hole in the sidewalk.
I fall in.
I am lost . . . I am helpless.
It isn't my fault.
It takes forever to find a way out.

I walk down the same street.
There is a deep hole in the sidewalk.
I pretend I don't see it.
I fall in again.
I can't believe I am in this same place.
But, it isn't my fault.
It still takes a long time to get out.

I walk down the same street.
There is a deep hole in the sidewalk.
I see it is there.
I still fall in. It's habit.
My eyes are open.
I know where I am.
It is my fault. I get out immediately.

I walk down the same street.
There is a deep hole in the sidewalk.
I walk around it.

I walk down another street.[15]

***

Piece of Paradise

No words can describe
The experience of the sunrise.
It's my piece of heaven, peace, and paradise.
It dances with all its fire and grace only to entice
The longing of my early morning desire to feel alive.
Because I can't live a life merely to survive.
No, because all my senses scream they are ready to grow and thrive.
My eyes are the entrance to the breathtaking rise of the pure liquid gold.
My eyes make the snapshot for my thoughts to hold.
My ears become the channel in which the music plays,
The rhythm of the lullaby sung by each wave.
The taste of pure open fresh salt air
Centers my soul and takes me away from any care.
The sand beneath my toes
Reminds me of every inch of my body and mind He not only made, but knows.

15 Portia Nelson, *There's a Hole in My Sidewalk (New York City: Atria Books/Beyond Words, 2012).*

Yep, it's hard to describe the beauty of the sunrise where the sand
   meets the sea.
But remember its grace . . . its love . . . never fails for you or for me.
May this day you cease to sleep,
But go out and embrace the life you want to have and keep.

***

The Beauty of The Mind

The beauty of the mind.
How fascinating is our mind that by grace we have been given?
Thoughts that freely flow will create death or a life worth living.
The mind, when enraptured by good thoughts and visions,
Becomes the key that unlocks men's and women's self-contained
   prisons.
We truly create our own reality with the thoughts we focus upon.
We can either create our lives to contain riches or create none.
Our thoughts reveal the reflection of our hearts and souls.
And if they're not positive, optimistic, and hopeful . . . they
   become our gravesite hole.
Our mind is so amazing that each second we have the opportunity
   to change the way we think.
Our perspective on life makes the difference just as quickly as one
   can blink.
The words say, as we think, we become.
Wouldn't you rather feel the pulse of life than go through life
   numb?

So today may you challenge yourself
to change your thoughts to happiness, love, and worry-free
So you can know what it is to have riches and health.
Remember, your thoughts are your freedom and they hold the key.

Pick Up Trash

I try to pick up trash when I can, if I'm not running (that would inter-fere—you know what I mean—inconvenience me . . . I might have to stop what I am doing . . . I mean, I have a goal set, you understand?). I've been convinced, once in a while, if I'm running, that I really need to pick up that one piece of trash that could be harmful to someone or wildlife . . . like a piece of glass or plastic. But, I'm ashamed to say, I'm not convinced to do so often enough.

This morning I was strolling along the water's edge when I dis-covered a piece of a fishing lure where the line had been cut, and three large hooks peeked up from the sand . . . looming . . . waiting for a bare foot to come along and rescue them out of the sand. Ouch! Okay, this is the third one this week. Anyway, it felt good to throw it in the trash and feel like my small action may have saved a surfer's foot . . . or that of some unsuspecting child running barefoot in the shallow surf.

It's amazing how something so minor can make us feel good. I mean, I would like to think that we all like to do good things. It makes us feel good, like we have a bigger agenda, other than ourselves. I like to help other people. I like to do things that make me feel like I'm mak-ing a difference in someone's life. It just feels so good.

But what about those things that are good—they don't feel so good, but you know it's for the best. What if it's getting up again after you've failed? What if it's moving forward in hope after you've lost the love of your life?

I believe that anything good or anything that will lead to better things for us or for others always disguises itself, especially in the beginning, as a challenge . . . as something that looks impossible to do. As a change . . . a change in what our days look like . . . a change in direction. As a sacrifice. And yes, sometimes, as pain and suffering. But I believe that as we allow ourselves to use these disguises as gifts . . . as a way to become stronger . . . a way to become our best for ourselves and others . . . that we begin to get a glimpse into joy, peace, hope, and faith.

This is what I can understand and what I've come to realize: that every time something is hard or painful or difficult, it's always for my best. I don't always want it or embrace it, but if I allow it to change me, I always become a better person because of it. In the end, it's always the best. Even doing something for someone else that makes us feel good demands some type of time, energy, thought, or sacrifice. It just does . . . but isn't the reward peace, gladness in the heart, joy?

You know, asking why this happened has never really gotten me very far. In fact, asking why to that age-old question just keeps me stuck. So I choose to believe that as horrific as some things seems . . . as painful as it may be . . . there is a purpose. Maybe our best isn't just for us. Maybe giving our best . . . being your best friend . . . being the best you can be . . . maybe becoming the best you can become is for a greater purpose. Maybe becoming the best you can become in your body, mind, and spirit is really for everyone's benefit.

What are you trying to avoid because it's hard? What are you trying to wallow in because it's too hard to accept it may be for your best? What are you not taking responsibility for because you don't want to have to drop that pride, even though you know deep down inside you made the choice and you need to accept the responsibility? Who and what are you wanting to blame for the pain? Is there a way to see that pain through a different lens . . . a lens that could give you the best view instead of a one-way view?

The Last Three Reps

"The last three or four reps is what makes the muscle grow. This area of pain divides the champion from someone else who is not a champion. That's what most people lack, having the guts to go on and just say they'll go through the pain no matter what happens."
—Arnold Schwarzenegger

You know, we all can't be Arnold, but we can be an Arnold in our own lives with what we've been given. Maybe your pain doesn't look the same as others'. Maybe you feel like it's worse . . . and maybe it is . . . but change only occurs through the pain. Growth only happens through that next tear . . . that next rep.

Maybe it's just deciding to get up one morning and start walking when you haven't walked in years. Maybe it's deciding to give up sugar for a day. Maybe it's deciding to ask someone for forgiveness. Maybe it's deciding to lose weight. Maybe it's deciding to think differently . . . to catch that toxic thought and turn it into something positive. Maybe it's deciding to become a next Arnold. Maybe it's to win the next marathon. Maybe it's deciding to go back to school. Maybe it's to become the next president of the US. Maybe it's to get through the death of a loved one.

Whatever it is, the only way to get there is by doing those things we don't feel like doing . . . going through the tough spots. That's the only way we change. It doesn't feel good. Maybe it's not what we want to do, but when you get up and do it anyway . . . when you make that decision in your mind, that choice that only you can make for yourself to go through the pain of those extra reps with courage, with persistence, with gratitude . . . that's when you become a champion. Don't stop because it's hard. Keep going because it will be easier on the other side. Freedom comes from the last three or four reps.

Maybe my champion won't look like Arnold, but I'll be a champion because I had the guts to go through the hard stuff . . . I decided the extra reps were worth the pain . . . and I did it with a smile.

Who Do You Follow

Who do you follow? Why do you follow them? So many to follow now and so many avenues . . . who do you follow and why? The options are endless. You have your buffet of platforms: LinkedIn, Twitter, Instagram, blogs, Facebook, Snapchat—the options are endless. Maybe it's not a person you follow. Maybe it's an agenda or a social cause. . .

But this morning I have a more reflective life-changing question for you. I want you to ask yourself this question: Would you follow *you*? Let me reiterate: Would you follow yourself? Why or why not?

I mean, are you eating the right foods? Are you moving your body and mind toward health and wellness? Are you investing your time and energy in personal growth? Are you a good influence on your children and grandchildren? Are you empowering others? Are you walking your talk? Are you making an impact in your community or at your work? Are you becoming better than you were yesterday?

Are you the pilot or the copilot of your life? Are you just along for the ride while others fly you on their agendas . . . where the media takes you where they want you to go . . . where time pilots your life? I don't know about you, but I'm not satisfied just being the copilot of my life. I want to fly that damn plane.

I want to look in the mirror and say to my reflection, "I would follow you!"

I want to walk the talk. I want to be better than I was yesterday. I don't want to wake up at the end of my life and say I wish I'd done this or that. I don't want to have regrets about how I lived my life . . . and I have a strong gut feeling that you don't either. I believe you want to look in that mirror of yours and say to your reflection staring back, "I would follow you."

I want to get more texts and messages that tell me to keep writing and speaking because it inspires them . . . that they've changed something in their lives because of my posts . . . that makes my purpose that much more solidified and my commitment not to quit that much stronger. That I'm on track with my dreams.

We have people watching us: our children, our grandchildren, our peers, our friends. And never think that your enemies aren't watching you too . . . to watch and see what you do with failures, how you take care of your body and mind. They want to see if you love or hate, get angry or stay calm . . . how you handle major crisis in your life . . . how you handle pain and loss. They want to see if you go after your dreams with passion, commitment, persistence, and courage or stay in your comfort zone because of fear. The world is watching you. Are you going to inspire them or discourage them?

People say to me, "You are so strong, Linda, and such an inspiration. How do you do it?" I do it because my passion is to look in the mirror at the end of the day—at the end of my story—and say, "I would follow you." Because I have dreams and passions that God gave me. He gave them to you too. I have a responsibility to fight for them . . . to become a warrior for Him, for the dreams so they'll be carried out for others. The big picture is not about just me or just you. The big picture is about serving all of us . . . doing something bigger than us so others will benefit from our dreams. Our dreams are about others. I have many, but I'll tell you about this one. . .

My figure contest. My third masters figure contest . . . taking my body and mind to a higher level. By doing that, I find I am unstoppable . . . that I can master anything if I can master my body. If I am strong physically and mentally, then I can handle whatever punches life throws at me . . . because life will throw them. I want to be able to punch back with force.

If I ask my clients to push through hard workouts or push through something they're going through, or if I'm preaching health and wellness to others, then I have to be able to do it myself. I can't tell someone to go the extra mile when I'm not willing to go the extra mile myself. I *am* going the extra mile.

If I'm strong both physically and mentally, then when times like this past May happen to me, I can look in the mirror and say to my reflection, "I would follow you." I lost my mom to a heart attack, my boyfriend broke up with me, and I totaled my Jeep . . . it was a bad month . . . but because I can see the bigger picture, I was able to get through the difficult circumstances. If I hadn't been strong both physically and mentally, I wouldn't have been able to serve as a pallbearer for my mom and help carry my mom's casket to her final resting place. Her spirit was already enjoying paradise. . . I wouldn't have been able to get through the hassle of buying a new vehicle in the midst of grieving.

I am determined not to quit. You see, this is just the beginning of our stories. We can start a new chapter any day we want. We hold the pen. I want to encourage others to live their lives richly and fully. I want my angels in heaven—my husband, Mom, and Dad—to look down and say, "I knew she could do it." I want God to say, "You have a lot of faith. . . Let me give you more to do." And I want my son to be proud to call me "Mom."

I made a decision when my husband died . . . that my new story had just begun. I'm not stopping until my dreams come true . . . and you can't stop until yours do. You have greatness within you that has not even been tapped into. Tap into it now. Go after your dream with a vengeance. Don't ever, ever, ever, ever, ever, ever quit.

When you come to the end of your life, what will your mirror reflect back to you? Regret or satisfaction? Would you follow you?

1, 140 Minutes, What Are You Going To Do With Yours?

The early bird will gain his minutes through a sunrise. You have been given by grace 1,140 minutes today to live out your day . . . some are already done. Those minutes are a valuable commodity . . . probably one of the most important commodities, besides two others:

What you decide to do with the minutes you've been given . . . how you invest them for greater dividends.

Your health . . . because without your health, it really doesn't make a difference what you do with your time. And we never appreciate health until it's gone.

So how are we going to spend our 1,440 minutes? Will they drive our agendas . . . our purposes . . . or will we drive them? There are two factors that will drive that decision today: looking for purpose and pleasure, or looking to escape pain. And they both look the same.

One thousand four hundred and forty minutes . . . the choice is in your hand.

My Little Buddy

My little buddy wants everyone to know that if they are stressed, anxious, or depressed, they need to look at the bigger perspective of life and realize: it's a beautiful day in the neighborhood. You are alive and it's a good day. You have purpose.

Stress: What are you going to do about it?
Anxiety: What are you anxious about?
Depression: What does it do for you?
"'Just living is not enough,' said the butterfly, 'one must have sunshine, freedom, and a little flower.'" —Hans Christian Andersen[16]

Serenade

———∞∞∞———

"There isn't any such thing as an ordinary life." —L.M. Montgomery

This guy was playing his guitar this morning, and it was beautiful. Serenade for the sunrise . . . and a dolphin was playing in the water. I can't make this stuff up. Sunrises and this beach are really magical. It's like God gives me a glimpse of heaven in the mornings. He's telling me, "Linda, you're right on track. Keep moving forward." It's a good confirmation. It's surreal some mornings. Life is extraordinary. Life explains to us that there is something bigger than us. When we become aware of the ordinary ... awake to the ordinary ... we understand that it really is extraordinary ... when we stop ... and look around us ... what are you missing in the ordinary that would lead you to the extraordinary life?

---

16 Hans Christian Andersen, *The Complete Hans Christian Andersen Fairy Tales* (New York City: Gramercy, 1993).

Contrast

———∞———

"There is no quality in this world that is not what it is merely by contrast. Nothing exist in itself." ——*Herman Melville*

Contrast ... is how we learn ... what contrast is. We have opposing experiences in life.

For example: love/hate . . . faith/worry . . . health/illness . . . sadness/joy . . . pain/pleasure . . . anger/calm . . . forgiveness/ unforgiveness . . . death/life . . . winners/losers . . . success/failure. . . People always wonder why we can't have health all the time . . . love all the time . . . pleasure and joy all the time. Well, we just can't because if we won all the time, we wouldn't know we were winning or how to win because we wouldn't understand or experience loss. Besides, it's been this way since the beginning of time. It's set in place while we are here on earth. It's not going to change . . . so get over yourself and learn to play these polar opposites. Embrace it and learn to fight for what you want more of in your life.

What I've learned is you really can't have two of these contrast happening at the same time. You're either feeding one or the other. You can't have a happy and sad thought at the same thought. You can certainly think a sad thought and then remember something happy and think about that in the next thought, but not at the same time. So whichever you choose to continue to feed wins the game.

You see, this is the game of life and you have to learn how to play it . . . especially since you don't want to lose. Because you know how it feels to lose . . . and to win.

You also have to learn when to draw the line. You know, when you're about to cheat instead of play by the rules of life's game. Yep, you have to know the rules and the consequences of not following those rules . . . of trying to cheat . . . because a cheater never really wins. You can't cheat the game of life, but you can learn to play the game strategically and have an advantage.

I'm such a believer in keeping your body and mind healthy because without these two players, you're automatically withdrawn from the game.

Say your body is craving veggies and you give it French fries. Do you think you're winning the game of health or losing? Say your body wants to get stronger . . . build bone up . . . gain some muscles . . . strengthen your heart . . . but you don't make the time. You don't feel like it. You don't have the money . . . and all other excuses. Are you getting stronger or weaker? You're getting one or the other. You can't cheat the game of life and expect to win . . . and be angry when you lose.

Optical Illusion

"What we see depends mainly on what we look for." —*John LuBock*

I love to look at optical illusion pictures because they force me to see a different side. In life, we tend to view things from one perspective. In fact, our outside world will reflect how we feel about ourselves on the inside and how we view the world and others.

Sometimes it's difficult to stretch ourselves to see another view. When we examine ourselves or another person or even our environment, we tend to see it through our inner world. This is why two people can look at the same picture and see something totally different. This is why we have debates. This is why people argue. This is why we get stuck in old habits. This is why relationships end. This is what keeps us stuck in the same old, same old. We will never change or grow if we can't recognize that there's another perspective. Even with ourselves and our image of ourselves. Are we really seeing the right reflection in the mirror? What illusion are we living with?

Maybe we need to gaze a little longer at the picture until we understand that our perception may have another side.

Fish Bowl

————

"Two lost souls swimming in the fish bowl year after year."
— *Pink Floyd*

The power, the adventure, the fun, the success, the freedom . . . it's all in jumping outside of your comfort zone. Away from the safety of sharing the same perception with everyone else . . . sharing the same fishbowl, circling the same waters with the same lookalikes, getting fed the same food by the same hands . . . sharing the same belief that this is all there is . . . that this is just the way it is. Make the jump into new waters . . . refreshing, clean water . . . with new, better responsibilities . . . new opportunities . . . greater success. Jump into an extraordinary life instead of the fishbowl of the ordinary. Because as long as you swim in another's fishbowl, they will create your environment and you'll be swimming in the same recycled water ten years from now.

Take the challenge and the risk and make the jump into a new and improved think tank.

But, It Rises Every Morning?

It was beautiful and calm out there this morning. You know, I was thinking about the sunrise pictures and the opportunity to witness sunrises and how grateful I am to be able to see this beauty each morning.

It's very difficult for me to miss a sunrise. It's ingrained in me now. The feeling I experience when I'm on the beach at sunrise just outweighs sleeping in.

Some people would say, "But it rises every morning, so you can miss it once in a while." However, just like some opportunities in life, the sunrises only come at a certain time of day, so you have to be there at that time to catch it—and every sunrise is different. Just like every opportunity is different. But if you miss it, you miss it, and that same opportunity will not come around again, just as that same sunrise won't. So you need to be awake to catch them.

The Flood, October 2015

"Alone we can do so little together we can do so much." — *Helen Keller*

Well, it's still gray and cloudy and rainy, but this morning I saw some rays trying to poke through. The sun will shine again. The waters will recede. Life will continue . . . maybe differently for some. In the midst of pain, loss, and damage, it's hard to see the light . . . but it will come.

I am extremely saddened by the damage and loss so many of my friends have experienced along with others I've seen and heard about in areas across our beautiful state of South Carolina. Prayers continue to be a source of strength and power in the midst of the flooding. May we all pull together and continue to pray for one another and encourage one another to stay strong and hopeful. Where there is more than one, there is always strength . . . so it's a great time to put aside differences and use them for strength, putting all the pieces back together again. Even though they may look a little different, it will be good . . . and the sun will shine again. It's always darkest before the dawn.

Rose Colored Glasses

"Are you still looking through rose colored glasses?" —*J.M. Madere*

Why yes, I am...probably always will.

It's still sunless in the neighborhood, but it's still beautiful because we have the opportunity to get stronger and better in this day.

When I woke up this morning, I was hoping to see the sunrise. I was excited. I ran downstairs, in the dark of the morning, to my car, and zoomed off to the beach. I parked my car and started the short walk to my piece of solitude and paradise . . . the shore . . . but when I looked up, there were no stars to be seen. A little disappointment set in with the realization that I wouldn't see the sunrise. And there's still more flooding that could take place as the waters shift and recede. (historic flooding in South Carolina)

So I started to be thankful for life and grateful for what I have. You know, a lot of people are still struggling and a lot of damage has not been assessed yet . . . and the water is still here. The sun refuses to shine this morning, but it will shine. The water will recede. We will rebuild what needs rebuilding and repair what needs repairing . . . because we are like that: resilient in hard times . . . determined to put our lives back together.

As bad as things may seem, it's part of life. The bad comes with the good, and you have to focus on the good . . . the solutions, not the problems. Focus on seeing what you want, not what you don't. That's how the process of rebuilding works, by focusing on the positive instead of the negative. And part of the positive is that our strength is always found in the midst of the struggle. I mean, I never get stronger swimming with the current. I never grow or get stronger using weight that gives no resistance. I've never found much of a solution to a challenge when I give up or quit. The solution always comes in trying one more time—differently. I have always found this incredible strength from deep within when I needed it the most . . . because strength is developed against the wind, in the resistance . . . the struggle . . . the pain.

The victory and the strength lie in the fight to become the victor over life's tragedies instead of the victim of life's hard strikes.

We learn to become a strong nation . . . a strong community . . . by becoming strong individuals who will take responsibility for our lives and attitudes. Then and only then can we help empower others in a common effort to build a strong and resilient community and nation. But we have to be willing to look at who we, as individuals, are becoming before we can help anyone else.

Blame never did win any victories. Self-pity never beat its opponent. Negativity never built a nation . . . for that matter, negativity never built anything but more negativity.

I don't know . . . maybe I like my rose-colored, optimistic, hopeful glasses because they give me a different perspective on an otherwise defeating glare.

Violin

"All we need to make us really happy is something
to be enthusiastic about." —Charles Kingsley

Isn't that the truth? I'm enthusiastic about life. And in the morning, nothing makes me get out of bed faster than knowing I have a purpose and a passion.

I believe faith and enthusiasm are like a violin. It takes both the violin and the bow. They just won't work unless the two of them connect. The violin won't play without the bow and the bow will not make music without the violin. If you're enthusiastic about life, then you have the faith that there is more to life than you can see. You realize that good things are happening and will happen. Because, if you have faith you can move mountains. That should be enough to make a person enthusiastic about life. All things are possible with God. I just believe it. And if you have faith, then that's the assurance of things hoped for, the conviction of things not seen. Wow . . . now *that* will make you enthusiastic about life.

You can feed into negativity and hopelessness. That's easy. Just turn on the news, listen to conversations around you, or go through your Facebook feed. You will quickly lose your faith and enthusiasm . . . and you know what amazes me? A lot of the negativity is from people who say they read, study, and know His word. Makes a person go . . . umm. . .

Or you can start your own enthusiasm about life and be different and maybe be strange to others. But you'll wake up knowing today is a good day because I have the faith to believe I can move mountains.

It is Done

It's a beautiful evening in the neighborhood, and it's been an awesome day of grace.

I love this legend. I hope it stretches us to become better than we were yesterday and to realize the answer always, always found from within. You always know where the answer lies. The only questions you have to ask yourself is: are you ready for the truth you find? And when are you going to be ready to seek it? The truth always sets you free.

In ancient times, the Creator wanted to hide something from humans until they were ready to see it. He gathered all the other creatures of creation to ask for their advice.

The eagle said, "Give it to me and I will take it to the highest mountain in all the land," but the Creator said, "No, one day they will conquer the mountain and find it."

The salmon said, "Leave it with me and I will hide it at the very bottom of the ocean," but the Creator said, "No, for humans are explores at heart, and one day they will go there, too."

The buffalo said, "I will take it and bury it in the very heart of the great plains," but the Creator said, "No, for one day even the skin of the earth will be ripped open, and they will find it there."

The creatures of creation were stumped, but then an old blind mole spoke up. "Why don't you put it inside them—that's the very last place they'll look."

The Creator said, "It is done."[17]

What Price Would You Put On Your Wellness?

A friend and I were talking the other day about health and wellness. He's in the same field as me. We're both passionate about empowering others to take care of themselves. We talked about the value of that for others. What kind of price would you put on health and wellness, on something that could add value to your life in so many ways? If you found someone who could empower you to change your life, what would you pay? He asked me what price I would put on my health and wellness. Of course, my answer was—as the old credit card commercials stated so clearly— "It's priceless."

He asked me what got me through all my experiences. I said, "prayer, my faith . . . helping others through my business . . . giving

---

17 Michael Neill, *Supercoach (Carlsbad: Hay House, 2010), 27.*

. . . physical exercise, working out and getting stronger . . . mental exercise, reading positive and motivational material . . . listening to motivational speakers . . . turning off the negative and worthless chatter on TV . . . staying away from gossip and negative people . . . eating healthy, nutritious foods . . . learning new things . . . getting out of my comfort zone . . . surfing . . . writing . . . doing my videos . . . speaking . . . making time for friends . . . getting coached . . . making time for meditation at sunrise . . . and daily affirmations." My health and wellbeing are priceless.

We were talking about how people always ask, "How much is personal training? How much is life/wellness coaching?" It's a fair question, because many of us have budgets to live within . . . but it fascinates me how we seem to put our health on the back burner of that budget when really, our health and wellness need to be on the front burner. Because without our mental, emotional, spiritual, and physical health . . . nothing else really matters. I mean, we may can go along for a few years . . . getting by . . . putting it off . . . but eventually what we do on the inside will show on the outside. You can't escape it. Life will catch up to you . . . unless you decide use your tool, called choice, to learn to defy your age inside and out.

I personally will spend whatever it takes to stay healthy because I understand the importance of health in a world that constantly tries to rob us of our health and happiness. I've learned it's priceless. It's hard to put a price on health, isn't it? Ask anyone who struggles with health or mental and emotional distress. Peace and wellbeing are priceless.

That doesn't mean it's easy. That doesn't mean you won't have difficult days. But it does mean that you'll find it easier to rise above it . . . easier to bounce back from sickness . . . easier to live your life on your terms, not on a circumstance's terms. You can take back control. Don't let your body dictate your life. Don't let your circumstances dictate your life. Take control of your health and wellness.

My health and wellness are priceless. I am worth it. What about you…I know you are worth it too!

CANCER SUCKS

I am sharing this because I understand the scare when someone comes in your room and says it's cancer. I had my five-year mammogram since my lumpectomy last week. I was a few months over in my scheduling of getting it done. I knew in my gut it would be clear and it was. I am so grateful.

You know I was very fortunate. I hate cancer. I hate the word. I have had friends and family members die from cancer, and friends who have beaten the odds. Cancer is a very serious disease. It is NOTH-ING to play around with. I am not telling my story for you to follow in my footsteps. I am telling my story because I want you to know there are options to every situation. Some of those options may be just as easy as a second opinion. So many people get scared and robotically follow the first opinion they receive. This opinion may not be in the person's best interest. My cancer was DCIS. It was hormone receptive which meant that I had too much of the bad estrogen in my body.

The doctors wanted me to have radiation treatment and a five-year drug treatment plan, an estrogen blocker called Tamoxifen. I choose not to do either one. I read the side effects on both. The side effects of Tamoxifen were so scary that I chose to study diligently about diet and the effects it had on curbing, stopping cancer. I talked to some of my friends who were on the drug and they were suffering from some of the side effect which included some of the following;

depression (then they had to take an anti-depressant), could cause liver and cervical cancer, (why would I trade one cancer for another?) (I had a friend who actually got cervical cancer from the drug), muscle weakness, hot flashes, (so one friend said the hot flashes were so bad they had to take something to curb those) and so much more. I chose not to do the drug therapy nor the radiation. (I DO NOT RECOMMEND THIS TO ANYONE) It is a personal decision. I had people, family, including Mark (my husband), tell me to do the radiation and drug therapy. I found out that if I did the radiation in that breast, that if the cancer came back, then I could not have radiation again in the same area. I had to ask myself if I wanted to risk that now, when the results indicated that my cancer was zero on a scale of zero to five, or if it came back, I thought to myself, I would rather have that ammunition in my arsenal then rather than use all my bullets now.

I chose instead to take dairy out, sugar out, processed foods (meaning anything with less than 6 ingredients that I understood the meaning of) and meat out of my diet, except for fish. I am so grateful that it was contained in one area and it was zero. Because to be honest with all of you it is a hard decision to make. I feel like when it came back zero that it was really pre-cancerous. I share this to say don't let others make decisions for you. You will know what is best for your body and your mind. Be pro-active in your health and don't just take one doctors opinion. Be sure to get two or three or more opinions if needed. Everyone is human and everyone can make mistakes, even your health care providers. You are in control of your body, your mind, your life. I was fortunate had my cancer been on a one on the scale and not contained I may have taken a different route. I know the scare when someone mentions the word cancer whether it is controllable or past that stage.

Let's support one another and let's find a cure. Let's learn to take control of our bodies our health. We can do this simply by educating ourselves on diet, exercise, and the drugs that our health care providers want to supply us with and the alternatives that may be available if any. Exercise and nutrition is huge in preventing many diseases. I could write a book about it. I guess the main point I want you to get out of this post is cancer sucks and you are in control of your decisions and your body. Do not let another person dictate your health and wellness. Life is precious and so are you. Take control learn about the drugs you are given and study the different options you have. Don't be embarrassed to ask for a second opinion it's your body. Don't' be afraid to ask questions and always research to find the best answer for you, because you are worth it. Yes, cancer sucks so let's work together to support one another, encourage one another, and find a cure. Let's let all the oncologist retire or find another career and drug companies out of business because we found a cure! We do thank the oncologist for their work and care of the patient . . . until the cure . . . then they can retire and I know they would be happy to lay that hat down and I know the drug companies would be happy to retire too . . . wouldn't they?

The Realist VS The Optimist... but really the Pessimist

An optimist is someone who always sees the bright side of any situation — a trait that can be either encouraging or annoying, depending on your frame of mind.

Could it be a happy Thursday? It depends, doesn't it?

I was talking with this guy last night. He said he was a realist. He had made a comment about how bad his life was. He didn't like what he was doing. I asked him what his passion was. He told me, but said, "I can't make money doing it." I said, "Sure you can. If we follow our passions, the money will follow." I believe this. I believe that's why we've been given our passions and gifts.

We don't have to hate what we do for work. We have lots of opportunities and possibilities to make money in our free world and make a great living doing what we love . . . if we choose to and if our attitudes and thinking are optimistic. I also believe that what we do needs to benefit others. I think that's the way the laws of the universe work.

He thought my optimistic view was a waste and that being a realist was a better way to view life. Well . . . differences are what make the world go round.

After listening to him, I thought to myself, He's not even a realist . . . he's a pessimist. Because everything was negative; too many "I cant's" and "never wills" . . . whew. . .

Well, I'm an optimist and I can pretty much guarantee that he'll be in the same place in his mind and career ten years from now, still saying he can't. Because guess what? Can't, never will, or never could produce results.

I prefer to look at the brighter side of life. I've had enough of the dark. I prefer to hope and believe that the impossible is going to happen. God tells me that with Him, all things are possible. I want to believe my life is going to get better and better—and I do. I prefer to believe that you don't always have to deal with things in a practical way . . . that sometimes it takes the impractical way to make a dream manifest into reality. We wouldn't have a lot of our modern conveniences if inventors had thought in realistic or practical ways. I prefer to see the good before the bad. This has helped me tremendously in getting through some very difficult times. Things will get better, and there is always something good that comes out of the bad.

I would much rather have optimistic thoughts running through my head than defeating ones. I mean, if you have a choice, why wouldn't you want to choose optimism? What could it hurt? Your mood? Your relationships? Your career? Your day?

Whoop Whoop

Give your desires, your dreams, your hopes, and your concerns to God. Leave them there for him to tend to. He's much better at it than you are. He simply asks that we trust Him. Believe He is. Expect He is.

Now that you've done that, step into action physically and mentally in concordance with that expectancy and watch the opportunities and peace unfold before your very eyes.

Look where you've never looked before. Believe like you say you do. Expect like you've already received the impossible. And then follow that with a great big, "Whoop whoop!"

Don't Like Sweat?

"No one has every drowned in sweat" —Lou Holtz

I'm going to gym to get some good old sweat going. Someone remarked to me one day that they don't like to sweat. I was like a dog cocking his head from one side to the other after hearing a strange sound. Huh? What? Those were strange words to my ears. Sweat is liquid drops from the fountain of youth...who wouldn't want to dive in the fountain of youth?

The Embers of Simplicity

"I would not give a fig for the simplicity this side of complexity, but I would give my life for the simplicity on the other side of complexity."
——*Oliver Wendell Holmes*

It's a beautiful day in the neighborhood, in the complexity called life . . . in the simplicity of the day.

We can stand, walk, run, or flee . . . but we cannot hide forever in the complexity of life. However, we *can* sit and meditate in the embers of simplicity, which bring peace. It's the simple things that make me smile. Enjoying the simplicity in the midst of the complexity. It keeps me sane. Thank You, God, for revealing Your grace to me yet again this morning. I need you . . .

It is Impossible to Fail

—⁂—

"You must act as if it is impossible to fail." —*Ashanti Proverb*

What would you do today if you knew it was impossible to fail? You know, you never really fail . . . you learn.

Make the Choice

—⁂—

The older I get . . . the more that life throws my way . . . the more difficult situations I find myself in . . . the more determined, passionate, and persistent I am to make it a challenge to overcome . . . to be better . . . to be stronger . . . to look for the good . . . just to be the good in this world . . . to be an encourager for another.

How do I do those things? By keeping my mind and my body healthy. By feeding my body and my mind with health-promoting foods, foods that fuel me. I'm not living to eat, but eating to live. By working my body, because it was meant to move. I look at food as my energy. By working it hard, but resting when I need to. By feeding my mind positive stuff, not junk, not propaganda, not hate, not gossip. By being around people who build me up, not tear me down—and if that means that I choose my friends wisely . . . well . . . that's what I do. That means having boundaries too. By learning new things. By using my gifts and talents to help others, to encourage them, to love them where they are instead of where I think they should be.

But the most important thing I do is make the choice each day to live a better life than I lived the day before. It is making a choice each day to love others. Making a choice each day to live life to the fullest. Making a choice each day to choose what I think about. Making a choice to keep moving forward.

You will face obstacles. You will be run off the path, but because you have motivation, because you have desire and a goal you want to reach, you will stay on your path. You will make it through to those dreams. You know from within what motivates you to keep on. Keep on.

Most

"Most people live, whether physically, intellectually, or morally, in a very restricted circle of their potential being." —William James[18]

Today is a great day to begin to separate yourself from "most."

Moment

What a difference a day makes. Cloudy, cool, and windy on the beach this morning. But what a beautiful morning. There is so much beauty in the quietness of the morning light. We just have to live in the moment to experience it . . . to be able to interrupt the reflecting thoughts

---

18 William James, *The Letters of William James* (New York City: Cosimo Classics, 2008), 253.

of yesterday and those of aspirations for tomorrow and allow the moment in which we are existing to complete us.

These moments of rest, seeing through our eyes of clarity, are when we discover the reflection of the one who gives us glimpses into our unique and extraordinary world. His world of purpose and design. His creation seen and His creation seeing. Peace and change always come to us in the present moment of clarity through the lens of the soul.

But I've found that the only way to truly see . . . to believe in where your path is guiding you . . . is by existing in the spotlight of the moment where you know there is nowhere for you to strive to get to . . . because you're just here.

Sweet Strength

"Make it Sweet and Keep it Strong…all day long…because life is sweet…and we are strong" —Linda McDandel

Since the death of my husband, Mark, a lot of people have remarked to me how strong I am. I find that fascinating really. I mean if you have faith and believe in everlasting life…. how else could you live? I live a rather easy life here in America. What do I really sacrifice? I think of all the widows, orphans, children that are trapped in sex trafficking (I cannot think of anything more horrifying) that have no one . . . no hope …. unless someone offers them hope. Unless someone rescues them. I think of people who have lost loved ones in war, poverty, women and children who have no rights, genocide, rape, natural disaster, hunger, health, my loss seems so little, because I have hope of being with Mark again, I am still among loved ones and still have a roof over my head and food on the table, and I know Mark is so loved right now. But, this is how I feel . . . I guess you could say it is my philosophy on life. I don't know if this will help anyone, but I would like to give you my thoughts on strength. It is what I believe strength looks like, what it looks like to me.

You only gain strength from adversity, from pain, from suffering, from failures. There is no other way to get stronger except through the struggle. You get stronger by looking at death . . . you are going to die and the only way to truly embrace life is to look at death. Strength to me is belief in the power of prayer, still, even when your prayers don't get answered in your way and your time. It is being able to say that my faith doesn't look the same and that is ok. My faith is stronger, but different. Strength is to believe in the impossible. Strength understands that after a loss of someone you love . . . your life is not the same . . . nor will it be the same . . . but it is finding the courage to find a new life a new way of living and being ok with that. It is being able to get up each day and be thankful of everything . . . everything . . . good and bad. Strength is looking for the good in all things. It is the ability to see things from another person's perspective. I am not always right. It is always the ability to swim against the current not with it. Swimming with the current takes no strength. It is the ability to say no and not have to give reasons for it. It is the ability to set your own boundaries so that you are not led around by others agendas. It is the ability to look at your weaknesses and accept them and build on your strengths. It is the ability to look at your failures and say to yourself. . . they weren't really failures they were learning experience. Strength is holding your head up, brushing your knees off, and moving on no matter how many times you fall or fail. You simply you get up, you get up, and you move with your head held high and your feet pointed to that goal. Strength is to realize that material things are just that material things . . . they can be taken from you at any time. You don't have security in anything

. . . that is an illusion. You don't need most of what you accumulate and you can live without more than you think. It is allowing your heart to be open to love someone else even though it may feel, look, and be different . . . but love is like that . . .and that is good. Strength is to love yourself . . . to know you are beautiful . . . not a prideful beautiful . . . but a humble beautiful . . . because you are . . . I am. Loving yourself means having the strength to take care of yourself, your body, your mind, and your soul . . . loving others . . . if you don't love yourself I am convinced you can't love God or anyone else. We were meant to move and that is part of strength, moving. Strength is being able to stretch yourself past your comfort zone . . . your perceived limits. It is to learn new things, to be curious, to face fears, because, we know that perfect love drives out fear. Strength is not being led by your emotions, but allowing yourself time to sit with them, because they will pass and new one's will come. Strength to me is allowing you to grieve over the loss of a loved one . . . but knowing that we really need to be grieving for ourselves . . . because we haven't made it home yet. I find strength in not taking myself too seriously and being able to laugh at myself . . . there is plenty to laugh at. Strength is never giving up, never, never, it doesn't matter what you may feel. You get up, you press through, and you know your spirit will give you the strength if you put the action behind it. It is to respect others opinions, but you don't have to be influenced by them. Oh . . . and don't put expectations on others . . . they may not or cannot live up to them . . . and then you will be hurt and rejected. Don't let others put expectations on you either, it just doesn't work, we all let each other down. Strength is being able to sit with someone in pain and not try to fix it. Because, only they know the pain they are in . . . you really don't have a clue. To remember your job is to love others. Your job is not judge them. You can't change others or save others . . . that is not your job . . . your job is to come along beside them and listen and empower them. You can change yourself though

. . . that is strength . . . changing you . . . not someone else. Strength is being able to release yourself to be someone different. It is looking through different lens. It is forming new habits. It is letting go with values and beliefs that are not benefiting you or those around you and be ok with that. Strength is to be determined not to stay the same . . . or not to be in the same place too long . . . mentally . . . physically . . . or spiritually. Strength is the ability to always be free from the opinions of others. That means . . . if someone tells you that you are beautiful and the next person tells you that you are ugly . . . both of those words could influence your whole demeanor for the rest of the day. It is just an opinion from their perspective. The question remains do you think you are beautiful or ugly? Strength is . . . letting go of the past and not rehashing it again and again . . . it's the past for Pete's sake . . . let it go. We were designed to move forward not backwards. Forgive others, because I somehow believe we have all done something . . . somewhere along the line that needs forgiving. Admit when you are wrong and extend forgiveness. Strength for me is being able to receive criticism and not let it cripple me, but move me. Oh, yeah and Strength is realizing that you are not above any temptation or sin . . . you will fall . . . but you don't have to stay there. Strength is realizing that just because you have money, success, beauty (external), status, whatever it is . . . it doesn't mean you are better or above anyone else. We need to always remember we put our pants on the same way everyone else does . . . one leg at the time. Strength is giving what you can to help others with whatever tools and gifts you have been given to do so. I don't know . . . do I always walk in what I believe about strength . . . no . . . but I am still on the potter's wheel. I am not giving up, I am not sitting down, I am running the race marked out for me. I am going to live and live it to the fullest. That, to me, is just plain Sweet Strength. How about you?

Part Three:

Photos

YOUR MINDSET IS EVERYTHING!
SWEET STRENGTH
MAKE IT SWEET, KEEP IT STRONG
WWW.SWEETSTRENGTH.COM

In Loving Memory of my Husband and Best Friend, Mark "the Shark"
November 13, 1958 - January 9, 2012

About the Author

Linda McDandel is a certified wellness coach, professional life coach, speaker, certified fitness professional, lover of life, and has competed in NPC Masters Figure contest, whose passion is helping others become empowered, take control of their lives and reach their dreams by defying their ages inside and out. Sweet Strength is her first book.

To Contact & Learn More About Linda:

Website: www.sweetstrength.com
Facebook: www.facebook.com/sweetstrengthcoaching
Email: linda.sweetstrength@gmail.com

Made in the USA
Lexington, KY
17 July 2016